Sourcing in China

Sourcing in China

Strategies, Methods and Experiences

By Guido Nassimbeni and Marco Sartor

First published 2006 by
PALGRAVE MACMILLAN
Houndmills, Basingstoke, Hampshire RG21 6XS and
175 Fifth Avenue, New York, N. Y. 10010
Companies and representatives throughout the world

PALGRAVE MACMILLAN is the global academic imprint of the Palgrave
Macmillan division of St. Martin's Press, LLC and of Palgrave Macmillan Ltd.
Macmillan® is a registered trademark in the United States, United Kingdom
and other countries. Palgrave is a registered trademark in the European
Union and other countries.

ISBN-13: 978–1–4039–9855–2
ISBN-10: 1–4039–9855–8

This book is printed on paper suitable for recycling and
made from fully managed and sustained forest sources.

A catalogue record for this book is available from the British Library.

Library of Congress Cataloging-in-Publication Data

Nassimbeni, Guido.
  Sourcing in China: strategies, methods and experiences / by Guido Nassimbeni
and Marco Sartor.
    p. cm.
  ISBN 1-4039-9855-8 (cloth)
    1. Purchasing–Management. 2. Materials management. 3. Industrial procurement.
4. Business logistics–China. 5. Commerce–China. 6. International business
enterprises–Management–Case studies. I. Sartor, Marco, 1974- II. Title.

HF5437.N28 2006
658.7′2′0951–DC22

2005051503

10   9   8   7   6   5   4   3   2   1
15   14   13   12   11   10   09   08   07   06

Printed and bound in Great Britain by
Antony Rowe Ltd, Chippenham and Eastbourne

Contents

Lists of Tables and Figures

List of Figures

List of Tables

Preface

In the worldwide economic debate, China provokes more conflicting attitudes than any other country. The detractors from the Chinese model criticize the absence of democracy, the social un-sustainability of too fast a transformation, and the absence of a complete legal structure that guarantees transparency and provides precise rules.

Many western enterprises complain about the difficulties in competing with manufacturing units in a country where the labour cost is much lower than in Europe, where the environmental cost is incomparably inferior, where the phenomenon of forgery is diffuse and uncontrolled.

On the other hand, the supporters of the Chinese model emphasize the extraordinary economic development that, following the reforms path started in 1979 by the Chinese leader Deng Xiaoping, has led the Gross Domestic Product to grow at an annual rate always exceeding 7 per cent and the trade exchange to increase four-fold in ten years: figures that have no comparison with any other country in the world.

The supporters still emphasize how China's appointment to the World Trade Organization in 2001 and the definition of commonly agreed rules have rendered this context still more attractive, given the investment opportunities it offers and the possibility of establishing favourable sourcing, manufacturing and sales bases.

These conflicting attitudes translate, on one hand, as the desire to take advantage of the opportunities that the Chinese market offers and, on the other hand, as the mistrust and fear of investing resources. However, behind both the will to accept the Chinese challenge and the fear that it subtends, there is a need for more knowledge. This is the reason why the first investment that a western operator must make is to know the culture of this country and its social and industrial reality.

Only a correct and complete vision can confer to every business approach the necessary strategic design capability, which is the essential element to the pursuit of any form of effective internationalization. This element has been specifically missing in Italy, which has established on Chinese soil an archipelago of individual experiences, mostly isolated and fragmented. As a result, several extraordinary opportunities have been lost expressed in recent years by China, authentic Asian sub-continent.

Perceiving this need I have created the Italy–China Foundation, an Institution which represents public and private energies and therefore provides a service to the entire Italian system. First, the Italy–China Foundation meets those expectations of a more articulated cooperation of the Chinese parties I have perceived several times, also at institutional level. Second, only an ambitious and concrete strategy suits the impetuous development of an immense and complex country like the People's Republic of China.

Moreover this publication, which derives from the European Project 'International Sourcing Strategies for China', promoted by the University of Udine in collaboration with the University of Magdeburg and the National Centre for Science and Evaluation Technology of Beijing, offers a contribution towards the better understanding of the Chinese context.

This study examines the problems and dynamics of sourcing activities in China, analysing their main typologies and characteristics. Besides the economic and managerial aspects, this work also gives space to cultural and social variables; it is necessary to comprehend them in order to understand an economic development which is the result of a precise political choice, of a lucid industrial project, of an ancient historical heritage, and of peculiar relational dynamics.

This study traces the guidelines to shape and plan sourcing activities in the Chinese market, assuming a two-fold analytical perspective, namely that of both the Italian buyers' and that of the Chinese suppliers. A sample Chinese manufactures has therefore been analysed.

This study offers interesting and valuable indications, especially for our system. The modern industrial enterprise is constantly solicited to extend its horizons beyond the domestic or continental borders. It must therefore demonstrate that it is able to operate on the global chessboard, moving its pieces to the most attractive squares. This structural flexibility, which translates into the ability to reshape continuously in order to take advantage of the opportunities offered by international markets, has now become a critical factor for success. Our system has already accumulated delays when compared to the most advanced systems. It now needs to recover quickly the time that has been lost.

Cesare Romiti
President of the Italy–China Foundation

Foreword

To compete in the global economy, companies must concentrate their operations on the core business and competencies and must outsource non-strategic processes and services to qualified, innovative and less expensive organizations. The crucial problem that surrounds top managers and supply-chain professionals is to source the world's best suppliers and to capture the best opportunities, taking into account the fact that today's top vendors will be overturned by others in a few years time. In 1980 Michael Porter defined enterprise as a 'floating factory' constituted by interdependent and interchangeable modules, envisioning today's supply-chain in its constant evolution. While, 25 years ago, such a concept might have appeared a bit fanciful, today it represents a tangible and unquestioned reality.

In the 1950s, given the simplicity of products distributed on the market, the selection of qualified vendors was quite easy; the possible alternatives were in fact limited and company sourcing was influenced by protectionist behaviour. Today's globalized environment has made everything more complex. The effect of materials on the cost of a product is much higher, the proliferation of technologies has infringed the company's autonomy generating a market dependency and, finally, globalization and internationalization have multiplied the supply markets making the low-cost countries very attractive. In such a situation global sourcing and purchasing partnerships represent the winning strategy.

As a consequence of all these changes, the roles and competences of the buyers are more complex and strategic. Instead of managing commercial transactions in domestic markets they have to deal with the integrated management of international supply chains involving market intelligence tasks, relationship management, and risk evaluation. They have to shift from short-term relationships, characterized by variables controlled by the parties, towards long-term collaboration programmes, influenced by events beyond their control. From simple meetings with local operators, they have to interface stakeholders of different cultures, laws and practices, who often forget the old but still valid adage: *'pacta sunt servanda'* (pacts must be honoured). Up to a few years ago these concepts were not acknowledged by the entire purchasing community; today, however, everybody recognizes that the reference scenario is the world and that the supplier base has to be international. Offshore sourcing is no longer the strategy of a few advanced organizations but the common contribution to the company's competitiveness and survival. The long-term profitability of most business organizations depends on the capability of their management to understand the ongoing changes and to act accordingly. The globalization of supply markets is by far the most important of these changes and nobody can ignore it. In the 1990s the decision to outsource production processes and source globally was often a measure to counterbalance the moves of the competition. Today it represents common practice and a fundamental strategy for those who wish to export their products worldwide. In some cases it represents an alternative to the realization of offshore factories.

In the 1980s most of the exchanges were made between the United States and Europe, due to their economic and cultural similarities. Today the vast majority of developing economies have established a valid industrial infrastructure and attract a significant portion of the market demand. Those who argue that imports weaken the national economy should consider that it is less painful to outsource part of the activities of a company than to close it completely. While offshore sourcing still represents an option for many manufacturing organizations, the situation within the distribution industry is rather different. In the non-food sector in fact, 45–50 per cent of the goods are bought offshore, against an average 17 per cent for the manufacturing industry.[1]

What is the magnitude of savings achievable through offshore sourcing? What can be bought or outsourced, and which are the most attractive markets? Should we buy abroad 100 per cent of our requirements or only a portion of them? Should we prefer direct buying or resort to intermediaries? Is it necessary to second our employees to monitor the outsourced activities or is it better to use to external auditing organizations? To answer these questions one should remember that companies buy offshore items that cannot be found on the domestic markets or that can be obtained offshore with substantial savings. Each time the supply risks are high, it is reasonable to buy locally part of the whole need. In general, companies choose to buy direct when dealing with repeat purchases of high volume, whereas for limited quantities or spot purchases they act through intermediaries. To monitor the appropriate execution of complex supplies, business firms can use their personnel or use specialized service providers. Nobody, in fact, can ignore that the respect given to quality standards is still a problem and that the replacement of scrapped materials is often rather problematic. But the real difficulties arise each time the buyer has to decide where to buy or how to find the best suppliers and opportunities, or each time the buyer has to assess the risks of the operation and evaluate the total costs of ownership. At such times supply professionals face complex issues, various independent variables, and rules which are often unclear and driven by exceptions. The only viable approach seems to be pragmatic and 'do it yourself'. In the case of outsourcing the classic questions faced by managers are: 'Is it better to buy or to establish a joint-venture?', or 'Is it better to adopt the win-win model based upon mutual trust, or to resort to a conservative approach and limit to the minimum the information provided?' To answer these questions one has to know the specific situation; each case has a unique story and there are very few gurus or masters.

The theme treated in this book by Guido Nassimbeni and Marco Sartor is therefore extremely actual and challenging. It helps supply-chain professionals to focus on strategies and tactics of global sourcing, and to understand their basic rules. Through the cases illustrated it is possible to connect the many pieces of a single puzzle which no one has yet completed or validated, but which will help to understand how to move and especially to understand what should not be done. How to buy in China is the most actual and crucial theme everybody has to face. China represents the most challenging offshore market which, despite its poverty and contradictions, is enjoying the highest growth rates in the world. It is the unique economy that offers a broad range of products and processes at very competitive prices.

China's success does not only derive from its low labour cost. It is the result of decades of accurate central strategic planning, the outcome of a logistic system that, if not perfect, is better by far than any other system existing in developing countries. China means strong internal competition, pride and the ambition to become the strongest economy in the world. Given the importance of the theme, the Italian Association of Purchasing and Supply Management has been honoured to lend its support to the authors, and has decided to promote the diffusion of the book among its members and all professionals interested in the management of supplies with Chinese businesses. Every day buyers look for information on how and what to buy in China. This book represents the first study that analyses systematically the strategies and tactics that have to be adopted by professionals who intend to buy in the Country of the Dragon. In the last few years China has been the subject of much debate. Economists and academicians have carefully analysed its development, its economic and financial aggressiveness and the opportunity of curbing its exports, and the reason for such interest lies in the high potential of the Chinese market and economy, in the receptiveness of its structures, flexibility and capabilities and in the low cost of its human resources.[2] The evidence of its growth is proven by its huge import of raw materials: since 2004 it has, in fact, has become the biggest importer of aluminium and steel.

The reactions of western companies to the rise of the new economic colossus have been interesting and diverse. Some have seen China's growth as a great market opportunity for their products and have opened manufacturing facilities and sales organizations in the most developed provinces. Others have realized that it is useless to compete on 'labour intensive' products and have outsourced to the local industry part of their manufacturing processes (hence the recurring use of the term *'rented economy'*). Many organizations have moved part of their supplies to China, while others have still to decide what to do. SMEs that cannot deal with large volumes have created consortia or buy through distributors.

The rose-pink picture we have painted of China should not induce anybody to think that buying or investing there is a risk-free tour and that every joint venture or productive investment will instantly give the expected results. Administrative bureaucracy and normative chaos reign everywhere and no one builds golden bridges towards the foreign companies that move there. Whoever goes to China must be ready to face unforeseen events, surprises, risks and delays. It is a country experiencing great transition and nothing should be taken for granted. Certainty about laws is not yet granted and the transparency of regulations sometimes leaves one stunned. Nevertheless, China is the country with the highest potential of growth in the world. Anyone who waits in the hope that shadows, doubts and risks will soon disappear could find himself out of the market. The so-called 'Chinese threat' will probably continue for another 15, 20 years. Martin Wolf, in a long article in the *Financial Times*,[3] has underlined that the current surplus of rural workforce amounts to 160 million units and, taking into account the poverty of peasants, he has foreseen that another 140 million could easily join those actually seeking work. Assuming as constant the current rate of growth, China should reach a satisfactory rate of employment by around 2025. From that date, according to Mr Wolf's estimates, every progress of its social–economic system should generate wage increases, partially reducing its competitiveness. Some American analysts have estimated that China should overtake the United States in terms of gross domestic product around 2020. Everybody makes forecasts and projections on the future of China, but most of them are scarcely reliable as people too often forget to consider all the variables involved and the relevant interdependency. Nobody, local experts included, is today in the position to make reliable forecasts beyond seven or eight years. The great concerns are whether the available natural resources will be sufficient to assure the current growth in the near future, and whether China will ever enjoy the standard of living of the most advanced western countries. In both cases the answer seems to be negative.[4] In the past 20 years fuel consumption has increased by one hundred times, steel consumption by 143 per cent and aluminium by 380 per cent. China has 21 per cent of the world population, but its reserves of fuel, natural gas and minerals are much lower than those necessary to guarantee the continuity of such development rates. It is clearly possible to import them, but it is not certain that the current surplus of hard currencies will continue to exist in the future.[5] The automotive industry keeps growing, but car owners total less than 2 per cent of the population.[6] To reach the American standard of living China should have one car for every two inhabitants, which means 600 million cars versus the current world fleet of 540 million. To achieve this target, however, China would need huge fuel resources and would have to sacrifice a good part of its farmland to build roads, service stations and parking, drastically reducing the agricultural output and increasing its dependency on the external world. Extending this analysis to many other sectors and activities, it seems reasonable to state that its development rate cannot continue at the current pace for more than ten years. Moreover, to enjoy the American standard of living China would need four times the resources available in the world today. It is true that progress and technology could make available alternative products and solutions, but it appears that the problem of scarcity of resources will limit the Chinese trend of expansion. Car prototypes using solar batteries are already on our roads. Their maximum speed slightly exceeds 50 kilometres per hour, but the average speed of cars at the beginning of the last century was lower than ten.[7]

This short summary underlying lights and shadows of Planet China could induce someone to take no action, and to wait for further stabilization of the Chinese economy. Supply-chain professionals should not make such a mistake. The perspective analysis of China's future shows some clouds, but there are many factors to consider and nobody can make reliable forecasts. There are some doubts but many certainties. The cost of labour, for instance, will continue to remain far below the European average for at least 20 years, and this will convince western companies to continue to use Chinese manufacturing capabilities or to buy locally for further decades. Following the Latin phrase *'carpe diem'* (seize the day) buyers cannot hesitate, and buying in China can provide their company with the competitive edge – the contribution to the company's competitiveness that is part of the mission of every purchase and supply department.

In 1990 we recommended *The Machine that Changed the World*,[8] an analytic and comprehensive study which introduced us to the reality of lean management.

Today we recommend this book as it shows us concepts of global sourcing that nobody can ignore.

Giovanni Atti
Chairman of the Education Committee I.F.P.S.M.[9]

Notes

1. In 1995 the average percentage of materials with an offshore origin was about 13%; today it is estimated at 17%, with peaks of up to 55%. The highest value was noticed for textiles, 23%, electrical and electronic components, 19%, metals, 18%, chemical products, 17%, means of transport, 9%, machinery, 8%, furniture, 7%, rubber and plastics, 6%. The incidence of foreign purchases on the sales price was 6%: Laura M. Birou and Stanley E. Fawcett – *International Journal of Purchasing and Materials Management* 1996. In 2001 the volume of international transactions

of electronic materials exceeded the textile sector, at around 29%: Sheila Finn C.P.P., 'Define your approach to globalisation'.

2. The hourly wage of a Chinese worker is $0.61 versus an American average of $16.14 (*Taipei Times 9 October*, 2003). In April 2002 the yearly cost of a worker in the big cities was: Guangzhou $2,750, Shanghai $2,630, Beijing $2,313, Tianjin $1,728 and Chonqing $1,150 (*South China Morning Post* 1 April, 2002). The yearly hours worked vary from 2,000 to 2,200. The average rate considered in the sales of finished products varies between 4 and 10 dollars depending on the company size and the productive assets available.

3. 'The long march to prosperity'. Martin Wolf, *Financial Times 9 December*, 2003.

4. In an article in the *Financial Times*, dated 25 May, 2004, James Kynge quoted and commented on a note from a Chinese governmental agency according to which China could not afford the model of development of western countries.

5. In the first two months of 2004 imports increased by 42% with respect to the same period of 2003, and the trade deficit amounted to about 8 billion dollars (data submitted to the Senate Policy Committee on 29 March, 2004).

6. In 2001 China had 18 million vehicles, of which 5 million were cars. Most of them belonged to governmental companies and organizations; about two million belonged to private citizens. In the period 2001–05 governmental plans foresaw the production of more than one million cars per year. These figures exclude imports, which totalled 172,683 units in 2003 (National Academy of Engineering, Washington, DC).

7. 'China's growing pains call for birth of green revolution', James Kynge, *FT* 25 May, 2004.

8. James P. Womack.

9. International Federation of Purchasing and Supply Management. It comprises 43 national associations and more than 200,000 purchasing and supply professionals.

Introduction

Given a GDP whose official growth rate is 8 per cent per year, 53 billion Euros of foreign direct investments in 2003, and two and a half million new entrepreneurs, China constitutes a true miracle. Unavoidably it provokes incredulity, if not perplexity.

An epochal transformation is in progress: from a 'planned' economy to the free market, from a mostly agricultural system to a fully industrial one, from an obstinately autarchic context to one interconnected with the rest of the world.

The sustainability of this transformation is often questioned. It involves the fast conversion of the huge public enterprise and the expulsion of millions of workers, a gigantic race towards urbanization which generates enormous territorial disparities, the explosion of public investments in order to finance an imposing infrastructures development plan. The capability of this country to maintain the current rates of development is questionable, as the fast growth of consumption has led to the deficiency of some fundamental production inputs. Another issue concerns the sustainability of the economic process of liberalization that, after legitimating entrepreneurship and private property, could induce the citizens to demand greater political freedom. The current peculiar combination of political authoritarianism and a free market may therefore collapse.

Thus, many questions surround the Chinese miracle, but this transformation is undoubtedly irreversible. The change has now assumed such proportions that a return to the past is impossible. We cannot guess the outcome of this process: it is difficult to make forecasts on a context that has made two presumed opposites compatible: a socialist economy and the free market.

However, China is also and especially an opportunity, if it is truly the most attractive country in the world as far as foreign investments are concerned. The adhesion of China to the Word Trade Organization, the current reforms that outline a more explicit legislative context, the institutional incentives that facilitate foreign investments, the strong engagement in Research & Development activities and the many cooperative projects with the most important Universities in the world are evidence of the extraordinary attractiveness of this market and its efforts to achieve a greater integration into the international economic community.

A presence in China more and more often represents a necessary dowel in company's internationalization strategies. Putting down roots in this country does not only permit access to a quadrant of the international chessboard characterized by low labour costs and the potentially greatest outlet market in the globe, but it also means entering a quadrant that occupies a barycentre position in the Far East basin and constitutes a natural bridgehead for the flow directed towards the American region. It means entering a context in which the 'rediscovery' of entrepreneurship and private property is accompanied by a capability to work that the 'fat' West has by now forgotten. China is a country *on the march* again, this time towards possible global leadership. It is a country where the business attitude is evidently part of the genetic code, and hasn't been weakened by several decades of socialist collectivism.

China is therefore a reality that no enterprise can neglect. Global competition requires a global approach to sourcing activities. China constitutes one of the most attractive sourcing basins, thanks to its low labour costs, the impressive qualitative improvement of local production, the availability of advanced logistic platforms, and the possibility of legitimizing a commercial presence in a market where the internal demand is quickly growing. This originates the febrile development of joint ventures, the fast activation of trading structures, the hasty exploration of the many supply opportunities and in essence the many initiatives that we have recorded in recent times in China. However, the constitution of a sourcing base must be the result of an informed, planned process. It must consider the risks and opportunities of this market, the characteristics of purchased items, the cultural and organizational problems. In addition, this process must be planned taking into account the most suitable strategies and the organizational and managerial solutions best adapted to such a distant and different context.

This book aims to provide information on these specific issues. Various studies have been published in recent years concerning the Chinese economic and political geography and themes related to Chinese (Asian) business (legislation, negotiating style, etc.) contexts. However, the literature lacks contributions that address the managerial aspects involved in the development of a production and supply base in China and the corresponding supply chain management issue. This development is a complex task in a social, cultural and normative context so distant from our own. A number of obstacles need to be overcome: the language, the cultural and geographic distance, the coordination of an international logistic net, the transfer of technological capabilities and managerial praxes, and quality monitoring at source.

The EU project 'International Sourcing Strategies for China' focuses on these aspects. This project was coordinated by the authors in collaboration with partners belonging to the 'Otto-von-Guericke' University of Magdeburg (Germany), the Beijing National Centre for Science and Technology Evaluation (NCSTE) (the main Chinese ministerial agency specialized in the assessment of scientific and technological programmes), and finally INNOVA, a leading Italian company for technological transfer and strategic advising. Aware of the growing importance of the Chinese market, the European Union has activated the programme 'Asia Information Technologies & Communication', whose aim is to promote the identification of organizational solutions and ICT instruments for the effective management of the supply chains that link Europe and China.

The project included the analysis of a sample of European enterprises, which were selected according to two criteria. These enterprises belong to industries where the EU–China interchange is the most relevant. In addition, these units are in some way representative in their ability to take advantage of the opportunities offered by the international chessboard, where the careful and systematic resort to the sourcing opportunities offered by emerging countries is at times responsible for major buying advantages, extraordinarily fast increase rates, and sometimes even for a radical modification of the business.

The book highlights the inducements, advantages and obstacles faced by the analysed enterprises in the development of a sourcing channel in China. A classification of the various types of sourcing is proposed. It then illustrates a normative model which, on the basis of some discriminating variables, suggests the most suitable sourcing choice.

This book then describes the paths leading to an effective sourcing channel and an International Purchasing Office in China. Finally, it proposes some concrete examples of sourcing in China. In greater detail, the structure of the book is as follows.

Chapter 1 reviews the papers published on international sourcing (IS). Determinants and problems, forms, development paths, and management practices of IS are illustrated following an extensive analysis of the literature.

Chapter 2 briefly describes the main events that have characterized the recent history of China. It then sketches a geo-economic picture of the country. It lists the most important economic indicators which reveal how this country is assuming a more and more important role in the international trading community.

Chapter 3 points out objectives and methodology of the project 'International Sourcing Strategies for China' from which this book draws its origin. After a short account of the samples, motives, advantages and obstacles underlying the choice of China as a sourcing base are described.

Chapter 4 shows a classification of the types of sourcing of the sample. Each type is described in terms of industry, purchasing code, organizational requirements, key competences, and characteristics of the relationship with the Chinese interlocutors.

Chapter 5 indicates some methodologies that could be useful when choosing and planning the establishment of a sourcing channel in the Chinese market. A normative model is proposed that suggests the best suited typology depending on the key context variables (company size and purchasing volumes, complexity of the Chinese industrial context, and the complexity of the purchase code). Then the sequence of steps and activities involved in the development of a sourcing channel and an International Purchasing Office are listed.

Chapter 6 details some of the most critical aspects of IS in China: the role of intermediaries, organizational decentralization, Chinese relational logic and negotiation style, the technology and know-how transfer.

Chapter 7 summarizes modalities and legislative constraints that discipline foreign investments in China. Main forms and historical course of foreign investments, fiscal facilities and instruments for the defence of the intellectual property are briefly depicted.

Chapter 8 gives a description of transport infrastructures in China. The evolution of the transport systems and the current situation of rail, air, road and naval infrastructures are illustrated.

1
International Sourcing: Literature

Introduction

The expression 'international sourcing' (IS) refers to the purchase of materials, components, and finished products from foreign suppliers. There are different types of sourcing according to the geographical extension of the supplying area, to the international distribution of the company production structures, to the existence of a strategy in which the production and business presence within the international markets match with the purchasing decisions. As described in this chapter, different names for this phenomenon correspond to different situations ('import sourcing' (Swamidass, 1993); 'offshore sourcing' (Kotabe and Swan, 1994); 'global sourcing' (Arnold, 1999); 'worldwide sourcing' (Monczka and Trent, 1992)) and each name is linked to a particular type of international purchasing.

IS represents a very topical issue. Market globalization, communication technology and transport system development, as well as the reduction of the international trade boundaries favoured purchasing abroad or, in any case, reduced some restrictions that hindered its relevant development in the past. Business experiences show how IS is now considered to be a strategic opportunity aimed at achieving a sustainable competitive advantage, while in the past it was just an occasional process linked to the need to reduce costs.

However, IS requires a proper organizational and information infrastructure, effective coordination mechanisms and logistics capabilities. Moreover, through IS companies have to face some recurring problems, such as: cultural and communication barriers; longer supplying lead times; higher transport costs; risks linked to business transactions with different contact people and different regulations. In spite of the increasing importance of this phenomenon, the literature on it lacks empirical studies and models providing companies with cognitive and normative references upon which they decide to adopt IS.

The literature can be divided into the following main research areas:

Determining factors and problems related to IS

Reasons, enabling factors, obstacles, and advantages are included in this area. According to the literature, IS is adopted because it represents a combination of several determining factors: the possibility accessing limited resources (raw materials, components, labour, technology) (Fagan, 1991; Monczka and Trent, 1992; Bozarth et al., 1998; Chadwick and Rajagopal, 1995); the possibility of accessing less expensive resources (Carter and Narasimhan, 1990; Herbig and O'Hara, 1996; Meijboom and Dekkers, 1997); the possibility approaching international sales markets (Chase and Zhang, 1998; Kotabe and Murray, 1990; Chung et al., 2004), and many other factors. In the literature, obstacles are often represented by problems linked to cultural and language differences, to the political instability of foreign countries, and to many additional costs relevant to transport, intermediation, personnel carrying out business transactions with foreign countries, import duties, logistics, etc. (Fagan, 1991; Swamidass and Kotabe, 1993; Birou and Fawcett, 1993; Carter and Vickery, 1989; Fraering and Prasad, 1999).

IS types and development paths

Many authors propose conceptual models which try to represent IS types (taxonomies) and the corresponding evolutionary dynamics (Kotabe and Murray, 1990; Monczka and Trent, 1992; Swamidass, 1993; Rugman in Chadwick and Rajagopal, 1997; Arnold, 1989, 2000). Some of these models have been empirically tested on European, Japanese, and American companies (Kotabe, 1990; Kotabe and Murrey, 1990; Swamidass and Kotabe, 1993; Wright and Burns, 1998).

IS management methods

Compared to *domestic sourcing,* IS involves management peculiarities linked to the different regulations, language, culture, contractual style, greater logistics complexities, etc. Therefore, this stream of studies deepens these differences and offers guidelines concerning the best way to manage foreign sourcing; for example: which products, suppliers, information sources, sourcing markets and agreement conditions are the best in a particular situation (Ellram and Billington, 2001; Andersen and Buvik, 2001; Caddick and Dale, 1987; Carter and Narasimhan, 1990; Babbar and Prasad, 1998). This stream includes studies related to IS strategies, that is, the methods used to select products to be purchased abroad, from which suppliers, and according to which agreement and relationship types. If companies own production plants abroad and are, therefore, internationalized at manufacturing level, these selections have a particular implication. In this case, the foreign premises can use local suppliers, or non-local suppliers who, however, have transferred their units (co-location) near to the customer assets, or, eventually, non-local suppliers. It is clear that this selection is linked to several variables: purchase code types, corresponding logistics requirements, decision-making decentralization related to foreign units, etc.

A further classification variable, overlapping the previous studies, concerns the geographical area to which the different studies refer. The bibliographic survey of Prasad *et al.* (2000) shows how 50 out of 150 articles about 'International Operations' reviewed by the most famous journals concern only specific countries. The United States, Japan, and the United Kingdom are the most analysed countries. A lower number of articles concern comparative surveys focused on the comparison between different industrialized countries, above all the United States and Japan. Even if Japanese companies are very internationalized at production level, these studies show that they have a more 'autarkic' attitude compared to American companies, namely they tend to favour domestic sourcing. On the other hand, American companies seem to favour purchasing labour-intensive materials and components from developing countries (South-east Asia and Mexico) where labour costs are much lower than in the United States. Few studies analyse problems linked to sourcing from eastern Europe, which today represents not only an interesting sourcing area, but also a market with high potential.

The analysis of the motivating and inhibiting factors will be the subject of the first part of this chapter, while the second part is dedicated to IS types and development paths. Both these parts are preceded by a section aimed at defining the meaning of the expressions used by the international literature to indicate international sourcing.

International sourcing: some explanations of this expression

In the literature, several authors used different expressions such as:

- *international purchasing* or *sourcing* (Fraering and Prasad, 1998; Babbar and Prasad, 1998);
- *offshore sourcing* (Kotabe and Swan, 1993);
- *import sourcing* (Swamidass, 1993);
- *global sourcing* (Murray *et al.*, 1995; Chadwick and Rajagopal, 1995; Meijboom, 1999; Meijboom and Dekkers, 1997; Arnold, 1999);
- *worldwide sourcing* (Monczka and Trent, 1992).

The meaning of these expressions are somewhat different. For example, Frear *et al.* (1995) and Kotabe and Swan (1993) use the expression *off shore* with reference to *overseas* purchasing carried out by American companies. Monczka and Trent (1992) distinguish between *international purchasing* and *global sourcing:* the former simply corresponds to the business transaction

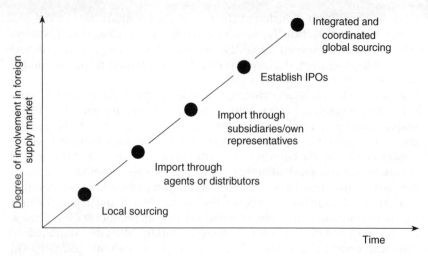

Figure 1.1   The Rugman Model (in Rajagopal and Chadwick, 1995)

between a purchaser and a supplier coming from different countries; the latter corresponds to the coordination at international level of sourcing and production activities between different units of a multinational company. In the same way, Murray *et al.* (1995) define *global sourcing* as 'the sourcing and production organisation of a company having activities distributed at international level'.

To understand better the meaning of these expressions, it may be useful to analyse the Rugman model (in Chadwick and Rajagopal, 1995) which defines different sourcing approaches according to two variables: time and involvement level in the foreign markets. (Figure 1.1)

According to this model, in the beginning the company purchases materials and components only from local sources (*local sourcing* or *domestic sourcing*). When the company needs to access foreign supply markets but does not have proper resources and capabilities (yet), it usually turns to intermediaries (agents or distributors). The next step is represented by the import through foreign subsidiaries. When the company involvement level in the international markets increases, the company creates purchasing offices abroad (*International Purchasing Offices* – IPO): structures created to manage international purchasing on site. Finally, *global sourcing* refers to companies that located production plants abroad and developed local supply networks around them.

These companies are therefore internationalized both at manufacturing and sourcing levels, and coordinate their supply networks from a global standpoint.

Ultimately the expression IS involves different situations whose shared element is the sourcing of raw materials, components, or finished products from suppliers located out of the domestic boundaries. These suppliers are, therefore, located in different countries from that of the purchasing company (or the headquarter, of the multinational company).

According to Figure 1.1, IS refers to all those situations that are different from the first one (local/domestic sourcing). Later on in the chapter, we will refer to IS with this meaning.

IS determining factors

Reduction of purchase costs

The search for less expensive materials than domestic materials is one of the most frequently-mentioned reasons (Frear *et al.*, 1995; Birou and Fawcett, 1993; Swamidass, 1993; Handfield, 1994; Herbig and O'Hara, 1996; Nellore *et al.*, 2001). Moreover, the factor of 'cost' is underlined by many authors in the analyses concerning IS evolutionary dynamics: the search for lower purchase costs is described by most models as the factor activating international sourcing. In the literature, a 'reactive' response method to the opportunities offered by foreign supply countries is often linked to cost advantages. 'Cost' remains a key motivation throughout the whole international sourcing development path up to global sourcing, in which purchasing coordination on a world scale is (also) one of the main reasons for achieving and consolidating economies of scale and for optimizing flows both within the country and internationally. A survey carried out by Trent and Monczka (2002) on a sample of American companies estimates that cost advantages resulting from the use of international supply markets correspond to a percentage ranging from 15 to 25 per cent of total costs.

Access to distinctive resources/capabilities

If cost often represents the starting factor, the access to suppliers having distinctive capabilities is the second most important reason underlined in the literature. Particularly, the search for the best quality or, anyway, for a better price/quality ratio is documented in different studies (Monczka and Trent, 1992; Herbig and O'Hara, 1996; Fraering and Prasad, 1999). Although in the past some authors (Caddick and Dale, 1987) pointed out a high risk of quality differences in international supplies, more recent studies underline how some sourcing areas have considerably improved, above all those located in the developing countries. This is the case with China, where the quality improvement has been considered 'unbelievable' by several companies analysed in this survey. It is also necessary to note how the quality risk reduction is indirectly linked to the development of transport networks and to the spread of modern information and communication technologies which means that possible unexpected quality differences can be coped with more quickly and efficiently than in the past.

Another distinctive resource that could be offered by international sources is technology, as shown by several studies (Swamidass, 1993; Hebig and O'Hara, 1996; Meijboom and Dekkers, 1997; Bozarth *et al.*, 1997). IS is justified by the search of technologies not available in the country of origin, or available abroad at a lower cost/with better service conditions.

Besides the technological aspect, the selection of the sourcing area also depends on the variation rate of purchasing codes, and, more generally, on the product life cycle. The literature shows conflicting opinions. On the one hand, some authors point out (Smith, 1999; Nellore and Soderquist, 2000), a technology which is subject to rapid changes requires frequent and direct interactions with suppliers. In this case, geographical distance can represent an obstacle. On the other hand, Swamidass and Kotabe (1993) point out that the product maturity is linked to a higher diffusion of technological knowledge. Therefore, the possibility of purchasing products from the domestic market increases. The empirical survey carried out by Handfield (1994) let us think that this second case is prevailing: on an empirical basis, the author shows that critical codes linked to products in the initial phases of their life-cycle are more frequently purchased from international sources, while codes linked to mature products are addressed to domestic suppliers.

Moreover, with regard to the distinctive capabilities of international suppliers, some authors also identified 'specializations' characterizing different geographical sourcing areas. Handfiedl (1994), for example, explains that Japan is the preferred sourcing area for electronic products, while Taiwan, Singapore, South Korea, and Hong Kong are the best sourcing areas for electro-mechanic and automotive components.

Possibility of increasing the number of the available suppliers

The exploration of international supply markets can significantly increase the number of potential suppliers. In this way, the purchasing company can achieve a greater variety and flexibility of production, being able to have more alternatives at its disposal. This advantage is shown by several studies (Rao and Young, 1994; Birou and Fawcett, 1993; Handfield, 1994; Humphreys *et al.*, 1998; Fraering and Prasad, 1999). In addition, the expansion of the geographical sourcing area offers useful terms of comparison to the purchaser in order to start or increase competitive dynamics between current suppliers.

Possibility of legitimizing or developing a commercial presence in foreign markets

The business penetration of a foreign market may be preferred by suppliers working within the considered market. First of all, the purchasing company can ask suppliers information about domestic demand, opportunities, and existing restrictions. Thanks to their support, cultural and procedural gaps in the local market can be better faced. In addition, the same purchaser working in the International Purchasing Office created by the company may prefer the penetration into the foreign market. Secondly, the use of a local industry system can legitimate the business presence: sometimes this can be an explicit requirement for sales. As we will see in the following chapters, imposed sourcing, namely the obligation to purchase domestic products, is a condition imposed by the Chinese government on foreign companies in some industries. Finally, management reasons (punctuality of delivery, just-in-time supply, etc.) require the creation of local supply networks around the premises of the company: the international distribution of activities also requires a global planning of purchasing sources and logistics flows.

The possibility of legitimizing or developing a market through IS is a reason underlined in several surveys (Cohen and Mallik, 1997; Giunipero and Monczka, 1990; Shi and Gregory, 1998; Frear *et al.*, 1995).

Trade barrier reduction and international agreements

The reduction of trade barriers within defined geographical areas – such as the creation of the North American Free Trade Agreement (Nafta) or the European Union itself – together with the creation of international organizations regulating and governing trade between countries (World Trade Organization) certainly favoured IS development within the involved countries (Prasad *et al.*, 2000).

The above-mentioned factors correspond to the determining issues most frequently discussed in the literature, even if the list is not exhaustive. To define its relative importance, it might be useful to point out the main results of a recent survey carried out by the author on a sample of 78 Italian companies (Nassimbeni, 2003). A 5-level Likert scale (1 = non-relevant factor; ....; 5 = very relevant factor) defines the importance assigned to the IS motivating factors by the purchasing managers interviewed. A factor analysis on the *items* of this scale has been carried out in order to define the underlying factors. The results are shown in the Table 1.1.

Access to the less expensive resources and to those resources not available on the domestic market represents the most important motivations.

The commercial implications of a foreign sourcing basis or the advantages offered (more advantageous taxation) are shown in the bottom positions of the table. Apart from their absolute value, it is interesting to understand how these motivations are linked to each other. This information derives from the factor analysis. The first factor, which explains 29.9 per cent of the whole variance and can be defined as 'Access to less expensive resources and intensification of the international competition', groups *items* linked both to IS economic advantage ('possibility of purchasing less expensive materials and components', 'possibility of accessing less expensive labour', 'more advantageous taxation') and to the global dimension of

Table 1.1 IS determinants in a sample of Italian companies.

Determining factors	Average	Factor 1	Factor 2	Factor 3
Possibility of purchasing less expensive materials and components	3.79	**0.654**	-0.320	0.126
Possibility of accessing resources not available in the country	3.56	-0.054	0.008	**0.823**
Possibility of getting less expensive labour	3.48	**0.729**	0.107	-0.206
Global competition	3.28	**0.650**	0.112	-0.052
Global company attitudes	3.11	**0.583**	0.264	0.228
Possibility of accessing advanced technologies	2.71	0.098	0.118	**0.829**
Reduction of trade barriers	2.62	**0.544**	0.367	-0.091
Possibility of developing a presence in foreign markets	2.26	0.134	**0.921**	0.096
Presence of manufacturing plants in foreign countries	2.25	**0.538**	0.239	0.170
Possibility of selling products in the countries from which you purchase	2.01	0.178	**0.896**	0.055
More advantageous taxation	1.84	**0.423**	0.357	0.098
% of the explained variance		29.9	14.3	12.4

the competition and of the company ('global competition', 'reduction of trade barriers', 'presence of factories in foreign countries', and 'global company attitudes'). The fact that these two aspects are grouped in a single factor is explained by some authors (Kotabe and Murray, 1990; Frear *et al.*, 1995) who declare that the international expansion of the company and the subsequent creation of international production plants and purchasing offices is a requirement in some mature industries. Here the limited innovation rate and a competition based on the best price foster the search for less expensive sourcing.

The second factor which explains 14.3 per cent of the whole variance and can be defined as 'Presence in new markets', groups items linked to the commercial valence of IS business ('possibility selling products on markets from which you purchase', and 'possibility developing a presence in foreign markets'). The third item which explains 12.4 per cent of the whole variance and can be defined as 'Access to distinctive resources' groups items which define an IS required by the search of suppliers having technology and/or materials and/or components not available on the domestic supply market. This reason, as for Monczka and Trent (1992), seems to be particularly important for companies working in 'dynamic' industries characterized by rapid and frequent technological developments and/or by reduced product life cycle.

The same survey compares Italian suppliers with the foreign ones with respect to the importance of several selection criteria; such importance is again defined according to a 5-point Likert scale (1 = non-relevant; ...; 5 = very relevant). The results are shown in Table 1.2.

First of all, it is important to observe that the first four criteria used in the selection/evaluation are the same as those used for domestic (Italian) and foreign suppliers. In other words, the characteristics defining the offer do not depend on supplier localization. However, the relative criterion importance changes. Criteria used to select domestic suppliers are more restrictive compared with those used to select foreign suppliers except for price, economic–financial reliability, and technological capabilities. As far as price and technological capabilities are concerned, possible reasons have already been explained. The use of less expensive suppliers – for example, thanks to their localization – or of suppliers having distinctive capabilities – namely technological capabilities – represents the main IS determinant. The higher selectivity related to economic–financial reliability may be linked to the relational uncertainty often connected to IS. By interacting with several and distant suppliers, the customer requires more guarantees assuring that the supplier can respect the commitments.

IS inhibiting factors

IS costs

Several surveys considered the total costs linked to IS (Meijboom and Dekkers 1997; Fawcett *et al.*, 1993; Herbig and O'Hara, 1996). Even if the

Table 1.2 Importance of domestic suppliers' selection criteria vs. that of foreign supplies in a sample of Italian companies

Supplier selection criteria	Domestic suppliers (average)	Foreign suppliers (average)	Δ
Punctuality of delivery	4.62	4.26	0.36
Suitable quality of the product	4.51	4.44	0.07
Meeting of required specifications	4.39	4.17	0.22
Price	4.23	4.49	−0.26
Proper technological capabilities	3.92	3.94	−0.02
Flexibility with reference to volumes	3.89	3.44	0.45
Economic–financial reliability	3.86	4.01	−0.15
Manufacturing specialization	3.85	3.76	0.09
Consolidated relationships	3.75	3.36	0.39
Technical assistance after sales	3.74	3.46	0.28
Terms of payment	3.7	3.28	0.42
Independent management of the complementary production aspects	3.3	3.25	0.05
Design capability	3.3	3.01	0.29
Geographical proximity	3.28	2.51	0.77
Large product range	3.1	2.79	0.31
Exclusive commitment	2.4	2.09	0.31

price of an item is lower, the IS can exhibit many other additional costs compared with domestic sourcing. For example, the risks of a longer lead time and of being out of stock, which require an increase in stock and, therefore, higher storage costs and obsolescence risks. Other additional costs are linked to import and export duties, customs duties, material transport and insurance.

Then there are costs linked to the management and coordination of the international supply network: supplier selection and auditing, conformity with different regulations and agreement terms, monitoring the material flow, costs linked to IPO. Moreover, these activities can be appointed to intermediaries, generating an intermediation cost. As already explained, the first international activities are often carried out through companies specialized in business transactions with foreign countries. If the company does not have suitable resources to carry out its activities in international markets directly, it refers first to intermediaries.

IS lead times

Several authors include the lead time extension among IS obstacles (Handfield, 1994; Mekjboom and Dekkers, 1997; Humpreys *et al.*, 1998; Nellore *et al.*, 2001). This lead time extension varies according to geographical distance, material type, and infrastructures of the countries through

Table 1.3 Logistics complexity of the continental areas
(1 = very low; ...; 5 = very high)

Area	United States	Germany
Asia	5	5
Australia/New Zealand	4	5
Central America	2	3
Eastern Europe	4	1
North America	1	2
North Africa	4	2
South America	3	4
South Africa	5	3
Western Europe	2	1

which the material has to pass during transport. Moreover, risk of delay and transport problems can occur, especially when intermodal transports are used. Other problems can be caused by packaging incompatibility between countries or between carriers, or by the higher risk of damage to products during transport. Tracking of the order is generally much more difficult.

It can be interesting to observe the results of a survey carried out by Kaufmann and Carter (2000) on 1,234 purchasing managers members of the American National Association of Purchasing Management (NAPM) and 800 companies belonging to the Germany Bundesverband Materialwirtschaft Einkauf und Logistik (BME). These authors try to classify the continental sourcing areas according to the logistics complexity (Table 1.3).

As far as sourcing directed to the United States and Germany is concerned, note how Asia – because of geographical distance and lack of infrastructures of many countries of this area – is considered the most critical continent. In this regard, it is important to observe that one of the reasons why China is preferred to other Asian countries is that it can offer important and modern logistics platforms.

Cultural and linguistic differences

As often shown in the literature, cultural differences and different languages play an important role when a company decides to engage IS. The studies proposed in this book show how these factors have an impact not only, and not so much on the negotiation step, but rather on the order management and on the transfer of (more) advanced management methods. Generally, the negotiation of the agreement is carried out by qualified personnel who are usually already familiar with foreign (western or eastern) contact people. Cultural intermediation is important when the supply relationship requires collaboration between the parties, namely

Table 1.4   Cultural difference between Italy and the other countries (Kougt and Singh, 1988)

Sweden	3.83	Greece	1.35
Singapore	3.59	India	1.35
Denmark	3.58	Turkey	1.21
China	**3.25**	Austria	1.18
Norway	3.03	Iran	1.10
Chile	2.43	Brazil	1.09
Portugal	2.38	Malaysia	0.95
Holland	2.36	Bulgaria	0.94
Hungary	2.36	Ireland	0.91
Philippines	2.34	Japan	0.89
Thailand	2.26	Spain	0.84
Venezuela	2.22	New Zealand	0.84
Hong Kong	2.13	Great Britain	0.81
Baltic area	2.13	France	0.74
Peru	2.12	Canada	0.57
Taiwan	**1.84**	Argentina	0.53
Pakistan	1.81	United States	0.51
Colombia	1.78	Australia	0.47
Czech Republic	1.67	Belgium	0.44
Slovakia	1.67	South Africa	0.33
Finland	1.63	Switzerland	0.29
Poland	1.58	Germany	0.22
Mexico	1.45	**Italy**	**0.00**
Israel	1.40		

when it is necessary to keep managing interaction and to redefine the production and management structure of the Chinese partner in order to adjust it to western standards. For this reason, Chinese personnel employed by local IPO are frequently involved.

It is interesting to show the results of a survey carried out by Kogut and Singh (1998). According to the famous Hofstede categories (1983) – power, uncertainty, individualism, masculinity – these authors define the cultural differences between 47 countries. With reference to Italy, the results are shown in Table 1.4.

China is the fourth most different country (3.25) from Italy at culture level preceded by Sweden (3.83), Singapore (3.59), and Denmark (3.58). Curiously, Pakistan, Iran, and Malaysia are the closest to Italy. If you consider the extraordinary development of some of these countries during recent years – particularly China – it is likely that some of these differences are overestimated.

Min and Gale (1993) analysed the negotiation strategies of 229 purchasing managers of companies adopting IS. From this study, the most critical factor is linked to communication and language, followed by time limita-

Table 1.5   Classification of the critical factors of the negotiations

Rank	Variable	Importance
1	miscommunication/language	1.987
2	time limitations	2.298
3	cultural differences	2.304
4	limited authority of the international negotiator	2.422
5	dishonesty of the international supplier	2.531
6	geographical separation	2.707
7	differences in conflict handling styles	2.862
8	size of negotiation team	3.484

Note: The average degree of seriousness is measured using a five-point Likert scale with 1 = very serious and 5 = no problem at all
Source: Min and Gale (1993)

tion and cultural differences (Table 1.5). It is interesting to observe how 'time' concept is not only a technical variable but also a factor linked to the culture and negotiation style. For example, some purchasing managers interviewed in this study underlined how Chinese negotiators have a different time concept, which means that they do not define and control it as a cost as in the Western context.

Knowledge/technology expropriation risk

Some studies (Min and Galle, 1991; Swamidass and Kotabe, 1992; Fraering and Prasad, 1998; Carter *et al.*, 1998) point out this factor as one of the most critical in IS dynamics. Geographical distance restricts the possibility to control the counterpart, while different regulations and institutional structures causes uncertainties about the result of a possible legal dispute. This variable plays an important role in the sourcing of some products from China, where 'copies' are traditionally produced. Again with reference to China, even if the risk of 'copies' still exists and has been often underlined by managers interviewed in this study, we think it will be reduced in the future. First of all, the entry of China into the World Trade Organization (WTO) offers western buyers higher guarantees concerning the respect of intellectual property and exclusivity rights. Secondly, today there is legislation actionable in case of disputes, while in the past transactions were carried out without fixed rules. Finally, experience has taught western operators the investment forms and the organizational structures that better protect these rights or, at least, limit the risks of violation. These issues will be considered later again.

(Political) instability of the foreign markets

Some empirical analysis include this factor among the obstacles of IS in some countries (Birou and Fawcett, 1993; Bozarth *et al.*, 1997). As far as

China is concerned, this played a very important role: foreign investments have increased, especially in recent years when foreign operators considered the economic and political change in China, to be credible and unlikely to revert. But some doubts about instability persist especially with reference to the ability of the Chinese State to manage not only the transformation in progress – from a collectivist economy to a free-market economy – but also the transition from an agricultural system (typical of the internal areas of the countries) to an industrial one (but focused on the coastal areas). Other doubts concern the ability to keep the current development rates when there is a lack of some important areas of production (eg. raw materials) which is generated by a fast increase in consumption.

Other obstacles to IS are linked to the need of operational interactions in order jointly to develop products or processes, to the data collection regarding foreign markets, to the possibility of defining a detailed and complete legal agreement, to the recruitment of qualified personnel carrying out business transactions with foreign countries, to the availability of intermediaries/business partners, etc. In order to evaluate the importance of these factors, it can be useful to consider again the survey of the authors on a sample of 78 Italian companies. Also in this case, a 5-point Likert scale (1 = non-relevant factor; ....; 5 = very relevant factor) defined the importance assigned to the different IS inhibiting factors by the purchasing managers interviewed (Table 1.6).

A first remark relates to the absolute value of the observed items: these obstacles are given average or below average scores, in any event lower than those given to the determinants previously analysed. The difficulty in managing logistics represents the main obstacle perceived by interviewees, followed by the difficulties in valuating actual supplier capabilities and in establishing a reliable relationship with them. In the last positions are regulation and agreement condition differences, political instability of the foreign countries, and lack of intermediaries.

Factor-analysis indicates a first factor which explains 38.6 per cent of the overall variance and that can be defined as, 'Information and relationship difficulties'. It includes items regarding which there is difficulty in establishing effective communication channels that can disseminate proper information about suppliers and supplying markets. The second factor which explains 11.4 per cent of the overall variance can be defined as 'Cultural and procedural differences' as it groups items mainly linked to differences concerning language, regulation systems, and administrative restrictions. In other words, these difficulties always involve communication issues, even if they do not fall within the negotiation topic but rather the regulations and corresponding procedures. It is important to observe that the relevance of these obstacles – valued as overall variance – is considered to be lower than that of the difficulties grouped by the first factor, even if the literature underlines the importance of the procedural barriers.

Table 1.6 Classification of the IS inhibiting factors (1 = very critical factor; ... ; 5 = non-critical factor)

Obstacles	Average	Factor 1	Factor 2	Factor 3	Factor 4
Difficulties in managing logistics	3.12	0.203	0.117	0.033	**0.908**
Difficulties in valuating foreign supplier capabilities	2.99	**0.729**	0.146	0.183	0.219
Difficulties in having reliable relationship with foreign suppliers	2.80	**0.670**	0.038	0.431	0.179
Difficulties in collecting information about foreign supplying markets	2.64	0.546	0.169	0.514	-0.035
Cultural and language differences	2.57	0.431	**0.578**	0.009	-0.116
Desire to favour Italian suppliers	2.55	0.144	0.170	**0.647**	-0.134
Lack of direct communication	2.50	**0.871**	0.134	-0.087	-0.041
Difficulties in recruiting qualified personnel	2.48	**0.521**	0.347	0.373	-0.048
Exchange rate instability/flexibility	2.37	0.233	**0.6796**	0.302	-0.015
Customs barriers	2.32	-0.075	**0.7646**	0.222	0.390
Administrative problems	2.31	0.043	**0.808**	0.082	0.161
Different regulations and agreement conditions	2.27	0.482	**0.6509**	0.236	-0.160
Political instability of the foreign countries	2.25	0.048	0.1809	**0.828**	0.253
Few intermediaries/business partners	2.24	0.460	0.136	**0.611**	0.066
Percentage of the explained variance		38.6	11.4	8.8	7.9

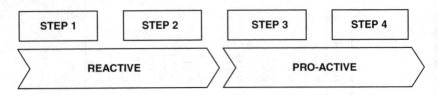

Figure 1.2   The four steps of the Monczka and Trent model (1991)

Logistics management difficulty represents a separate factor, while the third factor groups the remaining items.

IS types and development paths

This section shows some of the main models concerning IS types and development paths proposed in the literature.

The Monczka and Trent model

In a study carried out on a sample of American multinational companies, Monczka and Trent (1991) describe the international sourcing development according to a path divided into four steps, each of them linked to a different and more extended coordination level between the operating units of the company (Figure 1.2).

Step 1 – use of domestic suppliers.   In this step, the company does not carry out international purchasing activities directly: domestic sources properly meet its requirements. However, this does not mean that the company does not use foreign materials: if necessary, they are included in the components purchased from domestic suppliers. These domestic suppliers act as intermediaries if a foreign sourcing is required.

Step 2 – IS meets contingent requirements.   The loss of competitiveness by domestic suppliers or the competitive advantages achieved by competitors through IS, force the company to expand the geographical sourcing area. Companies often turn to this step after unexpected events, such as a rapid variation of the exchange rates, a loss of some important domestic supply source, or an unexpected increase in competitiveness. In other words, IS represents a reactive response to the external environment changes. In this step, the company is not usually well informed about the characteristics and opportunities of the foreign markets and is not able to face them.

Step 3 – IS is a part of a global sourcing strategy. Domestic and international sourcing are considered and managed jointly according to a consistent strategy. This step defines a prospective change: the company exceeds the domestic boundaries and considers the worldwide market in a pro-active way, being aware of the important performance enhancements that can be originated by IS. In this step, the company has developed neither integrated communication systems nor proper logistic networks among the operating units, yet.

Step 4 – Integration and coordination of the international sourcing activities. This last step of the internationalization process of purchasing is carried out when the global coordination of all facilities and activities is achieved. The central purchasing department defines how to centralize/decentralize processes and responsibilities: above all, it centralizes management of shared requirements (common codes), decides the general sourcing politics (supplier selection criteria, geographical areas, agreement conditions), distributes the management of specific codes and the responsibility for the corresponding flow management to decentralized units. Resources to be used can be extensive and, in addition to highly qualified personnel, it is also important to have information systems organized at international level and proper communication and coordination methods.

In a subsequent study (1992), these authors define five possible strategies that can be adopted by companies for the last steps of the above-explained path (steps 3 and 4). These strategies must always be considered as developing levels through a progressive integration and coordination process of the foreign sourcing activities. These strategies are described below.

First strategy – IS appointed to purchasing office staff (Step 3). The company defines one or more people within the organization to whom the responsibility for IS can be assigned. Generally, these people are already working in the purchasing office. This strategy is suitable for companies that do not have proper experience and structures or that do not need to use a higher level strategy. This step specifically corresponds to the shift from a reactive to a pro-active form of IS, and shows the main obstacles within the organization, mainly because: a) there are greater objective difficulties in managing international sourcing practices; b) dedicated staff do not have knowledge of the foreign language and, more generally, of international trade; c) staff tend to protect domestic suppliers and to maintain consolidated inter-organizational relationships; d) there are difficulties in developing and making operative decentralized units; e) there are longer lead times and more uncertainty about foreign supplies. To overcome these obstacles, Monczka and Trent (1991) suggest adequate training of the involved staff by teaching successful stories about companies adopting IS together with the positive support of top management, the possible use of intermediaries supporting initial purchasing and the creation of an office abroad.

Second strategy – Involvement of foreign subsidiaries or of foreign intermediaries (Step 3).   If the international purchasing volume increases so that central purchasing office is not able to cope with it, it is necessary to delegate at least a part of the responsibilities. In this case, the company can refer to foreign subsidiaries or foreign intermediaries supporting them in managing international transactions. These units, working on the foreign market, can better locate local sourcing opportunities by taking advantage of their language and cultural knowledge and the relationship they have (Monczka and Trent, 1992). The involvement of foreign units that have to carry out an additional activity (sourcing) compared with the main activity (production or sales), becomes rapidly limited when the purchasing volume increases not only in terms of quantity but also in terms of quality, namely when the complexity and peculiarity of codes require specific capabilities. Moreover, it is difficult to assign to them activities concerning international flow coordination.

Third strategy – Creation of the International Purchasing Office (Step 3). The company creates an office abroad which is mainly concerned with the international purchasing management within a defined geographical area, generally in the main supply markets.

IPOs depend on the central purchasing office and often employ local people. Their main activities are: identification of suppliers; the issue of requests for quotation and their collection; agreement negotiation; sample valuation; shipment management; coordination of information between head office and suppliers; technical support to suppliers; and management of the countertrade commitments. Companies that – at this level – do not have the necessary resources to create an IPO can opt to maintain some representatives abroad to manage sourcing activities and to monitor the main supplying markets (Monczka and Trent, 1992).

Fourth strategy – (Re)distribution of the responsibilities (planning, sourcing, and production) among foreign units.   A further step in the international expansion of the company shows that it is necessary to (re)structure the activities carried out by foreign units. These units, to which generally a specific initial task (for example a manufacturing one) is assigned, are also assigned other tasks (sourcing, product development). This means that they are used as footholds to develop other forms of presence (manufacturing, sales, etc.) in the market in which they are located. It is clear that a multinational structure that develops itself in this way can generate redundancies and inefficiencies. For this reason, it is necessary to reorganize the activities carried out by foreign units by specializing some of them in international purchasing within a defined geographical area. This step involves a further important coordination effort and organizational changes.

Fifth strategy–Integrated and coordinated international sourcing strategy: global sourcing. The last strategy requires the centralization of the shared purchasing (common parts) and the partially centralized coordination of suppliers of plants located abroad. A company entering this level can still use IPO or base itself on some foreign subsidiaries for product development, production, and sourcing worldwide. However, in this case the company integrates these activities in all relevant operating units adopting a global view. Integration can enable important performance enhancements, however, at the expense of a further organizational effort, in order to ensure coordination and synergies between different units.

Monczka and Trent (1992) describe the previous five steps according to: communication types and tools, coordination mechanism, personnel capabilities, managerial responsibilities, integration level between the planning, production, and purchasing activities. Table 1.7 provides an adaptation of their proposal.

This model was later (2002) submitted to empirical validation by the authors by studying a sample of American multinational companies.

The Rugman model

The model proposed by Rugman (in Chadwick and Rajagopal, 1995) and already mentioned with reference to the different names linked to IS (see Figure 1.1) is explained and examined more deeply in this chapter.

The model proposes a sequence of four different types of international sourcing defined according to the progressive involvement level of the company in the foreign markets.

1. *Import through intermediaries and distributors.* Companies tend to enter and explore international supply markets through specialized intermediaries and distributors. This sourcing type – which transfers the responsibility for negotiation and management of the supply relationship to

Table 1.7 Monczka and Trent classification

	Communication types and tools	Coordination mechanisms	Personnel capabilities	Managerial responsibilities	Integration between design, production, and purchasing
First strategy	Standard communication with suppliers Use supplier's monitoring systems	Processing of sourcing plans within the central unit/division	Knowledge of International sourcing practices Capability to select and use foreign suppliers	Completely assigned to purchasing personnel	Non-critical factor
Second strategy	Definition of official communication channels with subsidiaries or with other foreign intermediaries Use of suppliers' monitoring systems	Sourcing plans – processed within the central unit/division and communicated to the foreign units – take into account the opportunities of the international supply markets	International sourcing practices knowledge Selection and comparison of the foreign sources	Assigned to purchasing personnel activity with support from the foreign subsidiary units	Non-critical factor
Third strategy	Use of EDI or internet-based systems for communications with IPO Use of suppliers' monitoring systems	Periodical meetings of the IS staff Periodical audits to the plants of the main international suppliers Establishment of Commodity Managers to manage specific purchasing categories	International sourcing practices knowledge Deep knowledge of the international sourcing areas by IPO staff	Extended also to people responsible for IPO	The distributed manufacturing units of the multinational group start using the suppliers suggested by IPO

	Communication types and tools	Coordination mechanisms	Personnel capabilities	Managerial responsibilities	Integration between design, production, and purchasing
Fourth strategy	Use of CAD/CAM and Simultaneous Engineering systems Visibility on the production planning and on the product development projects between the manufacturing units of the group	Project Management tools Coordination of the activities at central level Organisation of periodical meetings between business units to monitor the progress of the 'global design-manufacturing-sourcing' projects	Capability to centrally manage purchasing requirements shared by the different operating units of the group Capability to coordinate purchasing requirements of the different manufacturing units	Involvement of the people responsible for international business units	Integration of the activities both within the company and between different business units
Fifth strategy	Use of a shared system to code purchasing items World-wide Data Base to which all units of the group can access World-wide Performance Tracking System shared by the units of the group Use of EDI or internet-based systems to communicate with suppliers	Periodical meetings with managers of the different operating units Coordinated and strategic support at central level Creation of groups (Material Commodity Teams) for the international sourcing management	Knowledge of the culture and contractual procedures of the various countries Knowledge and valuation of risks linked to various sourcing areas Full assimilation of the integration and coordination tools of the world-wide distributed business units Management of the worldwide map of the supplying channels	Definition of Corporate Material Executives for the integration of the purchasing sources at global level Managerial support to the operating units of the group	Selection at central level of the suppliers of common parts (shared by various manufacturing units) Complete integration of the design, production, and sourcing activities both within the company and between the different units of the group

intermediaries is simpler and less risky. However, the author points out that in this case purchase costs can be higher because they also include intermediation costs; moreover solutions defined by third parties may not always be the best for the company.

2. *Import through foreign subsidiaries*. In this case, the company uses its foreign – mainly manufacturing – units or subsidiaries. The main reasons are: a) the possibility of exploring the local market more easily and, therefore, of gathering more information about potential suppliers operating in that geographical area; b) experience gained with respect to local business practices; c) better capability of communicating and integrating with local contacts resulting in negotiation advantages; d) the possibility of monitoring the suppliers directly and starting collaborations with them. Rugman points out that this sourcing strategy becomes less effective when the purchase volume increases.

3. *IPO creation*. Purchasing office creation represents the third type proposed by Rugman. These offices are located in some countries in order to enter the supply markets and manage them better. Usually, they employ local personnel trained to manage business transactions and technical aspects concerning products, company processes, and purchasing codes. Main personnel tasks are:
   - to collect information and detect potential suppliers by carrying out direct inspections at their plants;
   - to manage the negotiation process. Rooting the IPO in the local environment and using domestic personnel enable a better cultural and language intermediation;
   - to monitor the legalities associated with the agreement conditions;
   - to act as representative of the purchasing company to foreign suppliers;
   - to track the purchasing codes during shipment and to manage possible logistics problems;
   - to look after technical aspects, to face non-conformity problems, to follow the technological and qualitative growth of the supplier;
   - to manage the countertrade commitments;
   - to guarantee that the foreign supplier fulfils conditions agreed in terms of price, quality, and delivery punctuality;
   - to assist the company in payment procedures.

4. *Integrated and coordinated global sourcing*. This last type of IS requires the highest organizational effort as companies want to integrate and coordinate the purchasing requirements of the whole international network. In this case, the main objective of the company is to maximize its purchasing power worldwide by centralizing the requirements shared by different production units and therefore reducing the inefficiencies due to order splitting. In this way, it is possible to generate economies of scale and reduce the total purchase costs (Rugman in Rajagopal and Chadwick, 1997).

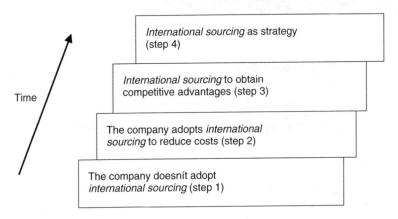

Figure 1.3   The Swamidass model (1993)

The Swamidass model

According to Swamidass (1993), the IS development dynamic is divided into four steps, each characterized by a different motivation (Figure 1.3). At the initial step, a company adopts international sourcing to reduce purchase costs by looking for foreign suppliers able to offer less expensive materials and components (step 2). In the following step, the search for better performances in terms of quality, time, and flexibility compared with the domestic market is added to the 'cost' reason (step 3). Finally, international sourcing itself becomes a strategic asset for the company (step 4), that is, it is considered a decisive competitive lever to support the presence of the company in international markets. Swamidass maintains that if a company skips the other intermediate steps, it is unlikely that it can reach the highest position of the development sequence: in effect, this position is the result of a progressive process.

According to Swamidass, cost was been the main objective of the first IS projects. Since the 1980s, new reasons have arisen, especially the search for better quality materials and the possibility to access resources not available in the domestic market. Finally, nowadays the awareness of the strategic importance of IS and the development of infrastructures to support the international trade represent the main determinants of IS.

The Monczka and Giunipero model

Monczka and Giunipero (1990) propose an international sourcing model divided into the following two steps:

- Step I: operating/transactional
- Step II: planning/managing

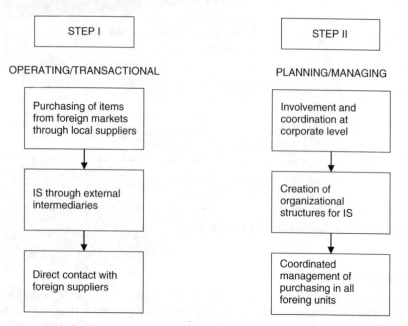

Figure 1.4   The Monczka and Giunipero model (1990)

In the first case, the company adopts IS primarily to reduce purchase costs and to overcome local supply market restrictions. The authors present an operating/transactional approach maintaining that in this step the company starts to face issues linked to the management of international operations and of transactions with foreign interlocutors. In the second step, IS is included in a strategic plan which involves the international development of the company; this plan pursues long–medium-term competitive advantages. For this reason, the company changes its organization creating units dedicated only to IS management (Monczka and Giunipero, 1990).

In detail, the sub-steps composing this model are as shown in Figure 1.4.

Step I: operating/transactional
Acquisition of codes from foreign markets through local suppliers or distributors.
According to the authors, companies adopt IS for the first time in an indirect way, sometimes even unaware that they are doing so, by using products purchased from local suppliers which, however, contain parts purchased abroad. Often, the origin of these items is unknown until it is necessary to change or substitute them.

Foreign purchasing through foreign intermediaries. In this step, the items purchased by the company are often commodities characterized by high labour content. Products are purchased by using intermediaries (brokers, trading companies ...) as the enterprise is not yet able to carry out business transactions with foreign subjects. In this step, the most important goal is to reduce purchase costs.

Direct contacts with foreign suppliers. After gaining experience, the company ceases to use intermediaries and interacts directly with foreign suppliers. Sourcing is extended to more complex products but the main objective is still economic advantage.

Step II: Planning/managing
In this step, IS – previously experienced at reactive level – becomes the subject of a strategic and planning analysis. The objective is to optimise sources and flows at global level, to establish long-term relationships with suppliers, to create organizational units addressed to the international purchasing management. Therefore, *foreign buying offices* (also defined as IPO) are created by involving also subsidiaries, divisions and plants in the sourcing activities.

The Carmel and Agarwal model

Carmel and Agarwal (2002) propose a model divided in four steps, called SITO (Sourcing of IT work Offshore). It summarises the results of a study on a sample of American companies working in the information technology industry. Even though it is a very specific industry, this model exhibits a number of similarities with the the previous models.

In this case, again, there are four developing steps (Figure 1.5).

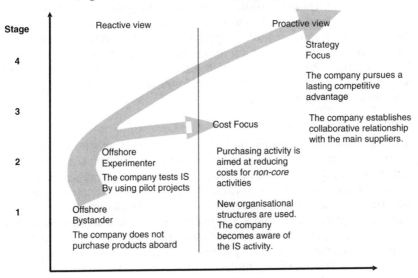

Figure 1.5   The steps of the Carmel and Agarwal model (2002)

Step 1: Offshore bystander. The company does not purchase products abroad. According to the authors, this decision – justified above all by the resistance to change of the personnel – depends on a corporate or divisional culture not oriented to international market and without the experience to manage worldwide projects.

Step 2: Offshore experimenter. The company tests IS projects. Generally, this decision depends on the need to reduce purchase costs. The company starts *ad hoc* projects in order to test IS opportunities and to identify capabilities and skills required within this scope. However, the supplier selection only meets immediate advantage criteria and is limited to the specific project (Carmel and Agarwal, 2002). It is a transient phase: depending on the result experienced, companies go back to the first step or go on to the third one.

Step 3: Proactive cost focus. The company pursues cost reduction objectives . Even if it knows IS advantages, the main objective is cost reduction for non-core activities. In the meantime, the management has developed proper capabilities and experience to manage international relationships efficiently and to create organizational units responsible for foreign sourcing.

Step 4: Proactive strategic focus. IS as a tool to achieve a lasting competitive advantage. The company recognizes international sourcing as a tool to achieve a competitive advantage not only in terms of costs but also to stimulate technological innovation, to develop new products, to favour the access to new markets and to grow at global level (Carmel and Agarwal, 2002). In this step, international suppliers are always involved in the development of new products and are responsible for process synchronization. Moreover, the company recognizes the need for a centralized purchasing coordination in order to achieve economies of scale and accelerate the time-to-market of new products.

Chadwick and Rajagopal taxonomy

Starting from the consideration that IS activities of a multinational company must be examined and structured together with the relevant international manufacturing organization, Chadwick and Rajagopal (1995) propose a taxonomy of the possible sourcing strategies according to two factors: the organizational coordination level of the international sourcing and the geographical distribution of the company manufacturing activities. To select these two factors, the Chadwick and Rajagopal referred to Porter (1986) and his famous taxonomy of the international manufacturing strategies. Figure 1.6 shows the four international sourcing strategies resulting by combining the above mentioned factors.

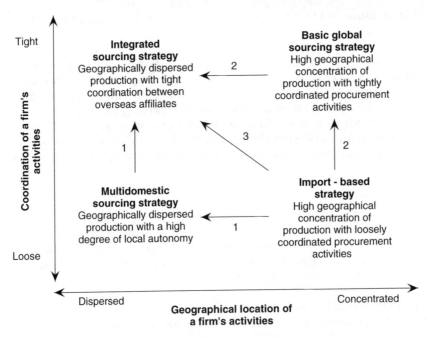

Figure 1.6 A classification of global sourcing strategies (Chadwick and Rajagopal, 1997)

1. *Import-based strategy.* This corresponds to a high geographical centralization of the production activities and a low level of sourcing coordination between productive units and foreign subsidiaries. The (central) purchasing office manages IS completely without creating branches in foreign markets. This structure can be justified by low volumes, by the limited complexity of foreign sourcing or, finally, by the use of intermediaries.
2. *Basic global sourcing strategy.* This corresponds to a high geographical centralization of the production activities and a high coordination level. The (central) purchasing office refers to the foreign units for sourcing and, in the meantime, coordinates overall requirements and flows.
3. *Integrated sourcing strategy.* This corresponds to a high geographical dispersion of the production activities and a high coordination level. It is also defined as 'global sourcing' with reference to companies working within international markets at production and sourcing level and coordinating the supplying networks from a global point of view.
4. *Multidomestic sourcing strategy.* This corresponds to a high geographical dispersion of the production activities and a low coordination level. In this case, the peculiarity of the local market inhibits purchasing integra-

tion forms and flow coordination which are managed by units control-ling single markets.

Moreover, the authors suggest three possible development paths of the IS strategy (numbered arrows in Fig. 1.6), from the 'import-based' to the 'inte-grated' strategy. This transition can occur gradually and the intermediate step can be represented by the 'multidomestic' strategy (the company grad-ually extends its presence in other geographical areas and then develops integration forms between them) or by the 'basic global' strategy (integra-tion and coordination are used to expand the geographical area of the activities).

Arnold taxonomy

Arnold (1999) distinguishes two different IS types according to the combi-nation of two variables: the international involvement level of the company and the centralization level of its organization. Both variables refer to the sourcing activity and to the company activities as a whole; this way four sub-variables are generated:

1. International involvement level of the company
   - International orientation of the company activities
   - International orientation of the company sourcing activities
2. Centralization level of the organizational structure of the company
   - Centralization of the company activities
   - Centralization of the company sourcing activities

By combining the first two sub-variables, Arnold obtains a first matrix showing four types of strategic approaches:

1. Global player (A): company activities, including sourcing ones, have a high international orientation level.
2. Global sourcing focus (B): company activities have a low international orientation level while the international orientation level of the sourc-ing is high.
3. Global sourcing deficit (C): company activities have a high international orientation level while the international orientation level of the sourc-ing is low.
4. Domestic player (D): company activities, including sourcing ones, have a low international orientation level.

By combining the other two sub-variables (organizational centralization level of the company and centralization level of the sourcing activities) the author proposes a second matrix showing four types of organizational approaches (Figure 1.7).

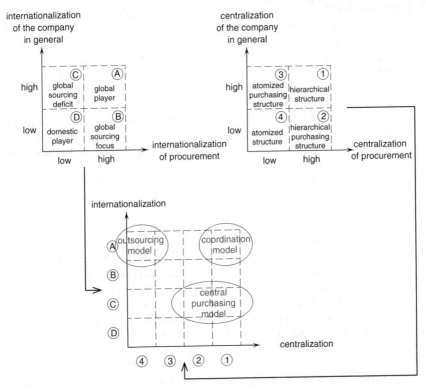

Figure 1.7 Analytical model for global sourcing organization (Arnold, 1999)

Hierarchical structure (1). The organizational centralization of the company is high as well as the centralization of the sourcing activities within the organization.

Hierarchical purchasing structure (2). The organizational centralization of the company is low, while the centralization of the sourcing activities is high.

Atomized purchasing structure (3). The organizational centralization of the company is high, while the centralisation of the sourcing activities is low.

Atomized structure (4). The organizational centralization of the company is low as well as the centralisation of the sourcing activities.

Finally, from the combination of the two above-mentioned matrixes, Arnold (1999) creates a third matrix in which three approaches to international sourcing are defined:

1. *Central purchasing model:* this kind of approach is used by companies characterized by very centralized organizational structures and even if they have global attitudes they are weakly oriented to IS. They assign the responsibility for purchasing management to a central department. By grouping material requirements shared by several manufacturing units, the company increases its market power, generates economies of scale and avoids functional redundancies.
2. *Outsourcing model:* this kind of approach is generally used by companies characterized by very decentralized structures and also having strong international attitudes with regard to sourcing activities. In this case, responsibility for international purchasing is decentralized: each operating unit of the group independently manages these activities.
3. *Coordinated model:* this kind of approach is used by companies characterized by a very centralized organizational structure and also having strong international attitudes with regard to sourcing activities. These companies look for high collaboration between the world-wide distributed units whose common parts and purchasing interdependences are centrally coordinated, even if each unit is given autonomy with regard to specific codes. Each foreign unit can offer an important contribution in managing the international sourcing activities of the group. Exploiting its direct presidium of the foreign market, the unit can easily gather information and keep better control thanks to the knowledge of culture, language, and local business practices.

The above-mentioned theoretical models and taxonomies exhibit evident similarities. For example, they share the IS initial type: the first sourcing from a foreign market is indirectly carried out thanks to intermediaries. Lacking in the right experience in international transactions, companies contact intermediaries and distributors. The main advantage of this kind of sourcing results from the possibility of rapidly creating a foreign sourcing channel, from the limited required experience and resources (appointed to the intermediary) and, finally, from the low or valueless organizational impact: this IS type does not require the creation of specifically dedicated organizational units. Almost all examined models set sourcing activity integration and coordination at global level as the highest step. This step is generally associated with the creation of dedicated structures (IPO) and an exact definition of the organizational responsibilities and tasks assigned to them, especially the decisions concerning the centralization/decentralization of the sourcing activities and the integration and coordination between purchasing functions and other functions (design and production) located within the world-wide distributed units of the multinational group.

With one exception, the described models are considered as inter-industry. In reality they have to be adjusted according to a number of factors, in particular the considered industry and product.

It is important to observe that the studies mentioned generally refer to large enterprises with activities and facilities distributed among several countries. For this kind of company it makes sense to identify a path which can reach the most complete structure of global sourcing by passing through several steps. On the other hand, it is unlikely that small enterprises can employ personnel in IS management, or create decentralized units to control foreign supply markets. Moreover, small enterprises seem to be culturally more linked to the area to which they belong and therefore are less inclined to explore other sourcing opportunities. In these cases, the use of intermediaries may be the right answer to the actual needs.

On the other hand, a large size does not ensure the capability and expertise required by the most developed IS types: creation of International Purchasing Offices, agreements for know-how transfer, coordination of production units abroad, definition of the best (societal) forms to be used in partnership agreements, as well as decentralization of the quality control directly at foreign sources, are processes that require an inter-cultural approach, great flexibility and mutual adaptation, knowledge of the foreign legal-regulating systems, equilibrium between centralized and decentralized requirements.

IS in China

China's opening to international trade and investments has encouraged many scholars to thoroughly analyse characteristics, opportunities, potentialities, and problems of this market. On the basis of a review of the literature, these main streams of research linked to sourcing activities in China have been detected:

- foreign direct investment (FDI). Subjects here analysed are for example: a) opportunities and threats for foreign investors (Luo, 1997; Haley, 2003); b) evolution of the legal norms which discipline these investments (Chadee and Qiu, 2001; Shi, 2001; Sun *et al.*, 2002; Chadee *et al.*, 2003); characteristics of these investments (duration of the agreements, localization of the Chinese partner, investor's nationality, etc.) and their impact on performances (Pan and Li, 1998; Luo, 1999; Chadee and Qiu, 2001; Shi, 2001); the changes they have induced in the industrial/social context (Wu, 2000; Li *et al.*, 2001);
- transfer and implementation of advanced management practices (total quality management, manufacturing resources planning, etc.) by western companies into the Chinese industrial environment (Chin *et al.*, 2002; Tseng *et al.*, 1999; Humphreys *et al.*, 2001; Chung *et al.*, 2004);
- logistic aspects (barriers, inner infrastructures, ICT tools, etc.) (Carter *et al.*, 1997; Daly and Cui, 2003; Lancioni *et al.*, 2003);

Beside these specific streams, other general, 'cross-sectional' topics can be detected:

- Social-cultural aspects connected to business relations with Chinese partners (Björkman and Lu, 1999; Selmer, 1999). Particularly studied in the literature is the influence of the relational nets and the interpersonal relationships ('guanxi') (Gao, 2003; Ambler *et al.*; 1999; Davies *et al.*, 1995);
- Technology transfer in China (influencing factors, opportunity and risks) (De Meyer, 2001; Thompson, 2002; Chen and Sun, 2000).

This literature, however, exhibits some important deficiencies; two in particular:

- there is a lack of studies focused on sourcing modalities other than those based on FDI. Other equally important modalities exist (i.e.: the resort to independent suppliers or to intermediaries), particularly for those (small) enterprises that do not posses adequate financial and managerial resources in order to establish equity participation in China. More generally, the various sourcing modalities are not characterized in terms of features of purchasing items and key competences and resources required in the supply transactions;
- aspects closely linked to organizational and managerial requirements of sourcing activities (selection of purchasing typologies and of Chinese vendors, establishment of an International Purchasing Office (IPO) in China, etc.) are rarely considered.

2
China: the Geo-economic Scenario

Introduction

The main difficulties in the interaction between western countries (in particular European countries) and China are often ascribed to the cultural gap existing among peoples with different histories and customs. The following section of this chapter on China's geo-economic scenario focuses on the historical events of this country. It gives an overview of the multimillennial Chinese culture and of the principal transformations that have led it from the imperialism of the Confucian era to the 'free market socialism' of today.

This chapter also provides some economic data on the so-called 'Chinese miracle'. China's GDP growth pace, which has constantly exceeded 7 per cent in the past few years (often with two-figure increases), and the trade exchange which has increased four-fold in 10 years (registering a hardly-equalled growth rate in the history of the world economy), are only some of the data describing China phenomenon.

The description of the geo-economic scenario concludes with some considerations on the sustainability of China's phenomenon in the future years.

Historical facts

The history of imperial China (also known as the 'Middle Kingdom') starts in 1520 B.C. (when the first official dynasty was historically traced) and ends with a slow decline in 1911. During these centuries, several dynasties followed each other in the govern of the wide Chinese territory; among them the *Ch'in* dynasty, which unified the country and the language in 221 B.C.

The most striking aspect for us as westerners is probably the duration of this boundless empire, which has survived undisturbed by the flow of time and events. The first extraordinary constant factor is the geography of the country: China's territorial boundaries have remained more or less unchanged so far despite the numerous foreign invasions. Another constant element is the cultural continuity: today, Chinese society is still strongly permeated with the Confucian ethic (which takes its name from the teaching of the philosopher Confucius who lived between 551 and 479 B.C.). Even now, Confucian philosophy affects the social and relational habits in this context.

Confucian philosophy condemns individualism, pursuing harmony and social peace: this balance can be guaranteed only if every individual accepts his role in society and identifies with it on the basis of precise dependency relationships and mutual respect (Weber 2003). This has resulted in clear consequences on characteristics and values of Chinese society:

- a strongly hierarchical society;
- the ongoing pursuit of compromise in order to satisfy the group in its entirety, rather than the individual;
- the fundamental and irreplaceable role of the family and clan;
- finally, the importance of the *guanxi*, a central concept in the Chinese society: the mediation of a third party, who acts as friendship guarantor, plays a fundamental role in order to create and preserve the bond between two people. This type of relationship turns into a mutual commitment that can be improved and consolidated through the exchange of gifts and favours (Lassere and Shütte, 1999).

The characteristics of the Confucian philosophy contribute to explain the unity thanks to which the immense Middle Kingdom has lasted for centuries: the creation of a powerful bureaucracy, organized according to a strict hierarchical structure and acknowledged by the entire population, guarantees the functionality and efficiency of the government system characterized by a strong administrative decentralization. China is indeed divided into several provinces; the intervention of the central authority is required only in case of important decisions. The bureaucrats (the so-called 'mandarins') are strictly selected based on their knowledge of the Confucian doctrine.

This articulate administrative system enabled the Chinese empire to survive for centuries and, at the same time, it forged a society model which had considerable repercussions on Chinese history and culture.

The Chinese Communist Party (CCP) gained absolute power over China in 1949, when Mao Zedong proclaimed the birth of the People's Republic of China (PRC). The republic was established after a long period of civil wars between communists and nationalists. Despite initial help from the United States and the numerical superiority of the army and weapons, the nationalist regime of Guomindang (led by Jiang Jieshi) was defeated. The victory of the communists was due to the decline of the Guomindang and to the fact that at the basis of the movement were the peasantry, the ideological power persuasion and the ability to win over the population's trust (Brancati, 2002).

Mao Zedong's China, which emerged from decades of civil wars was, a wrecked country, whose only resource seemed to be the peasant labour force. The new regime gave way to a strongly centralized government structure. The main objective of the new regime was a radical restructuring of the economy by resorting to strict measures to control inflation, organizing peasants in cooperatives and trying to increase the production in rural areas. In the meantime, the industrial production was gradually nationalized.

In those years, the high demographic density was considered such a strong point rather than a problem (as it would turn out to be in a few years) that the government introduced incentives for large families.

The CCP was characterized by the presence of a radical wing (more ideology-oriented) and of a moderate one (more concentrated on the technical aspects and advocating pragmatism), which in the course of time competed for power. The radical wing that in 1960 came into conflict with the Soviet Union initially prevailed. A series of ideological contrasts emerged between the two communist Powers; the Chinese were particularly critical of the Soviet leader Nikita Kruscev, who had been charged with revisionism and treason against the Marxist–Leninist ideals. Beijing openly proposed its leadership as an alternative to the Soviets in the communist world and this generated tension between the two Powers. Thus, the USSR's economic and technical support programme in favour of China was discontinued (Encarta, 2003).

The following period (1978) saw the rise to power of the moderate wing of the CCP led by Deng Xiaoping; this man became the father of the reform which revolutionized the Chinese economy and society. The stages that marked this process of radical change are to be found in the 'decollectivization' programme of the rural structure (1978), in the 'one-son' policy (1978), in the 'open door' policy (1979) and in the reform of urban areas (1984). This sequence of reforms was definitively confirmed in the concept of 'free market socialism' (1993), which marked the overcoming of the 'planned economy' model proposed (and imposed) by Mao Zedong.

The 'decollectivization' of the rural structure was the first step towards a reduced state control on the economy. Although it still wasn't possible to talk about private property, for the first time the concept of individual responsibility was used for land farming. This reform caused the yearly per capita income between 1978 and 1985 to be trebled (Weber 2001).

The real Chinese economic revolution was determined by the 'open door' policy, which preceded the definitive overcoming of the Maoist conception. The first step towards this reform consisted of the creation of Special Economic Zones (SEZs), initially (1979/1980) identified within the province of Guandong (in particular the areas nearby Shenzen, Zhunhai and Shanton), of Fujan (Xiamen) and later on (in 1984) by the island of Hainan. These first experiments were followed by the opening to international trade and foreign investments in a further 14 cities in the coastal area. Thanks to a very favourable rate of income tax (equal to 10–15%), trade and industry tax exemptions, the removal of customs duties for goods in transit, and regulatory improvements concerning the joint venture legislation, the SEZs attracted a record flow of foreign direct investments (according to some estimates, between 1978 and 1999 ones third of the world's total FDIs have flowed into China).

This radical opening to the external world, however, caused social and industrial imbalances. Foreign-owned enterprises offered remarkably higher salary levels than the average, thus underlining the inefficiency of the state-owned enterprises. A number of party executive cadres at the head of these state-owned enterprises were consequently replaced and lost much of their traditional prestige and social control. The most conservative communist leaders were the main mouthpieces of the resulting discontent, being in favour of keeping the strategic economic sectors centralized. In the meantime, disagreements between the moderate and the conservative wings of the CCP were rekindled and made harsher by the protest movement supported by Chinese students and intellectuals. They requested that the economic reforms that took place had to be followed by more democracy and a wider involvement of people in political decisions (Weber, 2001).

When the regime seemed to be on the point of collapse, the supreme head of the CCP (Deng Xiaoping) ordered the intervention of the army. On 4 June 1989, the Chinese government crushed the popular protest in the bloody Tienanmen massacre.

Despite the harsh criticism at international level and the doubts about the real ability of the CCP to sustain the programmed growth while preserving social cohesion, the economic development process did not slow down. On the contrary, it was supported by government initiatives to grant a higher tax autonomy to the provinces and enable the opening (1996) of the first stock exchanges (in Shangai and Shenzen).

The definitive political legitimization of the economic growth model introduced by Deng Xiaoping occurred with the declaration of the 'free-market socialism', which endorsed the coexistence of an (ever weaker) state-controlled economy with capitalism.

With respect to developments of recent years, at least three international events put the solidity of the Chinese model to the test: the crisis in Asia; the terrorist attack on the Twin Towers; and SARS (Severe Acute Respiratory Syndrome).

The financial crisis which hit Asia's economy after 1997 did not cause a slowdown of China's development as some analysts feared: the decrease in trade exchanges with the bordering countries that had been heavily struck by the crisis (Thailand, South Korea, Indonesia, Malaysia and the Philippines) was offset by the import–export growth with the western countries.

The events of 11 September offered the Chinese authorities the opportunity to confirm that they were open to international collaboration; China declared its will to collaborate with western powers in the fight against terrorism. The subsequent slowdown of the world's economy did not curb China's growth, which in 2002 and 2003 registered very positive values.

Moreover, the recent SARS crisis seems to have waned as well; the initial fears of a worldwide spread of the contagion have been overcome. The initial attitude of the Chinese authorities (who tried to cover up the seriousness of the problem) raised some doubts within the international community concerning the guarantees offered by this country. Once the problem had been stemmed, however, western enterprises returned to China to make investments, buy and sell just as much or even more than before.

Between the events of 11 September and the SARS outbreak, the Doha agreement, signed in November 2001, enacted the admission of the People's Republic of China to the World Trade Organization (WTO). Following the opening of this Asian giant's international markets, western countries have benefited from new market opportunities, thanks to the redefinition of the tariff barriers and the acceptance of acknowledged rules (related to contracts, balance sheets, debts, opening to competition, transparency, protection of industrial property, etc.). Thanks to this admission, the Dragon Country has experienced a further increase in direct foreign investments and international trade exchanges.

The macro-economic scenario

The economic prospects of China which, after 11 September and the SARS outbreak, is confidently getting ready for the Beijing Olympic Games (2008) and Shanghai's World Expo (2010), look generally optimistic, though they show a series of issues that will be dealt with in the following sections. The aggregate economic indicators (briefly illustrated in this section) show a country which plays an ever dominant role in the economy at international level.

The GDP

In 2004, the Gross Domestic Product of the People's Republic of China (PRC) reached 1,450 billion dollars with an annual growth of 9.5 per cent. This enabled China to be confirmed as the sixth economic power in the world.

No other nation has seen such a strong surge in the past 10 years: the Chinese GDP often showed two-figure increases (+14.2% in 1992; +13.9%

Table 2.1   Annual growth rate of Chinese GDP

1981–91:	10.2%	1991–95:	12.0%
1996–00:	8.3%	2001:	7.3%
2002:	8.0%	2003:	9.1%
2004:	9.5%		

Source: China Monthly Statistics, National Bureau of Statistics, World Trade Atlas, 1981–2004

in 1993; +13.0% in 1994) and was always well above 7 per cent (Table 2.1). Considering an average yearly growth rate of 8 per cent, according to some estimates China could top Great Britain, France and Germany by 2010, and Japan by 2020.

The trade exchange

Today, China is generally defined as the 'world's factory'. In some sectors in particular (such as the textile-clothing industry and toys) it is possible to combine local manufacturing skills with foreign technology and create good (in many cases even excellent) quality products at prices that are unfeasible in western countries.

In 2003, the Chinese market ranked fourth in the world for its size (Table 2.2), holding 5.5 per cent of the total trade exchange on the entire planet (5.8% of the exports and 5.3% of the imports).

China's yearly growth rates stand up to any comparison: the trade exchange showed a 21.8 per cent increase in 2002, 37.1 per cent in 2003, and 36.5 per cent in 2004, reaching the record value of 1,154.5 billion dollars (Table 2.3). In the light of all this, China is also setting the scene to become one of the key world powers in the trade exchange.

Table 2.2   List of the countries that performed the major trade exchanges in 2003

	USD bil.	Overall exchanges Rate 2003	Yearly % var. (03/02)	Yearly % var. (03/95)
Total	15473	100%		
1. USA	2027	13.1%	+6.%	+5%
2. Germany	1357	8.9%	+22.%	+5%
3. Japan	855	5.6%	+13%	+1%
6. China	**851**	**5.5%**	**+37%**	**+14%**
5. France	791	5.1%	+19%	
6. UK	698	4.5%	+11%	+4%

Source: WTO: International Trade Statistics, 2004

Table 2.3   China's foreign trade performance between 1993 and 2003. Data in USD bil.

	1993	1995	1997	1999	2001	2003	2004	% var. 03/04
Import	103.96	132.08	142.4	165.7	243.6	412.8	560.8	+35.7%
Export	91.74	148.78	182.7	194.9	266.2	438.4	593.7	+35.4%
Exchange	195.7	280.86	325.1	360.6	509.8	851.2	1154.5	+35.6%
Balance	−12.22	16.7	40.3	29.2	22.6	25.53	32.9	

Source: China National Bureau of Statistics and MOFTEC, 2005

In the past 10 years, the international trade exchange has shown an average yearly increase of 16.55 per cent, while in the past five years it rose by 21.85 per cent. Compared to 1993, the import and export volumes growth exceeded 400 per cent going respectively from 103.96 to 412.8 and from 91.74 to 438.4 billion dollars.

It should be noticed how the country's gradual export increase is related to a proportional import growth (although part of the imports is made up of raw materials and semi-finished products processed in Chinese factories to be sold later in the Western countries). Hence, China also represents a flourishing outlet market.

The data represented in Figure 2.1 shows how the Chinese economy does not seem to have been affected by the '11 September effects' (which caused a drop in business flows in several western countries) or by the health crisis that has recently hit the Asian world. Figure 2.2 illustrates instead the extraordinary business exchange acceleration from 1979, the year of the establishment of the 'open door' policy. In the past 20 years, after this

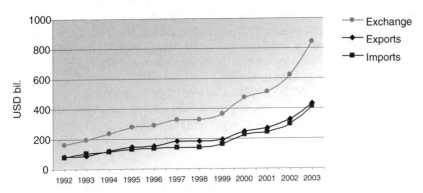

Figure 2.1   China's foreign trade performance between 1992 and 2003
Source: China National Bureau of Statistics, 2004

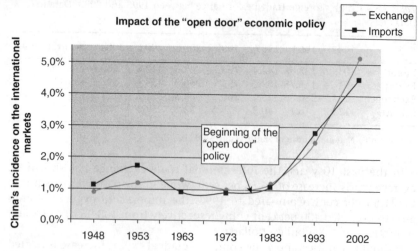

Figure 2.2   Effects of the 'open door' economic policy on the Chinese market incidence in the international trade context
Source: WTO international trade statistics, 2004

political reform came into effect, China has more than redoubled its incidence on the international market.

China's main trade partners are Japan, with a total exchange value of 133.57 billion dollars in 2003, the United States (126.33 billion USD) and the European Union (125.22 billion USD). These three economic areas account for nearly 50 per cent of the total transactions. They are followed by the 'Asian block', composed of the islands of Hong Kong,[1] Taiwan and the countries belonging to the ASEAN (which includes Indonesia, Malaysia, the Philippines, Singapore, Thailand and Vietnam). The 'Asian block' manages about 35 per cent of the total trade exchange.

China has a very favourable trade balance with Hong Kong (a country that still represents a fundamental trade joint), the United States and Europe. The balance is passive with Japan and the other Asian countries (especially Taiwan and South Korea).

Table 2.4 shows China's top 10 trade partners, their trade exchange in the three-year period 2001–03 and the corresponding variations, their rates (see Figure 2.3 for the graphical representation) and related variations. It also shows the trade balance between China and various countries.

Import

In 2004, Chinese imports, having increased by 35.8 per cent compared to 2003, totalled 560.8 billion USD. Japan proved again to be the first among China's suppliers (with 16.8% of the total), followed by Taiwan (11.6%)

Table 2.4 China's ten major trade partners in 2003. Data in USD bil.

Country (region)	Imp/Exp 2001	Imp/Exp 2002	Imp/Exp 2003	Trade bal. 2003	% var. 02/01	% var. 03/02	2001 Rates	2002 Rates	2003 Rates 02/01	Rates var.	Rates var. 03/02
Total	509.66	620.77	851.21		21.8%	37.1%	100.00%	100.00%	100.00%		
1. Japan	87.70	101.91	133.57	−14.76	16.2%	31.1%	17.21%	16.42%	15.69%	−0.79%	−0.72%
2. USA	80.45	97.18	126.33	58.70	20.8%	30.0%	15.78%	15.65%	14.84%	−0.13%	−0.81%
3. EU	76.64	86.76	125.22	18.57	13.2%	44.3%	15.04%	13.98%	14.71%	−1.06%	0.73%
4. Hong Kong	55.95	69.21	87.41	60.41	23.7%	26.3%	10.98%	11.15%	10.27%	0.17%	−0.88%
5. ASEAN	41.59	54.77	78.25	−17.07	31.7%	42.9%	8.16%	8.82%	9.19%	0.66%	0.37%
6. Taiwan	32.33	44.65	63.23	−40.51	38.1%	41.6%	6.34%	7.19%	7.43%	0.85%	0.24%
7. Korea	35.89	44.07	58.37	−23.57	22.8%	32.4%	7.04%	7.10%	6.86%	0.06%	−0.24%
8. Russia	10.67	11.93	15.76	−3.78	11.8%	32.1%	2.09%	1.92%	1.85%	−0.17%	−0.07%
9. Australia	9.00	10.44	13.56	−1.00	16.0%	29.9%	1.77%	1.68%	1.59%	−0.08%	−0.09%
10. Canada	7.37	7.93	10.01	1.12	7.6%	26.2%	1.45%	1.28%	1.18%	−0.17%	−0.10%

Source: China Council for the Promotion of International Trade, 2004

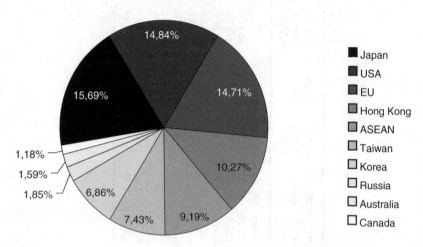

China's ten major trade partners in 2003

■ Japan
■ USA
■ EU
□ Hong Kong
□ ASEAN
□ Taiwan
□ Korea
□ Russia
□ Australia
□ Canada

14,84%
15,69%
14,71%
1,18%
1,59%
1,85%
6,86%
7,43%
9,19%
10,27%

Figure 2.3   The shares of China's ten major trade partners in 2003
Source: China Council for the Promotion of International Trade, 2004

and South Korea (11.1%). Germany (which saw its exports grow by 23.6% between 2003 and 2004), Russia and France are the top three European suppliers (Table 2.5).

In 2003, the foreign-owned enterprises held 56.2 per cent of the imported goods. In most cases, these goods came from the foreign investors' countries of origin, they were processed in China and then re-exported to their countries of origin.

In the commodity composition of the imports (Table 2.6) we see a clear predominance of instrumental mechanics to confirm the country's need for foreign technology. Furthermore, as already pointed out, a considerable percentage of the total imports is made up of semi-finished products that are processed in China to be re-exported to the countries of origin.

Export

China's exports in 2004 have increased by 35.4 per cent (compared to 34.6% in 2003), reaching 593.7 USD and proving not to have been affected by the general economic slowdown. China's exports have benefited from several factors, such as the local currency depreciation (the reminbi, RMB) and the lengthy procedures required to be admitted into the WTO (which occurred in 2001). A further factor explaining the results of these past two years can be identified in the nature of the exported products: compared to other Asian nations, China's exports are characterized by a higher presence

Table 2.5   Chinese imports: main supplying countries (1998–2004)

	1998	1999	2000	2001	2002	2003	2004	2004 Rates	% var. 04/03
Total	140.4	165.7	225.1	243.6	295.2	412.8	560.81	100.0%	35.8%
1. Japan	28.3	33.8	41.5	42.8	53.4	74.2	94.2	16.8%	27.0%
2. Taiwan	17	19.5	25.5	27.3	38	49.4	64.8	11.6%	31.2%
3. South Korea	15	17.2	23.2	23.4	28.5	43.1	62.2	11.1%	44.0%
4. USA	16.7	19.5	22.4	26.2	27.2	33.9	44.7	8.0%	31.8%
5. Germany	7	8.3	10.4	13.7	16.4	24.3	30.2	5.4%	23.6%
6. Malaysia	2.7	3.6	5.5	6.02	9.2	14.0	18.2	3.2%	29.8%

Source: China Monthly Statistics, 2001–03; World Trade Atlas – China Edition, 2005

of low value added goods, which were less affected than others by the crisis of the international demand (source: ICE Beijing, 2004).

Again the US market (with a 21.1% rate of growth) proved to be the main outlet market also in 2004, followed by Hong Kong (17.0%) and Japan (12.4%). The European Union holds more than 10 per cent of Chinese exports, registering a strong growth in 2003 thanks to the depreciation of the reminbi against the euro. Germany, Holland, the United Kingdom, France and Italy are China's main European customers (see Table 2.7).

With respect to the commodity composition (Table 2.8), the most significant rate is represented by the mechanical and electronic products sector (which alone represents more than 30% of the total exports of the country). Although such productions are mainly characterized by a 'mature' technology, the predominance of this commodity class shows how China is distancing itself from the economic industrial profile typical of the emerging countries.

From an analysis of the export companies emerges that over one-half of the exports originates from foreign-owned enterprises (54.8% compared to 31.5% of the state-controlled enterprises).

Direct investments

Mainly attracted by a low-cost labour force and an internal market of considerable size, a large number of multinational companies are currently investing in China. Attracting foreign investors is in fact one of the main objectives of the Chinese government, aware that only the transfer of capitals and technologies to China will enable the country to advance quickly in the process of industrial modernization.

The foreign direct investments (FDIs) allocated in 2004 equalled 66 billion USD. With these results China wins the first place in the world in terms of foreign investments attraction.

Table 2.6   Commodity composition of China's imports from the world

Commodity composition of China's imports from the world	Year 2001	Year 2002	Year 2003	Year 2004	% Var. 04/03
Total value of imports	243.6	295.2	413.1	560.8	+39.9
Machinery and mechanical instruments, machinery and electric equipment and their components; recorders and sound reproducer, televisions and parts/accessories of these items (codes 84 and 85)	96.5	125.4	175.6	233.6	+33.0
Mineral fuels, mineral oils and products extracted from their distillation; bituminous substances; mineral wax (code 27)	17.5	19.3	29.3	48.0	+63.9%
Plastics and similar items (code 39)	15.3	17.4	21.0	28.0	+33.4%
Iron and steel (code 72)	10.9	13.2	22.2	23.6	+6.3%
Optical, photographic, film, measurement, control, precision medical and surgical instruments and equipment: relative components/accessories (code 90)	9.8	13.5	25.1	40.1	+59.6%
Organic chemical products (code 29)	9.0	11.2	16	23.8	+48.7%
Vehicles (except railway and tram vehicles); airplanes, air space vehicles, their components and accessories (codes 87 and 88)	9.0	10.5	16.3	17.9	+9.9%
Copper and copper items (code 74)	4.9	5.7	7.2	10.5	+46.3%
Minerals, wastes and ashes (code 26)	4.2	4.3	7.2	17.3	+140.6%
Paper and cardboard; products made of paper or cardboard (code 48)	3.7	4.1	4.4	4.6	+5.5%
Other	62.8	70.6	88.8	113.3	–

Source: China Monthly Statistics, 2001–2003; World Trade Atlas – China Edition, 2005

Table 2.7 China's exports 1998–2003: main target countries

	1998	1999	2000	2001	2002	2003	2004	2004 Rates	% var. 04/03
Total	**183.8**	**194.9**	**249.2**	**266.9**	**325.6**	**438.4**	**438.4**	**100.0%**	**35.4%**
1. USA	38	41.9	52.1	54.3	69.9	92.5	125.0	21.1%	35.1%
2. Hong Kong	38.8	36.9	44.5	46.6	58.4	76.3	101.1	17.0%	32.5%
3. Japan	29.7	32.4	41.7	45.1	48.4	59.4	73.5	12.4%	23.7%
4. South Korea	6.3	7.8	11.2	12.5	15.4	20.1	27.8	4.7%	38.3%
5. Germany	7.4	7.8	9.3	9.8	11.3	17.5	23.8	4.0%	36.2%
6. Holland	5.2	5.4	6.7	7.3	9.1	13.5	18.5	3.1%	37.2%
7. United Kingdom	4.6	4.9	6.3	5.8	8.1	10.8	15.0	2.5%	38.3%

Source: China Monthly Statistics, 2001–03; World Trade Atlas – China Edition, 2005

Table 2.8   Commodity composition of China's exports to the world

Commodity composition of China's exports to the world	Year 2001	Year 2002	Year 2003	Year 2004	% var. 03–04
Total value of exports	**84.9**	**115.9**	**438.5**	**593.6**	**+35.4%**
Machinery and mechanical instruments, machinery and electric equipment and their components; recorders and sound reproducer, televisions and parts/accessories of these items (codes 84 and 85)	32.4	36.5	152.4	248.0	+43.8%
Clothing (code 61 and 62)	10.1	11.1	45.8	54.8	+19.7%
Shoes, gaiter and similar items (code 64)	9.1	11.6	13.0	15.2	+17.4%
Toys, sports items and objects; their components/ accessories (code 95)	8.5	8.4	13.3	15.1	+13.6%
Mineral fuels, mineral oils and products extracted from their distillation; bituminous substances; mineral wax (code 27)	7.6	9.9	11.1	14.5	+30.3%
Furniture: beds, mattress, mattress supports, pillows and similar upholstered items; lamps, lights and lighting accessories not included or specified elsewhere; light objects and plates and similar items; prefabricated buildings (code 94)	7.0	7.8	12.9	17.3	+34.3%
Optical, photographic, film, measurement, control, precision medical and surgical instruments and equipment: relative components/accessories (code 90)	6.7	8.0	9.5	16.7	+53.9%
Plastics and similar items (code 39)	6.5	7.4	10.0	13.1	+31.3%
Other	103.9	109.0	156.4	189.1	–

Source: China Monthly Statistics, 2001–03; World Trade Atlas – China Edition, 2005

Table 2.9 Main forms of investment in China 2001–03

	2001		2002		2003	
	Value	% of tot. no.	Value	% of tot. no.	Value	% of tot. no.
Total	46.85	100%	52.74	100%	53.50	100%
EJV	16.25	34.7%	14.99	28.4%	14.66	27.4%
CJV	6.06	12.9%	5.06	9.6%	4.01	7.5%
WFOE	23.55	50.3%	31.73	60.2%	34.19	63.9%
Holding	0.46	1.0%	0.07	0.1%	0.05	0.1%

Source: China Ministry of Foreign Trade and Economic Cooperation, US–China Business Council, MOFTEC

In 2003, the number of new enterprises financed by foreign capital was 41,798, making a total of 465,994 companies since the 1978 reform.

As regards the types of investments made, the establishment of wholly foreign-owned enterprises (WFOE) represents the most common type of foreign direct investment. In the last three years, it was worth more than 60 per cent of the overall investments, followed by joint ventures in the 'equity' (30% of the FDIs on the whole) and 'contractual' forms (less then 10%). As shown in Table 2.9, the holdings are still not numerous (an in-depth study on issues related to foreign investments is contained in Chapter 7).

Hong Kong continues to be the first investor in China, holding one third of the direct investments. Its incidence on the total FDIs has however has dropped since 1997, when this ex-British colony was returned to China.

The mid-term analysis (Table 2.10) shows a strong rise in the capital inflow from industrialized countries. These data represent a sign of maturity of China's economy and industrial system, which seems to be increasingly opening to the international markets. Thus, investing in China seems to be less difficult now for all companies (even for use that are more dissimilar from the Chinese culture and business practices).

The results are also interesting in terms of outbound FDIs: Chinese companies registered abroad reached 6,796 units at the end of 2002, with a total of 97.2 billion dollars of investments.

Other economic parameters

Industrial production

In past years, industrial growth has been substantial. The industrial sectors that have mostly contributed to such growth are electronics, telecommunications, transportation and chemical industry.

Table 2.10   Main investors in China. Amounts in billion USD

Country	1997	1998	1999	2000	2001	2002	2003	% 1997	% 2003
Total	52.4	45.6	40.4	40.7	46.8	52.7	53.5	100%	100%
1 Hong Kong	21.5	18.5	16.4	15.5	16.7	17.8	17.7	41.03%	33.08%
2 Virgin Islands	1.7	4.0	2.7	3.8	5.0	6.1	5.78	3.24%	10.80%
3 South Korea	2.2	1.8	1.3	1.5	2.15	2.7	4.49	4.20%	8.39%
4 Japan	4.4	3.4	3	2.9	4.3	4.1	5.05	8.40%	0.40%
5 U.S.A.	3.5	3.9	4.2	4.4	4.4	5.4	4.2	6.68%	7.85%
6 Taiwan	3.3	2.9	2.6	2.3	2.9	3.9	3.38	6.30%	6.32%
7 Cayman Islands	0.2	0.3	0.4	0.6	1.06	1.1	0.87	0.38%	1.63%
8 Singapore	2.6	3.4	2.6	2.2	2.14	2.3	5.05	4.96%	9.44%
9 West Samoa	0.2	0.1	0.2	0.3	0.5	0.87	0.99	0.38%	1.85%
10 Nederland	0.4	0.7	0.5	0.79	0.78	0.57	0.73	0.76%	1.36%
11 Deutschland	1.0	0.7	1.4	1.0	1.2	0.92	0.86	1.91%	1.61%
12 United Kingdom	1.8	1.2	1.1	1.2	1.05	0.89	0.74	3.44%	1.38%
13 Australia	0.3	0.3	0.3	0.3	0.3	0.38	0.59	0.57%	1.10%
14 Canada	0.3	0.3	0.3	0.3	0.4	0.58	0.56	0.57%	1.05%
15 Mauritius	0.1	0.1	0.2	0.26	0.3	0.48	0.52	0.19%	0.97%
16 Macao	0.4	0.4	0.3	0.35	0.3	0.46	0.42	0.76%	0.79%
17 France	0.5	0.3	0.9	0.9	0.5	0.575	0.60	0.95%	1.12%
18 Malaysia	0.4	0.3	0.2	0.2	0.26	0.36	0.25	0.76%	0.47%
19 Italy	0.2	0.3	0.2	0.2	0.21	0.17	0.32	0.38%	0.60%

Source: Data from China Statistical Yearbook 1997–2003[2]

Local joint-stock companies have registered the best results (with a production growth of 14.1%), followed by foreign companies (+13.3%), state-owned companies (+11.7%) and joint ventures (+8.6%).

The growth rates of heavy and light industry are comparable. The former, especially boosted by the new infrastructures works, experienced a growth of 13.1 per cent (231.2 billion dollars); while the latter saw a rise of 12.1 per cent, due to a higher demand for consumer goods by families (148.1 billion dollars).

Per capita income

In terms of wages, China is characterized by marked differences between the inland and costal areas (in particular the Special Economic Zones, SEZ). The main development boost comes straight from these areas (Guangdong, Beijing, Shanghai, Zhejiang) where the yearly average per capita income of the population exceeds 1000 euro (as against an yearly average income of about 300 euro in rural areas), and where wages have reached levels comparable to those in the west.

Retail sales

In 2002, retail sales exceeded 484 billion dollars, an 8.8 per cent growth compared to 2001. As a result of a reduction in customs duties (following China's admission to the WTO), the car industry achieved the most significant growth (+73% on an annual basis). With 1.1 million cars sold, China represents the third largest world market in this industrial sector. The telecommunication industry ranks second following the car industry in terms of expansion (with an increase of 69.2% compared to the previous year.)

General retail price index

The positive performance of retail sales has had a remarkable affect on the consumer prices trend, which exceeded 3 per cent in 2004 (see Table 2.11). This high rate of price growth is casting doubts over the government's effort to rein in the booming economy.

Table 2.11   The Chinese general retail price ratio

	1998	1999	2000	2001	2002	2003	2004
General retail price index	−2.6%	−2.9%	−1.5%	−0.6%	−1.3%	−0.1%	+3%

Source: Data from China Monthly Statistics, 1998–2004.

Employment

Unemployment and under-employment represent important issues in the ongoing debate on the future of China's economic reforms (see conclusions below). The modernization and change of China's economy and its industrial system have brought wealth, but at the cost of unemployment for many. According to data circulated by the Chinese Ministry of Labour and Social Security, in 2003 approximately 4.4 million workers coming from publicly-owned companies were hired by the private sector. An important part of the workers sacked by publicly-owned companies, however, has not succeeded in being hired in the private sector, causing a slight increase (+0.3%) in the official unemployment rate (in 2003 this reached 4.3%).

Research

An aspect of the Chinese territory which arouses interest is its lively scientific and technological development: research in China is a national priority since it attracts 63 billion dollars of investments per year (given these figures, China ranks third in the world behind the USA and Japan). The results of years of heavy investments in this sector are taking shape in the technological corporate profiles, which in some cases are even more advanced than in Western countries.

Current transformations and related problems

The reform of the Chinese industrial system

Before 1978, the Chinese industrial system was extensively supported by the SOEs (state-owned enterprises), which covered about 75 per cent of production (the remaining 25% was supplied by joint ventures); the SOEs did not limit themselves to dealing with the aspects related to production, but also carried out some fundamental social functions. Besides receiving a wage for their work activity, the employees also enjoyed accommodations at a 'political price': health care service and retirement benefits.

This welfare system managed by the SOEs was strictly connected to other Chinese social life areas. The reform of the industrial system entailed substantial changes to a series of structural factors related to it.

At the beginning of the 1990s, when the Chinese government decided to restructure China's production structure, over 300,000 SOEs employed about two-thirds of the industrial labour force; according to some estimates, around one third of the workers were made redundant. These companies' productivity was very low (in 1995 they contributed to only 35% of the industrial output). Furthermore, the SOEs had to carry the burden of the general incompetence of those managers who held the most prominent positions because of political merit rather than for their real technical and managerial skills. They proved unable to introduce innovations and to manage the changes required by the increase in activity volumes.

Moreover, the lack of managerial quality and preparation was worsened by spreading corruption.

As a result, almost all the SOEs had to close at a loss.

It is easily understood that any reform capable of tackling the problems relating to the transformation of the industrial system should have been introduced gradually. Indiscriminate liberalization would have caused uncontrollable social crumbling.

One of the first interventions made by the Chinese government regarding the structure of its own industry was agglomeration: the industrial system was and still is strongly fragmented with a number of small-sized units incapable of supporting development investments and often burdened with balance sheets problems. Hence the need (depending on the industrial production) to merge some SOEs according to the production industries, to sell some others to private individuals, and to adjudicate a state of bankruptcy for enterprises with excessive debts.

The government decided to count on about 500 SOEs; they represented less than 0.5 per cent of the total SOEs but produced more than 65 per cent of the profits (Weber, 2003).

To understand the deep transformation that took place, it should be noted that 11 large Chinese enterprises were ranked in the 'Fortune' 500 (Atti, 2003).

The social effects of the SOE's restructuring process

This process of industrial modernization, although gradual, caused the dismissal of numerous redundant labourers; subsequently, after joining the WTO, this trend seemed to intensify, to the point that the restructuring process of the SOEs has now caused the dismissal of 26 million state employees (source: Italian Embassy in China, 2003).

The problem of unemployment is heightened by the crisis in the rural sector, which is causing the migration of a large number of workers from the rural areas to the big cities.

To face over-manning, the Chinese government:

- has taken measures aimed at favouring the activities of private enterprises and increasing the inflow of foreign investments;
- has increased state investment in infrastructures;
- has introduced a welfare system for the labourers dismissed by SOEs (or by JVs).

Clearly these benefits cannot be compared to the European social security cushions, but they represent an initial step for stronger labour protection (regulations required by the admittance to the WTO).

The pension reform strongly connected with the restructuring of SOEs seems to be still under discussion: the opening of China to international competition has led the Chinese government towards a more westernized view of pension expenses, which are based on a threefold support system constituted by the state, the enterprises and the individuals. As a result, China opened its doors to numerous foreign insurance companies, which proposed pension funds, health and life insurances.

A further issue related to the SOE's reform concerns labourers' accommodation which, as mentioned before, was provided by SOEs: this caused further demands on their budgets. This situation also determined a lack of labour mobility. In recent years, several initiatives have been launched to enable the renting or buying of houses; furthermore, since 1999, SOE employees have been unable to obtain accommodation on preferential terms, but at the same time they are able to contract loans for the purchase of houses.

Uneven growth

The deep transformation brought about by Deng Xiaopingh, suggested the adoption of a gradual approach by the Chinese government: initially, the opening to foreign investors involved only special economic zones (SEZs). This enabled the Chinese authorities to control the process of economic growth, to evaluate its effects, to take suitable corrective measures; at the same time, however, it created big gaps between the 'open' areas (the SEZs and subsequently the 14 coastal cities) and the rest of China.

Some data can explain these gaps: the industrial production growth rate granted by the SEZs between 1984 and 1991 amounted to 282 per cent of the country's average, the GDP/population ratio was 9,810 reminbi against a national average of 1,570 reminbi; although the 14 coastal cities included only about 3 per cent of the population, they produced 10 per cent of the national wealth (Weber, 2001).

Within a few years, egalitarianism, as an essential element of Maoism, has been replaced by an increasing disparity between the cities and the rural areas: in 2004, the yearly income in the cities exceeded 1,000 dollars, three times as much in the rural areas. This factor, along with a more generalized crisis of agrarian production, has induced the population to migrate to the cities.

The infrastructures

The capillarity and the quality of the transport network in China has registered a rapid growth in the past few years.

Until 20 years ago, most products were produced locally for local markets according to plans and rules of the planned economy. This hindered the development of suitable transportation and distribution channels in the rural areas. In this regard it should be pointed out that until no more than

10 years ago, 25–30 per cent of agricultural products perished before reaching the target markets. Deliveries from Shanghai to Guangzhou (1,945 km) took on average 25 days to reach their destination. From Shanghai to Beijing (1,462 km) they took at least 21 days. Deliveries to internal areas were even slower: from Shanghai to Xian (1,511 km) the time required was 45 days (Speece and Kawahara, 1995).

With respect to the railway system, for a long time Chinese development plans assigned a very low priority to the construction of the rail network. During the first 10 years of reforms (1981–90), the investments in favour of this transportation industry only amounted to 1.4 per cent of GDP, about half as much as the figures shown by the other developing countries (Speece and Kawahara, 1995).

The quality of the Chinese road system, despite its great importance, was not satisfactory (in 1999, 75% of nearly 130 million tons of shipped goods were transported through the road network). In 1993, only 20 per cent of the 1.08 million kilometres of Chinese roads were paved and about one quarter of the roads could not be easily used in rain and bad weather (Speece and Kawahara, 2001).

The current situation is very different from that just described. Recent development plans have invested considerable resources in the improvement of the transportation system. Today, therefore, the situation is more suitable for the requirements of foreign investors, both from the point of view of the capillarity and the quality of the main transportation routes.

A problem which is still unresolved concerns the infrastructure difference between the coastal the inland areas. In recent years, important projects have been launched with the purpose of creating main roads capable of connecting more easily both the internal and coastal areas and also the Northern and Southern areas.

(An in-depth analysis of this issue is contained in Chapter 8 of this book, dedicated to the transportation system in China.)

Pollution

The industrial production growth in China has also brought the problem of toxic gas discharges into the atmosphere.

The emission/energy ratio produced in China is much higher than the European standards. This is due to the almost exclusive use of coal (extracted from local mines), which covers about 75 per cent of China's energy requirements and which is burnt in particularly inefficient small thermal plants.

The government, however, is taking special measures to curb environmental pollution which has become unsustainable in some area and is causing sharp disagreements with neighbouring countries (in particular with Japan). New plans have been recently approved for the exploitation of new energy resources, in particular methane (of which there are fields in

China's Sea and in nearby northeast Russia), and hydroelectric energy (the famous and disputed Three Throats project, which environmentalists believe could cause blatant eco-system transformations along the Yellow River).

Evidence of the Chinese government's good intentions is given by the endorsement of numerous international conventions on environmental protection, such as the Prime Minister's declaration to subscribe to the Kyoto Protocol (although China is still considered a developing country and therefore is not obliged to ratify the Protocol).

However, despite the official declaration, the environmental problem does not actually represent a priority for the Chinese government.

Price increase of raw materials

The price increase of raw materials since 2002 has been considerable and, in some sectors, it has exceeded a 60 per cent annual growth rate (source: Goldman Sachs's general index).

Among the reasons for such a decisive price increase, the main cause can be ascribed to China's extremely rapid economic development and the related strong rise in domestic demand. This growth affects different sectors: from wheat to cotton, from soy to maize, from oil to carbon coke for steel production. For example, the price of wheat increased by 20 per cent in the last half of 2003, while the price of cotton experienced a 60 per cent boost, driven by the abundant supply activity of the Chinese textile industry 'eager for production' (Figure 2.4).

These sensitive rises of raw materials' prices have heavily affected whole industrial sectors, which have faced huge costs increases in the span of a few months. In some cases, due to a shortage of raw materials (exhausted by the Chinese market demands), some supplies have been denied to western companies.

The situation of the iron and metallurgical industry is particularly serious. Since China, as the world's first producer of raw steel, is increasing

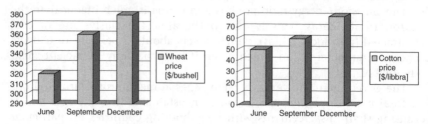

Figure 2.4   The trend of wheat and cotton prices in the second half of 2003
Source: ChartBook, 2004

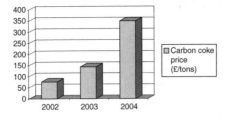

Figure 2.5 Price trend of carbon coke
Source: Federacciai, 2004

its production capacity at a pace of 30–40 tons per year (the Italian yearly production is 26 tons), the supply of carbon coke is beginning to run short. In the world market, carbon coke quotations rose from 79 dollars per ton in 2002 to 143 in 2003 to 350 in the first half of 2004, showing a 343 per cent increase (Figure 2.5).

Furthermore, the rapid increase of the Chinese domestic demand is causing strong price rises and serious problems of availability of raw materials, which tend to be used to meet the country's domestic needs. This phenomenon is not only undermining the iron and steel industry, but also the whole international industrial structure linked to the use of semi-finished products made of steel, cast-iron and non-ferrous metals (for example car and building sectors).

The difficulty of sourcing raw materials and their price increase is the most recent problem that China's ongoing development is causing at international level. Among all the problems we have analysed so far, this represents one of the events which is most strongly affecting the supply strategies of western companies.

Conclusions

The data provided in this chapter give an idea of China's extraordinary economic development. Today this country is the fourth key player in international trade and the sixth economic power in the world. This rapid development is the result of a transparent economic and industrial project, started 25 years ago with the 'open door' policy and carried on with some temporary setbacks (Tienanmen) until today. Quite often, the analyses have only considered the cost differentials allowed by this market. The cost variable is certainly important, but taken alone it cannot justify the two-figure growth rates and the capacity to attract foreign investments which remains unrivalled in other countries. In fact, other Asian markets are just as attractive or even more enticing from this point of view.

The difference finds its origin in an economic and industrial policy based on some distinctive resources, which have gradually prepared the ground for new developments. The first resource is undoubtedly the number of population living there. Over 1.3 billion inhabitants compose the main labour force reservoir (which is very competitive and so will remain for a long time), which represents the main potential sales market in the world. Moreover China is a sub-continent with a large quantity of raw materials (placed in a key position taking into account the other Asian markets) and relying on a consolidated tradition in some industrial sectors and on an ancient trade attitude.

Based on these resources, the State has introduced special incentives for foreign investments. It has created special economic areas, developed massive logistic platforms to facilitate inter-continental transportation, and offered mutual exchange conditions to foreign operators to favour local industry development and the transfer of technology from Western countries. For a long time China turned a blind eye to the issues of forging and counterfeiting trademarks and ignored the strong environmental impact of certain technologies and production processes to which it resorted to support its initial turbulent industrialization phase. To enter the WTO it has also wrung out preferential conditions which were accepted by the western pasties eager to control this country as soon as possible.

Today, we witness a second development phase requiring higher rigour and discipline in order to recognize China as a reliable partner for western countries. In this new season, a significant role has been played by the recent visits of the Chinese premier who has concluded important trade agreements and underwritten his commitment to respect trademarks and patents. China has developed specific regulations on this matter (along with the one related to company law) offering more guarantees to foreign operators. The Olympic Games of 2008 and Expo 2010 also represent occasions eagerly pursued by the government to boost the development further and to make the 'made in China' image renowned in the world (an aspect which is probably the weakest point in Chinese production at the moment).

Some further data which should induce reflection on the government's precise design relate to the investment efforts in research and development. According to some estimates, China can count on 750,000 operative researchers: this number has doubled in the past 20 years. Academy of Sciences alone, the backbone of the Chinese research system, employs 60,000 scientists in basic and technological research. Research is a national priority; 63 thousand billion dollars have been invested. This puts China in third place in the world for research investments behind the USA and Japan. China, which in the past was considered the country of trademark counterfeiting, is now becoming very competitive in research and innovation, the very activities in which western countries would have to invest to distinguish themselves from the Asian market.

The basis of the Chinese success is a clear long-term development project. We think that this different planning ability is the real distinctive aspect of China compared not only to other Asian countries, but also to Europe, or at least to some of its countries.

In this overall positive picture, however, some shadows are looming.

Social inequalities are huge and are becoming bigger year by year; development is completely heterogeneous in the territories; unemployment has increased following the restructuring process of the SOEs; the welfare system is basically missing. The legal system is still flawed under in different areas and there is real risk of a crash in the banking system: the big four banks of the country (the Big Four) have to tackle serious solvency problems due to excessive credit carelessly granted in the past.

Furthermore, the country still lacks infrastructures: the road network is still insufficient, railway transport is inadequate as is the river network. Other problems concern pollution and environmental protection, irrigation and purification of the water supply systems, public healthcare, corruption and infringement of tax liability.

Undoubtedly, this country still has many problems to tackle. However, if we look at the results it has achieved in the past few years and the path covered, the impression is that China has the potential to advance further. More than its recent history, what gives us this conviction is the analysis of some researchers we have checked in the course of this study. Nowadays, China is characterized by a widespread awareness of a new destiny for the country, a new future. Its population feels 'on the march' again as part of a collective project that raises hopes for a future common welfare, and that today generates that social consensus indispensable for leading the massive transformation at which we are looking.

Notes

1. Although part of China, Hong Kong is still a special region which maintains its cultural, geographical and economic identity.
2. The table considers only investments with effective utilization.

3
The Research

Introduction

The data concerning the China phenomenon reported in the previous chapter clearly explain why enterprises are looking at this market with a growing interest. Notwithstanding its importance, only a few studies have been conducted on IS from China. Various studies have been published in recent years on Chinese economic and political geography issues. Other contributions analyse juridical themes with reference, for example, to Chinese company law and to the opportunities and restraints linked to the realization of foreign direct investments. Nevertheless, only a few works consider the decisive issues linked to the problems related to the management of sourcing activities.

The research project *International Sourcing Strategies for China* has focused exactly on these topics. It has been co-financed by the European Union and coordinated by the authors in cooperation with the partnership of the Otto-von-Guericke University of Magdeburg (Germany), the National Center for Science and Technology Valuation (NCSTE) in Beijing (a Chinese institution specialized in the valuation of scientific and technological development projects) and finally INNOVA S.p.A., an Italian company leader in technological transfer and strategic consultancy for innovation.

Being aware of the increasing importance of the Chinese market, the European Union has activated the 'Asia IT&C' programme, which aims to promote IT research and organizational solutions capable of managing International Supply Chain relations between European and Chinese SMEs in the best way. The following section provides an overview of the project's objectives and methods, and the companies that we examined. Some evidence which emerged from the analysis of the case studies is then shown, while the results linked to the sourcing typologies observed in the sample and the main IS critical points in China will be further discussed in the next chapters.

Objectives and methodology

The objectives of the research project were as follows:

- To analyse IS choices within the company's path to internationalization. One of the possible types of internationalization is that concerning sourcing. In the first chapter IS determining factors, advantages, obstacles and forms are pointed out, highlighting how this choice must be consistently integrated with those concerning other functions, in particular that related to *international manufacturing*.
- To qualify the IS choices in general and those related to IS from China in particular, with reference to the selection criteria of supply markets, the suppliers' selection criteria, and purchase codes.
- To analyse the cultural, contractual, and logistic issues associated to sourcing from China. In particular we tried to identify the peculiarities of the negotiation process, of the purchase contracts (terms of payment, know-how transfer, duration). As far as logistic issues are concerned, the analysis considers transport modes, delivery terms, obstacles linked to the geographical distance, if any, and additional costs deriving from the coordination of logistic flows on an inter-continental scale.
- To identify the organizational and management solutions used in sourcing from China, and their development path. We have tried to isolate the phases through which a purchasing channel from China has been set up: information sources, organizational responsibilities and their possible decentralization to peripheral units (IPO), supply chain control and monitoring tools.

Finally, we check whether the developed solutions identify a ruling strategy and a common path or whether there is a variety of strategic options dependent on context factors, such as: business size, industry, type of purchase codes, development stage of the IS.

The methodology we have chosen is that of case studies, since the aspects analysed were not suitable for a standard survey tool, but rather for a quality analysis of single experiences and situations.

For this reason, a check list has been prepared subdivided in four sections:

1) *General characteristics of the company*. Information about juridical form, turnover and employee number, organizational structure and characteristics of the market and the products manufactured.
2) *International sourcing areas*. This section contains information about: value of the international purchases and their geographic distribution; criteria for the supply market choice; type of codes bought in China and

on the other foreign markets; success factors and failure to resort to foreign supply areas.

3) *Organization of international purchases.* This section contains information about the organization of the purchasing function, in particular about the use of personnel specialized in transactions with foreign countries, the creation of an IPO (International Purchasing Office), the resort to intermediaries, the criteria for the work division among buyers (geographical area, product class, etc.).

4) *Management of international purchases.* This section contains information about: information sources used; selection criteria of the Chinese suppliers; negotiation process and contractual agreements; areas and intensity of buyer–supplier operational cooperation and integration (i.e. in product development and flow synchronization); transport modes and logistic issues; vendor control and monitoring; development steps of the supply relationships; supporting ICT infrastructure.

The sample

The companies on which the analysis was conducted were selected within industries in which the China–Italy trade exchange is more developed.

The sample includes different-sized companies in order to investigate the possible effects of dimension on the IS process considered here. With respect to the possibility of small and medium-sized enterprises having access to international supply markets, the literature offers conflicting indications. Some authors (Arnold, 1989; Min and Gall, 1991) highlight that SMEs have insufficient financial and management resources for international growth; on the other hand others (Scully and Fawcett, 1994) argue that the reduction of transport costs and the development of communication systems have reduced entry barriers to the international supply markets, making them more accessible.

A common element among all the investigated enterprises is the existence of a direct or indirect purchasing channel from China. Table 3.1 indicates the composition of the sample according to the industry and the sourcing area from the Far East.

Of the 11 cases analysed, 10 are 'buying' enterprises, namely enterprises which manufacture products using materials purchased in China. One of them (ZenAsia) is an intermediary offering IS services and cannot be directly compared with the other cases; we therefore decided to include it in a second phase of the research in order to understand better the intermediation-related issues. All the buying enterprises are limited companies, whose turnover varies between 23 million and 1,000 million Euros (2002 data).

The incidence of international purchases on total purchases amounts to between 15 per cent and 100 per cent. De-Ta is the company that resorts to

Table 3.1 The sample: industry and Asian markets

	Industry	Asian Sourcing areas
Asem	Information technology	Taiwan, China
Campagnolo Commercio	Textiles	China, Bangladesh, Pakistan, India
DE-TA	Office furniture	China
Danieli	Engineering industry	China
Geox	Footwear industry	China, Vietnam, Indonesia, Sri Lanka
Safilo	Eyewear industry	China (Hong Kong)
Savio	Textile plant engineering	China, Taiwan
Thun	Home furniture	China
Trudi	Toys	China, Vietnam, Indonesia
Black and Decker	Woodworking machinery and tools	China
ZenAsia	Tools, mechanical and electrical components	China

foreign supply markets (office chairs) the least, which is partially explained by the fact that the company is located in the Manzano area (Udine – Italy), the area with the highest concentration of chair manufacturers in the world. This concentration clearly continues to represent an important sourcing area, even though the transfer of production to foreign countries has now become an important phenomenon. At the extreme opposite we find Campagnolo Commercio and Trudi, whose purchases are exclusively international.

As we will better see later, Trudi has delegated its whole production to its Asian suppliers (80% of volume is manufactured in China), while the activities concerning product development, marketing, and logistics are currently kept in Italy. Campagnolo Commercio represents an interesting case of an international trader which, once becoming familiar with international markets and taking command of the internal and foreign factories, has progressively developed product development, marketing and logistics capabilities to put itself forward on the final market with its own products.

Geox has a strong propensity to IS. East Europe is still the most important sourcing area, but the supply from Asia (and from China in particular) is nevertheless continuously growing. As a matter of fact on the one hand, the company is willing to exploit the indubitable cost-related advantages guaranteed by this area; on the other hand it intends to catch the enormous opportunities offered by a continuously expanding market.

Campagnolo Commercio and Geox provide excellent examples of the ability to exploit the opportunities offered by the international chessboard, where the systematic use of manufacturing outsourcing located in the most attractive geographic areas represents the basis for an extremely rapid growth (Geox) and for a radical business change from simple intermediary to developer and seller of products with the company's brand (Campagnolo Commercio).

International sourcing has an impact on Thun's purchases too. The company from Bolzano has kept in Italy the production of the stove division and the manufacturing of the large ceramics objects, whose transport from China is particularly difficult and onerous. On the other hand, the small and medium-sized ceramic objects have been partially transferred to China to exploit, besides other advantages, the consolidated Chinese tradition for these products.

The other cases studied offer other specific and interesting insights. Danieli, as we will see, offers a peculiar example of imposed sourcing; that is a sourcing imposed by Chinese legislation in order to facilitate the growth of an industry (steel plant production) considered as strategic.

Safilo represents an advanced example of operational integration with international supply sources, and of the adoption of supply chain management-evolved tools. Savio operates in one of the main industries in which Chinese business has grown in the last years: textile plant design. This industry has recorded a number of forgeries and copyright violations in recent times. Facing the extraordinary growth of some Chinese operators, Savio has chosen an interesting synergy policy with some of them.

The percentage of purchases in China in comparison with the total purchases in the sample has varied from some percentage points to about 90 per cent. The average value is near 45 per cent. If we only consider the Danieli case, the percentage appears to be modest (2%), but it only considers the purchases made in China and directed to other markets; this means that it doesn't take into account the previously mentioned imposed sourcing, which represents a considerable part of the value manufactured and sold in this market.

Black & Decker Italia represents the only unit whose headquarters are not in Italy. This is a not a minor diversity factor: the location of the strategic centre of a multinational company can notably influence its approach to internationalization. Actually, Black & Decker Italia represents the only European manufacturing facility surviving the drastic process of group reconfiguration that has moved a large part of production to the emerging countries. The Italian manufacturing facility is the only European one still existing by virtue of the excellent results obtained thanks to an expert combination of the advantages of the local supply base (essential to create 'lean

Figure 3.1 Geographical location of the Chinese suppliers of the sample

production') with the advantages deriving from the use of an international base (and in particular a Chinese one). The Italian unit thus had the chance to exploit the advanced organizational infrastructure created and consolidated by the whole group in China.

ZenAsia represents, as indicated, the only intermediation company of the sample. It cooperates with enterprises oriented towards an IS form that needs moderate investments and limited risks. By specializing on the Chinese market, ZenAsia has obtained extraordinary growth results.

Figure 3.1 shows the geographical distribution of the sourcing bases (suppliers or owned units or participated units) of the sample companies.

It is immediately evident that these bases are mainly distributed in the eastern coastal area. One main reason is logistic. The most used form of transport is shipping: millions of containers leave from the Chinese ports every year. In order to support the continuous growth of the volumes embarked, Chinese authorities have created efficient and flexible harbour infrastructures, and have speeded up the customs formalities, reducing transport time. Meanwhile the lines of communication that link harbours with the areas immediately in the shelter of the coast have been improved. In these areas the road links are therefore modern and efficient, and also the airport infrastructures have been subject to a noticeable improvement in recent years.

The accelerated development of the coastal areas is also motivated by a second, political, reason. They have been subject to industrial policy interventions that determined a differentiated development in comparison with other territories, emphasizing the heterogeneity of the country's economic and social geography. The first movements towards regional differentiation go back to the end of the 1970s, when the SEZs were created in the munici-palities of Shantou, Shenzen, Zhuai and, after that, of Xiamen, and Hainan (D'Agnolo, Dal Colle, 2003). Central government grants SEZs special poli-cies and flexible measures, allowing them to utilize a special economic management system (special tax incentives for foreign investments, greater independence on international trade activities, etc.).

Together with the SEZs we have subsequently witnessed the development of other special area types (for example the ETDZ – Economic and Technological Development Zone). It is easy to guess how the opportuni-ties offered by western operators to the single regional realities can vary significantly, for example in terms of fiscal and customs treatment. In the past, coastal areas have been able to attract almost all of the foreign invest-ments. Nevertheless today the Chinese state is trying to develop the most underdeveloped areas through incentives to foreign operators and infra-structure investments. At the same time, the most advanced areas (for example Shanghai or Guanzhou) have saturation problems of the available resources and significantly higher costs than in the past. It is for this reason that today a growing number of western operators are looking with greater interest at different regions than those that have been the actors in the first phase of the industry transformation process.

The choice of Chinese area

For what reasons have the sampled enterprises decided to create sourcing bases in China? What are the context variables considered, the advantages and the obstacles met? In the following sections some evidence coming from the interviews is briefly reported. Many of the elements introduced here (geo-political situation, transport infrastructures, cultural and linguis-tic elements, organization of purchasing activities, legal agreements) will be considered again in the following chapters, in which they will be set within a taxonomy of the sourcing types, and a methodology for the development of supplies in China.

Purchase code type

Many of the surveyed firms have chosen the Chinese supply market mainly on consideration of the cost advantages they could achieve. The first char-acterizing element of the purchasing codes bought in China is therefore the relevant labour content, a factor which is strictly linked to the cheapness of the purchase. As a matter of fact the progress made in technology and quality by the Chinese industrial production are extraordinary in some industries, as it has been stressed by all the interviewed managers. In China the deep-rooted presence of foreign OEMs for the production of hardware IT components indicates unequivocally the interest in this market even in industries which are not exactly labour intensive. According to Safilo's own experiences the quality levels of the components manufactured in the Far East today can be absolutely compared with those from Europe. In some cases, the comparison is in favour of the Chinese suppliers, in particular if we consider the most recent technologies. While for traditional products the manufacturing quality of western companies is still higher (also considering the learning curve which needs time to develop), for the new products (titanium glasses) the gap will be filled by Asian producers.

All in all, the purchases in China of the sampled units concern a variegated number of products, from those with low technology and high labour content, to those with exactly the opposite composition.

Information sources and search for suppliers

Several approaches have been used by the sampled units to get in touch with Chinese vendors. They are: a) participation in trade fairs; b) use of the word-of-mouth method between enterprises that have already experienced this market; c) contacts with and visits from commercial representatives of Chinese manufacturers; d) the internet. With the only exception of a company that has created a joint venture with a Chinese manufacturer, and therefore has tied itself in a stable link with a single interlocutor, the sampled companies are still selecting new suppliers in China. Where one exists, the IPO manages this activity, and it is addressed and coordinated by the central purchasing department. A growing number of Chinese companies have been developing or consolidating commercial bases in Europe, in order to place themselves directly on the western market. Moreover, all the interviewed managers have pointed out that direct auditing is necessary, notwithstanding the travel costs. Visiting the premises of potential suppliers is therefore an obligatory step to check their manufacturing and technological capabilities.

Suppliers' selection criteria

Table 3.2 shows the average evaluations assigned by the sample to each of the following suppliers' selection criteria. The score follows a 5-point Likert scale (1 = not important … 5 = very important):

Quality obtains the highest score, and therefore represents the most selective criterion. The supply quality has been estimated as more than satisfactory, even though in various cases buyers have required a strong reorganization of the suppliers and asked them for the transfer of know-how in order to ensure the required standards.

Quality growth has been and still is ever more monitored by the organizational infrastructures (IPOs) developed by the buyers in this market. It's not by chance that control is frequently transferred on-site with procedures that will be discussed in the following chapters.

Table 3.2 Average valuation of the suppliers' selection criteria in China

Factor	Average valuation
Quality	4.8
Price	4.2
Vendor's financial solidity	3.8
Delivery punctuality, timeliness, and completeness	3.5
Know-how and product uniqueness	3.3
Research and technological development capability	3.0
Access to advanced technologies	3.0
Product mix	2.8
Terms of payment	2.7
Relations consolidated over time	2.5
Geographical location	2.3
Post-sale services	2.3
Certifications from recognized institutions	1.7
References	1.3

Price is the second most important factor: the research mentioned by Trent and Monczka (2002) indicates that the cost advantages potentially obtainable by using international sources are on average between 12 per cent and 25 per cent with respect to the utilization of domestic sources. These values are in line with those observed in this research: the estimated advantages are about 25 per cent with peaks of 70 per cent (net of the higher charges concerning control, transport, and stock of materials coming from Chinese sources). Almost all the investigated enterprises have decided to source in China in order to gain cost advantages, mainly thanks to the low labour cost and the high availability of production capacity in some industries.

Delivery reliability is considered essential and is one of the most important selection and monitoring parameters.

Terms of payment represent a medium/low-importance factor. The main payment method is based on the letter of credit (commercial instrument through which a bank or other financial institutions authorize the bearer to draw a stated amount of money from the issuing bank, its branches, or other associated banks or agencies); nevertheless it depends on the nature of the customer–supplier relationship and past history. Payment is generally in dollars: thanks to the recent appreciation of the Euro against the dollar, the investigated companies have obtained further cost advantages.

Geographical location receives a moderate score. The data is influenced by the fact that the supply relationships analysed are positioned in the coastal area of the country, and are therefore well served from a logistic point of view. Only Trudi considered this factor as critical, to the point that the company is concentrating its Asian supply sources in the Shenzhen area (Guangdong). This choice is essentially justified by logistics reasons: the closeness of Shenzhen to Hong Kong not only simplifies the shipments to Europe, but also the recruitment of qualified local personnel for quality control.

Certification is not a relevant criterion when selecting Chinese suppliers. Nevertheless, the progresse China is making is notable: according to ISO data, at the end of 2001 China ranked first in the world in terms of the increase of certified enterprises (10,548) and fifth in terms of the number of certification institutions operating in the country (41).

Political stability

The modernization process started by the country and the image resulting abroad are such that none of the sampled companies has considered the risks of political instability as relevant. It is a current opinion that China has nearly reached a satisfactory level of stability if compared with the other states of the Asiatic region. For example, the Indonesian market is considered more risky from a political point of view and less convenient from an economic point of view, also taking into account the strong inflation dynamic of the last years. Nevertheless, it must be said that the investigated companies started to source from China only quite recently: apart from one enterprise, none of them was actively sourcing from China before the second half of the 1990s. As a matter of fact, it is in recent years that the opportunities of this market opened up to foreign investors, even though the 'open door' policy was started a quarter of a century ago. But a certain risk remains, not linked to (non)reversibility of the political path that China undertook, but rather to the ability of the central government to control the epochal transformation which is under way.

Trade barriers

The reform of the customs system was launched in China in 1996, and has determined since then a total reduction of duties on foreign imported goods of 35 per cent, bringing the imposition of duty from an average of 35.9 per cent to one of 23.3 per cent (Comba and Schapin, 1997). The reform was part of a more general strategy of progressive adjustment to international customs standards which China was required to undertake for entry into the WTO. Moreover, its admission required the redefinition of the customs restrictions on equipment, materials and components for those companies having partial (joint ventures) or total foreign participations (wholly foreign-owned enterprises).

China's entry into the WTO has determined (and will continue to determine) a further reduction of the barriers that limit both the incoming and outgoing commercial flow. It is not by accident that the investigated companies, and more generally the foreign direct investment flow, have been massively aimed at the Chinese market starting from the end of the 1990s, that is when many reforms had already been carried out in the expectation of China's admission to the WTO.

The close commercial integration of China with the other Asian countries (Indonesia, Malaysia, Philippines, Singapore, Thailand, Brunei, Vietnam, Laos, Myanmar and Cambodia) must be mentioned: in 1996 an agreement was signed concerning the creation of a free-exchange area (CCIC, 2002.)

Transport

As observed, the enterprises analysed are currently keeping supply relationships with companies located on the coastal area, where the industrial growth of recent years was concentrated. In these areas the infrastructure endowment has been considered adequate. The use of suppliers positioned in different areas will determine further costs linked to transport difficulties and shortage of infrastructures. On the other hand, transport management within China's territory is delegated to the supply companies themselves (most of the agreement are FOB (free on board): the seller has an obligation to deliver goods to a named place for transfer to a carrier).

The development of the transport systems in China has not followed the growth rate of the economy, and in any case it shows marked territorial heterogeneity. In the past, the majority of products were manufactured and sold on site; as a consequence the need to create transport channels among the different areas of the country was not so important (Speece and Kawahara, 1995). Moreover, foreign investments historically concentrated in the eastern and south-eastern coastal regions of the country, which from the 1980s saw the creation of the five Special Economic Areas, the Economic and Technical Development Areas and the Free Areas, that grant an exemption from customs duties, VAT and consumption tax (Padolecchia, 2003). Fujian, Shanghai, Jiangsu, Beijing, Guangdong are the areas where the highest inflow of investments has been recorded, determining an improvement of the infrastructure conditions. Nevertheless, the new five-year development plan includes the improvement of the rail and road network mainly in the central western regions in China. This is intended to create conditions for a better distribution of investments in the territory, also because with the increase of the cost of labour the incentive to invest in the coastal areas is declining.

With reference to the flow of materials coming from China, the most used means of carriage is by sea, with an average transport time of about one month (higher if there are trans-shipment necessities, usually in Hong Kong and Singapore). Many of the investigated units use planes as complementary carriers; this usually happens when particular emergencies and the need for specific products arise. For example, Asem uses planes for processors, memories and mother boards, while using ships for the remaining products. The valuation of the means of transport comes essentially from the following factors: quantity and volume, obsolescence, management of possible delays.

Moreover shipments are conditioned by the terms of payment: in case of pre-payment, air transport is usually used in order to avoid the financial burden deriving from long lead times.

Organization of purchasing activities

The management of international sourcing can require an organizational change of the purchasing function, mainly the specialization of purchasing personnel for supply markets and the decentralization of responsibilities to peripheral units (IPOs).

In our sample these choices seem to be linked to a company's size. Small units resort to intermediaries, delegating to external units the management of the international sourcing activities, or rely on one or a few internal buyers that specialize according to the supplied geographical areas. In any case, in small units the work distribution criteria is mainly by commodity or geographical area. As the size grows we observe organizational units expressly dedicated to the international purchase activity: the central purchasing department becomes subdivided into areas specialized according to the geographical sourcing basin (purchasing for Asia, purchasing for Europe, etc.). In other cases peripheral units are created to manage the local supply market (IPO). Among the small and medium-sized investigated businesses, only Trudi has its own purchasing office (Virgilio) located in Singapore, which governs the whole Asian area. In the beginning this office enjoyed a large autonomy in the management of the purchasing activity, from the search for new suppliers to the negotiation and transfer of orders. Recently, however, the office has been completely reorganized and its autonomy has been reduced: responsibility for negotiations has been partially brought back to Italy and today the order transfer follows a triangular path (the central planning interfaces not only with the IPO, but also with the suppliers). This example demonstrates how critical the choice concerning the centralization-decentralization of responsibility is, and how the profile of competencies assigned to the IPO must be attentively configured by balancing the control and supervision needs of the central bodies with the IPO's needs of autonomous operating ability.

Among the large businesses, Danieli is currently involved in the establishment of a purchasing office in Beijing, to which the purchasing responsibility will be delegated. The project was started at the beginning of 2003 with the transfer of Italian personnel to the Chinese capital city. The IPO will also coordinate the purchases from Vietnam by virtue of the geographical closeness between the two countries. In Safilo the sourcing activity from China is managed from Hong Kong through the purchasing office responsible for purchases in the Asian area. The office uses technicians, whose function is to assist the vendors in the management of the manufacturing activity in order to guarantee product quality alignment, and in the choice of the most critical materials. Also Campagnolo and Geox have also developed IPOs in China.

Communication

Table 3.3 shows the evaluations of the interviewed purchasing managers on the communication problems with the Chinese suppliers (5-score Likert scale; 1 = not important problem ... 5 = very important problem).

The cultural differences prove to be the main obstacles in the interaction dynamics with the Chinese sources. That's the reason why many investigated units are strengthening the use of local personnel in purchasing or representative offices. A second problem is the lack, or at least the insufficiency, of a 'vis à vis' communication; this problem emerges in particular when the relationship is based on strong functional interdependencies in the product development or in the manufacturing process definition. The mobility of the western personnel in charge of training the Chinese personnel, has been considered essential in order to obtain an effective knowledge transfer.

Communication between the western and eastern personnel (employees of the IPO or of the supplier) is in English. Language is perceived as a problem of medium importance thanks to the fact that different companies have developed a local techno-structure able to carry out an efficient linguistic mediation.

None of the companies has considered the time zone as an important factor in the management of the sourcing activities from the Asian areas. On the other hand, communication from Europe to China is mainly by e-mail.

Advanced ICT systems are scarcely used for the management of the international supply chain. Safilo has developed an internet-based tool for the information integration of the supply network. Today even the main Chinese vendors of Safilo are able to interface with this system, and have in turn developed enough evolved information systems so that the buyer is able to control the production progress status remotely (through passwords). Moreover, since 1998 Safilo has developed a marketplace that oper-

Table 3.3   Main communication problems with the Chinese suppliers

Factor	Average
Cultural differences	4.0
Lack of 'vis à vis' communication	3.1
Language	2.6
Time zone	2.1
Availability of ITC systems and their compatibility	1.7

ates at international level in order to support the information exchange among the units of the production chain. Once a common language in terms of type and structure of the exchanged messages has been defined, the technological platform OptoIDX has been developed to operate as an integration service provider, intercepting document flows among the partner companies and translating the different formats. The exchanged documents include orders, order confirmations, transport documents, debit and credit notes, requests for delivery against open orders, price lists and invoices. OptoIDX manages the transmission problems through a complete mechanism of reminders and alerts and the documents can be sent over backup channels (for example through FAX) or they can be looked up through a Web interface. Danieli has an e-sourcing system through which it searches for new suppliers using the internet-based completion of a specific form for the selection.

Contractual elements

The cultural differences and the divergent contracting habits represent the main obstacle during the negotiation phase. That's the reason why the investigated companies tend more and more to involve local personnel during this phase, if possible organized in an IPO. Some other difficulties emerge and they are related to the comprehension of the specifications and the technical agreement, which can be partially due to the different design conventions used, and to the fact that the Asian companies have often matured a technical–productive experience in the copy market. This therefore means that the negotiation must often start from the sample study rather than from the description of the technical specification. Many interviewees agree in indicating that the Chinese suppliers are often unable to propose their own offer only according to the specifications, and they tend to focus the negotiation on prices and volumes. It is exactly this difficulty of negotiation agreement that convinced some companies to resort to specialized intermediaries.

Generally speaking, no particular formalities in the purchase agreements with China in comparison with other countries have emerged. Nevertheless, the complexity of these agreements vary both according to the types of product and the industry to which they belong. Conciliation seems to be the preferred Chinese way to solve disputes. According to some managers interviewed, the diffidence with which Chinese people consider the law, seen as an abstract (legislative or jurisprudential) convention imposed by the State, is almost commonplace. Very frequently a contractual clause (arbitration clause) is stipulated, devolving to international arbitration the resolution of disputes with the Chinese partner, if any.

4
Types of Sourcing in China: a Classification

Introduction

The enterprises we have analysed show that sourcing activities in China may depend considerably on some structural characteristics: the presence of governmental limitations in vendor selections, the presence and the kind of possible (inter)mediation forms (third parties), the content of the customer–supplier interactions, the establishment of equity agreements between western and eastern parties. Therefore some distinguishable types arise, tied to a series of conditions relating to context: purchasing code features, company's size, industry. These conditions will be considered in greater depth in the next chapter, where a normative model will be proposed which suggests the proper type of sourcing according to the conditions. This chapter, however, introduces the basic types, classified in such a way that recalls to some extent those presented in the first chapter:

- imposed international sourcing;
- intermediated international sourcing;
- direct international sourcing.

Actually these types represent conceptual categories well established in IS literature – see for example Monczka and Trent (1992). However, our classification extends previous studies by characterizing these categories with respect to a number of contingent factors such as: types of purchased material, organizational infrastructures required, buyer's and supplier's key capabilities, critical factors in the relationships, formalization and time horizon of the relationship. Moreover, we classify these categories specifically in the Chinese sourcing context, where important characteristics exist concerning the profile of local industries, contractual constraints, the negotiation process affected by the peculiarity of this social environment, among other factors. Table 4.1 summarizes the main characteristics of these types of sourcing described in the following paragraphs.

Imposed sourcing

By this term, we mean sourcing imposed by Chinese law (in the past) or a Chinese customer (today) to acquire the opportunity to sell products in the Chinese market. In other words, the resort to local suppliers is a counter-trade condition for allowing the sale of western products in China. Western firms operating in those industries labelled as 'strategic' by Chinese legislation must therefore select local suppliers from the list of imposed sourcing alternatives provided by the Chinese client. This list includes public (SOE, State Owned Enterprises) or private companies.

As is well known, the Chinese structure underwent a process of great change in the wake of the economic reform policy which characterized Chinese history of the last two decades. The big and solely state-owned enterprises gradually gave way to private enterprises, which went towards rapid technological, organizational and managerial improvements in order to be able to work in a regime of market economy.

In order to promote a gradual transition, the Chinese state imposed local sourcing in some industries, which means a sort of 'protected' market for SOEs as well as local enterprises where conversion to the private regime is in process. The technological and organizational profile of these businesses is likely be anything but acceptable: the objective of this kind of sourcing is precisely the transfer of know-how from leading western companies to the local industrial system.

Since China has become involved in the WTO, most of these legal limitations are disappearing, but in some sectors some industrial compensation will still be required that will have similar characteristics or final effects on the market.

The almost 20-year systematic application of these obligations enabled China to acquire key competences in some industries and, at the same time, improve the professional skills of the local labour force. This type of sourcing integrates into a more general policy aimed at acquiring Western technologies and know-how to support the economic growth. It involves a wide number of industries, the so-called 'strategic' or 'encouraged' industries, usually connected to *high-tech* and *engineer-to-order* (*ETO*) products.

The skills a buyer is required to have are high and diversified. In particular:

- *Negotiation capability.* The phase of negotiation with the customer, which is critical in all identified sourcing typologies, presents in this case specific complexity factors. In fact, the interests of the partsie are generally in opposition to each other when selecting the (local) supply base and managing the (advanced) know-how. Moreover, the formalization level of the transaction is higher since it is disciplined by strict local regulations and subject to institutional control, given the 'strategic' importance of the industries involved;

- *Supplier development capabilities.*   Western companies responsible for the whole product/project realization have to enable 'imposed' suppliers to perform the work assigned to them. This implies also the transfer to the suppliers of technological know-how and production methods, necessary to reach the quality standards agreed with the Chinese customers.
- *Ability to coordinate the local supply network.*   The western company can be required to play the important and complex role of main-contractor, i.e. to lead and supervise the entire international supply network, as the local (Chinese) party usually has poor technological and organizational skills.

   Hence the need for 'integrating' and 'systematic' capabilities. They include first of all the ability to acquire and transfer competences to different actors and coordinate the material and component flow among members of the network. Furthermore, the western enterprise must own an 'architectural competence', which means it must combine and integrate the technological and productive contributions of the different manufacturers into the whole project.

Production control and scheduling, as well as the control of the correct working progress, may require the western company to locate its own staff with the suppliers, in order to monitor their quality and time. Furthermore, the possible location in China of organizational facilities may facilitate sales service, order management, and post-sales services. On the other hand, the screening of the suppliers is less relevant since this activity is subject to the above-mentioned constraints.

The type of sourcing here briefly described is one of the reciprocity (counter-trade) conditions demanded by Chinese government of western companies. However, even in the absence of explicit norms, western companies decide to use local sources in order to legitimate their presence in China and to gain tax incentives, simplification of bureaucratic procedures and permissions and social consensus.

The continuous changes to the legislation which disciplines this kind of sourcing should be emphasized. Its characteristics, in fact, depend closely on the political orientations: the adhesion to the WTO has, amongst other things, progressively relaxed the hindrances and limitations imposed by Chinese legislation.

The western companies operating in 'strategic' industries must thus prove that they are able to respond quickly to changes in the regulatory context governing this sourcing, by seizing new opportunities which arise.

Intermediated sourcing

By this term we mean the presence of a third party that interposes between the two ends of the transaction (supplier and buyer). The empirical cases highlight two types of intermediation: traditional intermediation and outsourcing of international sourcing services.

Traditional intermediation

In this case the intermediary is an international wholesaler who buys products on the Chinese market and resells them on other markets. His profile is essentially commercial, even though the type of service provided requires the capacity to manage duly all the variables connected to the international transfer of goods (logistic, customs obligations, etc.). Thus, the western buyer is not in this case directly visible to, and does not subsequently interact directly with, the eastern supplier. The products bought are usually standard. Indeed it is not advisable to use this form of supply to buy specific or complex products, as there is not a steady and direct relationship between the parties. The possibility to give technical explanations or ask for any project and productive changes is indeed difficult as the intermediary plays a typical commercial role.

Outsourcing of international sourcing services

In this case the intermediary provides a set of services: analysis of the Chinese offer, identification of potential suppliers, agreement definition, quality inspection, screening of international carriers, monitoring of the suppliers.

The role of the intermediary is particularly relevant in the initial phases, i.e. when the potential suppliers are identified and the preliminary contacts are made. Thanks to his experience and the operating base he has on the Chinese market, the intermediary can select the most suitable information channels and screen the supply opportunities. He can manage the trading phase even better by controlling any opportunistic behaviour by the Chinese party, at the same time making it understand the advantages of the supply relationship. As a matter of fact, the western operator exploring the Chinese market is often bewildered by the various offerings provided, by the surplus of information available and by an unusual contractual style.

The experiences we analysed show how during the first phases the provider of international services usually represents the sole link to the Chinese party, by concealing the identity of the potential Chinese suppliers until the pilot productions. But later, mainly when there are products requiring a technical and technological interaction between the parties, the buyer and the supplier interact directly and directly finalize the contract. Yet the intermediary often continues to maintain the whole responsibility of international sourcing. His expertise in international business and his local network of intermediaries cannot indeed be easily substituted. That is why the use of outsourcing of international logistic services is probably an inescapable choice for small purchasing companies. They rarely have suitable resources and expertise to sound out the foreign market, control the suppliers on site, or track the progress of the order. In many respects, the intermediation company acts as the international purchasing office of the purchasing companies. The setting-up of a Chinese office implies investments only to be contemplated when adequate purchasing volumes are involved. By focusing on these activities for a variety of customers, the intermediary is able to obtain for them economy of scale and specialization. At the same time, his cultural mediation can make the Chinese party more flexible to any change to the production agreed (e.g. in the event of defects or unsatisfactory quality) and for the joint development of new products (according to the specifications provided by the western customer) and, more generally, more open to the introduction of advanced production and management methods.

From the managerial and operational point of view, the intermediated sourcing represents the simplest and quickest sourcing strategy. The creation and management of the relationship with the supplier is indeed delegated to the intermediary and no specific purchaser's skills are needed.

The intermediation can be an effective way and one with relatively little risk to test the Chinese market, anticipating choices of direct sourcing. The disadvantages are the intermediation costs and – as far as traditional intermediation is concerned – the difficulty or impossibility of interacting directly with sources.

In both these forms of sourcing, the intermediary qualifies for his effective presence on the Chinese market through his own structure of buyers. The main assets of the trading companies lie in the network of relationships and the knowledge of local business practices. However, in the case of outsourcing of logistic services, the local base has a more structured skill profile and often 'location-oriented' characteristics, i.e. the buyers are constantly located at one or more suppliers and control their quality and delivery times.

In the past, intermediation was allowed only to a limited number of authorized Chinese companies. Today, the great changes involving the Chinese industry have significantly changed the reality and characteristics of intermediation. The openness of China towards international markets and the subsequent progressive privatization of the huge and, usually, inefficient state-owned companies have put an end to the monopoly of international activities enjoyed by the Chinese foreign trade companies. There were two consequences: on the one hand many private companies (those of greater size and attitude to internationalization) succeeded in directly relating with foreign customers; on the other hand new types of intermediation were created.

According to the experiences surveyed during this research, the Chinese foreign trade companies are seldom considered as a valid sourcing opportunity by the western companies. They are sometimes used where it is necessary quickly to activate a sourcing channel from China or to reduce time and costs for vendor selection: the relationship with the trader ends when the western purchaser has found, through them, qualified suppliers and has established direct relationships with them. This relationship with FTC still survives in those industries where local supply is pulverized in a myriad of businesses characterized by limited size and managerial profile.

It is worth observing how frequent is the resort to Korean and Taiwanese enterprises as intermediaries. Evidently these enterprises operate in economic and industrial contexts that for historical reasons have a higher affinity and familiarity with western managerial customs.

Finally, intermediaries located in the west but with organizational appendices in China are quickly developing. This way they offer a more accessible and receptive interface to European customers, at the same time the operating base in China is specialized in the management of the local supply relationships. The topic of the intermediation will be resumed and considered in greater depth in the next chapters.

Direct sourcing

By 'direct sourcing' we mean the sourcing with neither intermediation nor constraints connected with the choice of a supplier. On the basis of empirical evidence, it is possible to distinguish these forms of direct sourcing:

- *Traditional.* The supply relationship occurs when there are no operational integration forms between the parties. The western buyer turns to a Chinese contact according to an approach we could call 'pure market': the code is standard, i.e. it is available in the catalogue without specific adjustments (limited switching costs). Therefore there are limited risks of unreliability of supplies. Quality control exhibits no particular problems as these are repeated orders of standardized items. It is often carried out or completed in the buying plant. The western firm does not intend to guarantee long term relationships: the relative facility in finding new sources suggests choosing from time to time the most favourable opportunity in the Chinese market or in other markets.
- *Collaborative.* In this case, the relationship provides for the operative 'collaboration' between the parties. There is abundant literature on forms and advantages of buyer–supplier collaboration. Briefly, this collaboration develops first of all in the design and production-logistic ambit, and aims respectively at joining product development and at a better material-flow synchronization. At the bases of these synergies there is the awareness that competition does not depend only on the single enterprise, but on the whole chain or network in which it is placed (De Toni and Nassimbeni, 1999, 2000). The supply unit, even if

located offshore, becomes part of a production system internationally distributed but integrated and interconnected.

The cases analysed confirm the presence of wide buyer–supplier collaboration–interaction forms: the anticipated transfer of production plans, the joint-definition of product specifications, the sharing of engineering and industrialization choices, the adoption by suppliers of agreed capacity planning tools and manufacturing, quality control, packing, and transportation modalities. Purchasing items involved in this kind of sourcing present relevant technological or qualitative contents or stringent service requirements. In other cases they are characterized by a short life-cycle: collaboration between buyer and supplier is solicited by the frequent product portfolio turnover that requires flexible and reliable suppliers, ready to comply promptly to new specifications. The western buyer is interested in encouraging and supporting the supplier's growth. Therefore he can undertake supplier development programmes, transferring a correct *modus operandi*, which can lead to the complete re-organization of the supplier and the training of local work force and executives.

In the sample surveyed, these forms of collaboration sometimes go together with equity agreements, i.e. forms of capital participation. The Chinese laws ruling these agreement forms are rather complex and steadily changing. This topic will be discussed more in detail in the following chapter. We can anticipate that there are essentially three investment forms used in China by foreign subjects (Weber, 1995; Padolecchia, 2003; ICE, 2003):

- *Equity joint venture* (EJV): this type of company is typical of a limited company, constituted and managed jointly by two or more partners who share risks, responsibilities, losses and profits, according to the capital share invested;
- *Contractual joint venture* (CJV) or co-production company: in this case the foreign investor usually contributes with money, advanced equipment and technology, while the Chinese contribution can be limited to the building, the equipment present in China, and the right of use of the land. It differs from the previous type of venture, since it does not necessarily require the constitution of an autonomous legal company structure. This configuration has the advantage of a higher managerial flexibility and ease of administration.
- *Wholly foreign-owned enterprise* (WFOE). The foreign investor forms a company with limited liability according to Chinese law, wholly owned and managed by him. In the past, the law established that the WFOEs had to be 'advanced technology-oriented' or had to produce for export. Following recent amendments these requirements have been practically eliminated. This kind of enterprise has to comply with the same consti-

tution, managerial, fiscal and accounting principles of equity joint ventures.

The WFOE has recently become the preferential choice of foreign investors. The main advantage of a WFOE is control. EJV experiences often showed that Chinese equity participation may be very difficult to manage. Moreover, WFOEs permit greater guarantees of intellectual property protection. On the other hand the absence of a local partner can cause bigger problems regarding introduction into the local industrial context (activation of business relations) and a greater vulnerability in legal cases. Moreover fiscal benefits and, more generally, government relief for WFOEs can be considerably lower.

The cases examined show how direct sourcing is often accompanied by the use of an IPO whose role is to manage the main operating activities supporting sourcing from China. The following activities are typically delegated to them: a) selection of new suppliers; b) negotiation of purchase contracts; c) management of communication with suppliers; d) quality control, eventually by Chinese personnel permanently employed in the production units.

This classification can be compared with the only other classification that we have identified in literature: that proposed by Wang (2004). The author distinguishes the types of sourcing according to the foreign buying subject (Table 4.1):

- manufacturing MNCs that have production and supply bases in China. Wang cites the examples of General Motors and Siemens, for a long time present in this market with manufacturing joint ventures and well-rooted supply networks;
- trading companies which represent western clients and manage their local (Chinese) sourcing basin. As an example, McDonalds acquires through third parties the famous 'surprises' and toys included in the food products sold;
- retailing Giants, such as Wal-Mart and Carrefour, that have long resorted in a big way to Chinese supply market. Many of their own brands are indeed produced in this country;
- procurement professionals and agents, who usually interface small western customers, acting as international sourcing providers.

While our classification mostly relies on the nature of the customer–supplier relationship (imposed, intermediate, direct with or without equity agreements), Wang's classification is based on the profile of the foreign buyer. These two variables are evidently correlated (see Table 4.2).

The trading companies are oriented to greater purchasing volumes and commercial form, of mediation, therefore achieving what we have previ-

Table 4.1 A classification of sourcing strategies

	Imposed	Intermediated	Traditional	Direct IS	
	IS	IS		Collaborative non-equity	Collaborative equity
Industry	'Strategic'	Not strategic	Not strategic	Not strategic	Not strategic
Purchased material's characteristics	ETO, High tech	Standard	Standard	Complex, Short life-cycle	High-Tech Registered Need for interactions in NPD or in productive-logistics activities
Buyer's key capabilities	Negotiation, supplier development, local network coordination capabilities	None (delegated to the intermediary)	Wide and updated knowledge of (Chinese) market opportunities	Thorough knowledge of local culture, language, work customs and legal system. High relational attitudes and supplier development capabilities	
Suppliers' key capabilities	Not highly developed	Intermediary: capability of developing effective local relationships. Knowledge of local business practices	Manufacturing efficiency, volume flexibility	Capability to absorb western operational and managerial practices. Relational and integration attitudes. Product, mix and volume flexibility	

Table 4.1 A classification of sourcing strategies – *continued*

	Imposed IS	Intermediated IS	Traditional	Direct IS Collaborative non-equity	Collaborative equity
Buyer's de-location of organizational units	Local personnel for commercial activities and legal consulting	Not necessary (substituted by intermediary's units)	Local personnel with sourcing responsibilities	IPOs with responsibilities for supplier selection and monitoring. Location of personnel in the suppliers' plant for the control of activities and the transfer of operational and managerial competences	
Critical factors in the relationship	Negotiation; know-how transfer; expediting; quality control	Intermediary: comprehension of buyer's requirement	Supplier selection	Partner selection; negotiation; know-how transfer; quality control	
Technological and know-how transfer	Imposed	Absent	Absent	Agreed	
Level of relationship formalization	High	Low	Low	Medium	High (Chinese legislation on equity agreement)
Time horizon of the relationship	Low (single project)	Decided by the intermediary	Spot transaction	High	

Table 4.2 Wang's classification

	Intermediated	Direct IS		
		Traditional	Collaborative non-equity	Collaborative equity
Manufacturing MNCs			✓	✓
Trading companies	✓			
Retailing giants		✓		
Procurement professionals and agent	✓			

ously defined as 'traditional intermediation'. 'Procurement professionals and agents' on the other hand, focus on that specialist, customized service we have previously called 'outsourcing of international logistic services'.

The Manufacturing MNCs cited by Wang (2004) prefer direct sourcing, with or without equity agreements, often supported by solid IPOs in China. The sourcing of retailing giants is based on traditional direct modalities, because the role and the profile of these subjects is basically commercial.

Examples

In this section we will supply some examples to define the context of the above classification. Some of them will be further reconsidered in the case studies at the end of this book. It is necessary to observe that many types of sourcing can coexist in the same enterprise: as we will see in the next chapter this choice (also) depends on the type of product and on the industry considered. It can happen that for some products the enterprise chooses a traditional method, while for others a direct or intermediated form is preferred.

Imposed sourcing

Danieli, one of the world leaders in the steel production systems industry, provides an example of this type of sourcing. China is for Danieli one of the most important markets, since it represents about 20–25 per cent of its turnover. The Chinese market is considered 'excellent' in terms of sales prospects, so that among the 50 main orders obtained in 2002, 20 came from the Far East. However, like other international customers the Chinese imposes precise conditions to the sales: about 85 per cent of the order value must come from local supplier. Danieli develops internally the whole design of the steel production systems and the manufacturing of the most critical parts; the rest is committed to the local (Chinese) supply base.

Imposed sourcing has allowed the Chinese government to support the growth of the local manufacturing system with velocity of growth absolutely greater than the official annual average of the country, as far as the steel industry is concerned (7–8%). This industry, like others, is facing a gradual and growing privatization. Besides being a technological and management growth tool, imposed sourcing ensures a protected market for the enterprises, that allows a gradual conversion to the private regime. It is therefore easy to understand why the western operator can today choose within the imposed list the Chinese supplier considered as the most suitable, while in the past the state pre-assigned production to companies according to scheduled planning.

Since Danieli is completely responsible for the projects it carries out in China with the participation of local developers, it is generally necessary to supervise the suppliers directly, so the location of personnel at their premises is necessary. Danieli has therefore created a representative office in China, whose main duty is to control the production cycle and to ensure the control of each phase. Other functions of the representative office are: a) sales support; b) legal support; c) order management support; and d) local post-sale service support.

Intermediated sourcing

De-Ta SpA, the largest Italian producer of office chairs and the second largest in Europe, provides an example. Since 2000 De-Ta has purchased spring suspensions for office chairs from Korean and Taiwanese companies, which have relocated their production to China.

De-Ta negotiates price, quantity, terms of payment, and delivery times with the intermediary. The intermediary then asks his Chinese suppliers for these services in order to ensure deliveries according to the agreed scheduling and to the required technical specifications. Intermediation was effective mainly for the management of two activities: the negotiations, and the monitoring of the execution of the technical specifications. During negotiations the Chinese suppliers often feel tempted to try continuously to reduce prices, aiming at changing some specifications in order to meet the agreed target price. From this, the need arises for an interlocutor able to establish suitable relations with the manufacturer and, at the same time, to offer adequate warranties to the Western customer. It is evident that the Taiwanese origin of the intermediary plays a decisive role: on the supplier's side the intermediary can speak Chinese and knows the relational context of the country, on the customer's side he is familiar with western practices.

Another example of intermediation is offered by Savio SpA, a company which is part of the most important world-group in the yarn finishing machine sector, ranging from wool, cotton, linen and silk to synthetic fibres. There are two main reasons for sourcing in China: the presence of important economies for some components (estimated as about 30%) and the possibility of eliminating, or at least better controlling, the Asian producers, who operate on the 'parallel market' of the non-original components. The intermediary used by Savio is a Taiwanese company, which in turn represents about 20 small Chinese manufacturers. It seems therefore mandatory to use intermediation to interface with these producers. Moreover the Taiwanese import–export company is able to ensure a cultural intermediation with the Chinese manufacturing world. The main difficulties in the relationships and the major misunderstandings with eastern reality derive from the fact that the local enterprises are still mainly employed in the 'copy' market. Negotiations must therefore start from the 'study of the sample to be manufactured, rather than from the description of the specifications, as it happens with a western supplier.'

Another example of intermediated sourcing is given by Asem, one of the Italian leaders in the production of industrial personal computers and the first national server producer. The Taiwanese supply market alone represents about 30 per cent of the purchase value for the office division and deals with containers, feeding units, and mother boards. At least half of Asem's Taiwanese suppliers have created manufacturing facilities mainly on the Chinese coastal areas in order to facilitate handling and logistic flows. There is another decisive reason for the investment in China, besides the advantages deriving from the low labour cost: the presence on a market which is already today the first in the world for PC sales. Moreover it must be said that over time Chinese producers have developed abilities and capacities which can hardly be found in other contexts thanks to these processes of manufacturing transfer. Finally, this area is almost always the preferred sourcing region for this industry. As far as some products are concerned, Asem has developed direct contacts with Chinese manufacturers; however the Taiwanese intermediation is absolutely preferred, since it offers warranties of quality and reliability that direct sourcing has not been able to offer.

An interesting example of an international sourcing service provider (that allows for the execution of a collaborative intermediated IS) is represented by ZenAsia, an Italian company specialized in intermediation with Chinese suppliers. The services offered are mainly directed at small and medium-sized enterprises able to support the investments connected to direct sourcing from China. The activities carried out by ZenAsia are suppliers' selection (identification and auditing), negotiation and contracting, product development in OEM mode, online and pre-shipment quality control, time monitoring, management of the shipments, post-purchase support, and legal support. The agreement that ZenAsia draws up with western customers is subdivided into three different parts. The first part controls the identification of potential suppliers. The second part describes the procedure for the manufacturing, control and delivery of the first production lot. The third part controls the continuing relationship between the parties. ZenAsia uses Chinese employees for all activities that require a constant presence at the producers. The most critical aspects (e.g. the negotiation or the definition of the contractual terms) are defined by ZenAsia's headquarters.

Direct sourcing

An example of this type of sourcing is provided by Trudi SpA, leader of the Italian market of soft-toys, with a catalogue containing more than 500 models. Trudi has transferred most of its manufacturing activities to China. Only the most value-added activities (marketing, product and prototype development, engineering) have been maintained in Italy. This transfer has been determined by two related factors: the low cost of labour (these are labour-intensive productions) and the 'remarkable manual skill of the Chinese workers' (soft toys require an almost exclusively manual processing). If we exclude the manufacturing process of some components, the product does not have a particular technological complexity. Nonetheless it requires a significant methodological precision and then the ability rapidly to reconfigure the manufacturing system to introduce the new collections. As a matter of fact the soft toy is a product that, apart from some exceptions, has a short life cycle and must be rapidly renewed at the most important annual deadlines (beginning of the school year, Christmas, Easter, etc.). These requirements and the competitive positioning of Trudi (high quality) suggested the transfer of technical know-how to the Chinese suppliers and the careful assignment of quality control responsibilities. This control takes place in three phases: first of all it is made by the Chinese company, then by a Trudi quality controller (located within the supplier and managed by the Chinese office) and, finally, in Italy. Trudi also created a purchasing office in Singapore that controls quality, selects new suppliers and manages the sourcing activities of raw material in China. The allocation of orders and the negotiations are made jointly with the central (Italian) units.

Safilo SpA, the second manufacturer of eye-wear in the world, has started to consider the Chinese market in order to gain cost advantages. The Chinese suppliers have been able to grow very rapidly in terms of quality and technological ability, so that their offer is sometimes more advanced than the European one.

The company uses some important suppliers, who have separated, even from a geographic point of view, the sale function (situated in Hong Kong) from the manufacturing plants (situated in the Shenzen area). The creation of a real technologically state-of-the-art 'eye-wear district' has been witnessed here, and this district has attracted foreign investments from other various international manufacturers. The purchases from China (generally of finished products designed by Safilo itself) have been carried out through a purchasing office that works in cooperation with the business centre in

Padua. In this case too, the main task of the office is the coordination of quality assurance activities. Moreover, Safilo has established an equity agreement with a Chinese supplier located in the Shenzen area. This choice was justified by the need for a higher control of the supplier's manufacturing, but mainly by the will to develop a 'Chinese' foothold in order to promote sales in this market. The use of a local partner to support market penetration objectives is quite a common practice.

The case of Campagnolo Commercio highlights the evolution of a wholesaler which has reformulated its own business and changed its organizational structure in order to exploit the opportunities offered by the Chinese supply market. This market ensures considerable cost advantages even though limitations on export quotas exist.

Campagnolo Commercio operates in the low–medium segment of the textile sector, where international competition is quite aggressive. In the beginning, the company operated only as an international wholesaler, by purchasing products in some markets and selling them to others. By seizing the opportunity of manufacturing in China and activating direct and collaborative relationships with some suppliers, the enterprise has developed internal product development and marketing activities. In other words, if in the past the company carried out only trade activities, today it develops the products, sends them to the Chinese suppliers for their manufacturing, and then manages their marketing and sales.

Campagnolo Commercio has a Chinese office, in which eastern employees work. They have to manage the relationships with the suppliers, transfer the technical specifications, monitor their realization, and control quality. Their activity is carried out under the supervision of the (Italian) people responsible for foreign purchases; they frequently travel to the Far East in order to take part to industry trade fairs, to get in touch with new suppliers, to stipulate manufacturing agreements and, sometimes, to control the production batches before their shipment. To better synchronize manufacturing with other activities, the company notifies sales data to some suppliers.

5

Is Strategy and Planning in China

Introduction

In the previous chapter various types of sourcing were explained. On the basis of this classification it is now our intention to provide some useful suggestions for the choice and design of a purchasing channel in the Chinese market. The failure or the difficulties that enterprises meet during realization of such a channel derive from the absence of a planned strategy together with inadequate knowledge of the peculiarities of the Chinese context. The strategy should take into consideration the following: the constraints, the risks, and the opportunities of this market; the enterprise's capacities and resources; the characteristics of the purchase codes; and the profile of the relevant industry. An adequate cognitive exploration and a planned project can reduce the inevitable difficulties associated with the establishment of a sourcing and manufacturing base in China: disorientation due to an enormous market or to numerous supply opportunities, to different negotiation practices, to more unsure legislative contexts. Purchasing from this country, if considered in context of the internationalization of the overall enterprise and configured considering some contextual factors that will be described below, offers opportunities that can rarely be found in other markets.

In the first part of this chapter a model is indicated, which suggests the most suitable sourcing type among those previously identified according to three context variables (the business size, the complexity of the industrial environment, and the complexity of the purchase code). The purpose of this model is therefore regulatory, even though the indications it offers do not have strictly prescriptive aims.

The second part of the chapter illustrates the sequence of steps in the creation of a purchasing channel. This sequence also derives from the analysis of the business cases; this analysis has highlighted, even in the diversity of the single situations, shared critical aspects and development paths that are common in many respects. In particular, similarities have emerged in the

Chinese vendor's selection, in some negotiation and relationship aspects, and in the formalization of the final agreement that foreshadows continuous manufacturing.

Finally, in the last section some methodological suggestions are proposed, which are useful to create an International Purchasing Office (IPO), which is mainly decisive for some sourcing types.

Type selection: a model

The types of sourcing previously described are linked to a variety of subsidiary conditions, which can be traced to these main three conditions:

- the business size (or the exchanged volumes)
- the complexity of the purchase code (component/product)
- the complexity of the industrial supply context.

These are the three context macro-variables (enterprise, product and industry) that influence the policies and the dynamics of any kind of sourcing, not necessarily at an international level, and which in this case are defined with reference to the purchases in China.

Business size (or exchanged volumes)

Many studies demonstrate that international sourcing does not represent a prerogative of large corporations, but rather an opportunity open to small and medium-sized enterprises. On the contrary we could affirm that these units, in particular those operating in many traditional industries of *Made in Italy*, often prove themselves to be more exposed to international competition, and are therefore urged to find favourable sourcing opportunities in the Eastern countries. Having said that, it is evident that the size of the business affects the ways in which the company faces the internationalization challenge. Managerial ability and culture, and availability of financial resources are in the first instance linked to size, and they determine the possibility of accessing the foreign market and the type of presence on it. Think, for example, about the possibility of investing in shareholdings or in the creation of IPOs, but also about the level of human resources specialized in international trading, the ability to process information concerning the international markets and therefore the ability to analyse the complex environment.

The variable 'purchase volumes' is separate from the business size, even though clearly linked to it. The total value of the purchases realized or realizable in China suggests sourcing choices binding and challenging in different ways. Small volumes do not justify the investment for the setting-up of a Chinese office or the suppliers' development, unless they are part of a strategy aimed at exploiting the opportunities and the supply and/or sale potentialities of the market in the medium–long term. On the other hand, volumes affect the supplier's behaviour towards the buyer, and therefore the range of sourcing options that can be used.

Code complexity

The types of sourcing analysed in the current research cover a wide portfolio, from low-added-value and notably labour intensive codes for which therefore the Chinese sourcing is essentially justified in terms of cost, to high-added-value codes which require important technological abilities and sophisticated monitoring tools. It is evident that different complexity levels of the exchanged code correspond to various source availability levels, negotiation power, relation and interrelation forms, that is, different types of sourcing. The variable 'product complexity' includes a number of attributes:

- *The complexity of the technical specifications required.* First of all there is a comprehension problem, not only linked to language, but also to the project-graphical conventions and other information tools that support and make the technical drawing clear. Some of the parties interviewed have observed that the product sample often represents a reference for the Chinese supplier, which is more important than the technical specification. Therefore, rather often the sample reproduction, improved and refined several times until it corresponds to the item required, traces the path followed by the vendor in order to satisfy the customer's needs.
- *The need to transfer technology and knowledge* in order to attain the desired standards.
- *The need for specialized personnel to be used in quality control and in the support during the manufacturing phases.*
- *The product life cycle.* Short life cycles, which are for example typical of the clothing industry (the Campagnolo case) and of the soft toys industry (the Trudi case) demand from the supplier a wide flexibility, since they ask for the ability rapidly to renew the offer and to continuously introduce changes.
- *The product mix.* The characteristics of the supplier–customer relationships (and as a consequence the sourcing method adopted by the buyer) also depend on the number, and on the variety of the exchanged articles. Also the variety of the requested *packaging* contributes to the determination of this complexity.
- *The architectural complexity.* The purchase code can be configured as part of a whole composed of multiple lower-level components. In this case the manufacturer requires 'architectural' abilities, that is, abilities to integrate a variety of elements by interacting with multiple sources. On the finished product side, the architectural complexity becomes symmetrically the manufacturer's ability to give his own contribution to the

project. It is an important ability, particularly in some sectors of the instrumental mechanics or in the plant-engineering industry.
* *The creativity and innovation level requested to the supplier.*

Complexity of the industrial supply context

This variable is intended to capture the heterogeneity of the Chinese industry context, in terms of production ability, technological state of the art, familiarity with western practices, the possibility of penetrating the relational 'guanxi' by establishing profitable trade relationships, geographical concentration, facilitations and incentives for the Western operators. In other words, there are differently attractive industries and territories in a country as large as a continent in which, as it has already been indicated, the industrialization process has developed in a non-uniform way. There are industries and companies that are more inclined to change than others, that is to follow the western partner in a development path based on cooperation. In the same way there are fossilized, less flexible, and still strongly bureaucratized companies (most of them state-owned). There are realities with scarce or no experience in international trading or in which this experience is or was mediated by the 'old' foreign trade companies.

The ability to create relationships with the western companies differs between territories and industries, and even within the same industry. An example is given by the sport shoes industry that was born after the delocalization of western enterprises and that has already developed a more than decennial advanced manufacturing tradition. A large part of the world production comes from China, where it is often organized in generally well logistically-served districts. Establishing trade relationships with these manufacturers is easier than in other industries. Another example is represented by the textile industry, or at least by many of its sectors. In this case too they are already consolidated industries, in which there is a technostructure able to interact without any difficulties with western partners and equipped with advanced manufacturing-technical structures. On the other hand they are productions in which the Chinese competitive force is well known and not linked only to cost advantages. China also has a particularly appreciated tradition in the ceramics industry (Thun).

Other industries, for example plant engineering, may have a technological delay in comparison with the supply opportunities existing in other markets and at the same time may have a higher 'environment complexity'. Nevertheless it must also be considered that in the established industries, in which there are several qualified suppliers that offer their products to the western buyers, the problem concerning the selection of suitable suppliers is still present. In fact the Chinese party tends to satisfy any needs of the customer, accepting even very noticeable price reductions, even though in reality he doesn't have the necessary abilities and know-how to do it.

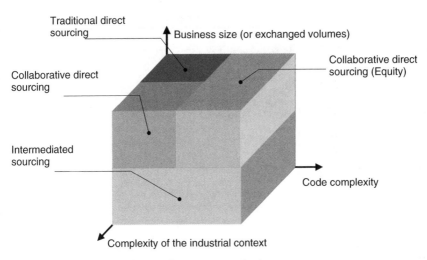

Figure 5.1   Context variables and sourcing typologies

Finally, it must be said that the quantity and quality growth of the Chinese industry as a whole is surprising, and a clear public investment project in research structures and partnerships with important international university institutions is rapidly destined to refute the commonplace saying that the Chinese are 'very good copiers, but insignificant innovators'.

These three context variables affect the sourcing strategy as explained in Figures 5.1 and 5.2.

The model proposed in Figure 5.1 associates types of direct *sourcing* to a medium-sized or large purchasing company (and to considerable exchange volumes), while it suggests the use of intermediaries in the case of a small company with low purchase volumes. The direct sourcing, especially if collaborative, requires infrastructures and investments that are hardly within the small units' reach or in any case is only justified by proportional volumes. In the previous chapter we explained the differences between the traditional trader, who is an international wholesaler, whose profile is mainly a commercial one, and the provider of international logistic services, who continuously substitutes the customer in the supplier selection and management and in the control of the order cycle. As can be seen in Figure 5.2, this intermediary figure appears to be more and more appropriate with the growth of the product and context complexity, that is when a higher production specialization by the third party and a higher commitment and control in the tracking of the material sources and flow are required. On the other hand, for standard purchase types, no specialized knowledge is required to support the technical interaction with the supplier. In this case the intermediation of the traditional trader can be sufficient.

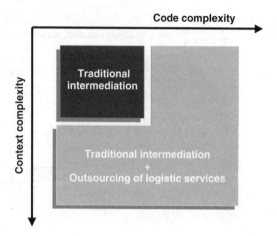

Figure 5.2   Sourcing types for small companies (low volumes)

Where the sizes (of the company and of the purchase volumes) are more significant, the choice of proper sourcing types becomes wider. Generally speaking, a collaborative direct sourcing type is associated with a high product complexity, since the sourcing requires the transfer of the knowledge concerning product-process and quality control to the suppliers. Cooperation can be supported by equity agreements, in case a higher control of the Chinese party is needed, for example to better protect intellectual property or to limit the risks of the supplier's opportunistic behaviour. More generally the manufacturing and organizational integration between buyer and supplier with the subsequent higher information (and knowledge) exchange and the supplier's gradual improvement process are favoured by the joint shareholding.

The equity agreement in a direct and collaborative IS relationship is strongly motivated by the high complexity of the industrial supply context. As a matter of fact, the Chinese partner can start in an easier way and manage more efficiently the relationships with the external local subjects (suppliers, customers, public institutions) and the internal ones (personnel). From interviews carried out it has repeatedly emerged that negotiations produce different results according whether they are carried out with the Chinese rather than with people of different nationalities. The presence of a local partner (equity agreement) especially in highly complex contexts becomes therefore essential in order to enter better into the local relationship network (*'guanxi'*), developing that reciprocal knowledge and trust that often constitute the prerequisite to operate with the local subjects.

Safilo provides a useful example of equity agreement motivated by high complexity of both product and context. The company has realized a direct investment through the acquisition of a capital share of a Chinese supplier, in order to develop with him a collaborative interaction, which is not limited to the production area, but extended to the activities of product development. Since the supplier operates in the Shenzen district (a purchasing area used by the main international competitors attracted by low prices, but mainly by the excellent quality level and the high technological content of the offer) Safilo believed that the equity agreement could determine a higher cooperation by the partner and offer more control opportunities as to his behaviour.

Conversely, the traditional sourcing type, that is without integration forms between the buyer and the supplier, has been considered in the model as a low complex type as far as both the environment and the product are concerned. In this case we are talking about *standard* products, for which different and consolidated procurement possibilities exist, and which are mainly chosen due to cost advantages. In other cases this type of sourcing concerns products manufactured in China by multinational companies, whose reliability level is considered excellent. An example of this is the De-Ta case that uses this type of sourcing for the supply of gas springs: the supplier is a Korean multinational company, a world leader in the production of these products that has located some productions in the Chinese territory.

The model, focused on the sourcing types, doesn't appear to consider another option: that of foreign investment with complete foreign participation. This option, which in the past was not allowed or was very limited, represents today the privileged way of entering the Chinese market. As a matter of fact, in recent years the entry barriers to foreign investors have notably decreased, together with the great need of the State to offer employment opportunities to the growing mass of workers that leave the countryside or are fired by State enterprises. In this case we are no longer talking about sourcing (buy), that is, no longer purchasing from a supplying company (possibly participated), but rather of the 'delocation' of production activities (make). The advantages and disadvantages of this option will be better investigated in a subsequent chapter. From the point of view of the context characteristics that better qualify it, the choice to create a wholly foreign-owned enterprise is linked to business size (being large enough to allow execution of the investment from a financial point of view and justification of it from a manufacturing point of view), and to high product complexity (so that to suggest the creation of an internal manufacturing unit integrated with the enterprise's international manufacturing system). Vice versa the whole foreign ownership and therefore the absence of a local partner can generate problems for introduction into the local industrial context with possible purchasing, recruiting, social legitimization and legal safeguard difficulties. It is the preferred method in contexts characterized by a low level of complexity.

The creation of a purchasing channel in China

In Figure 5.3 the main steps for the creation of a purchasing channel in China are described, as they emerge from the business cases investigated.

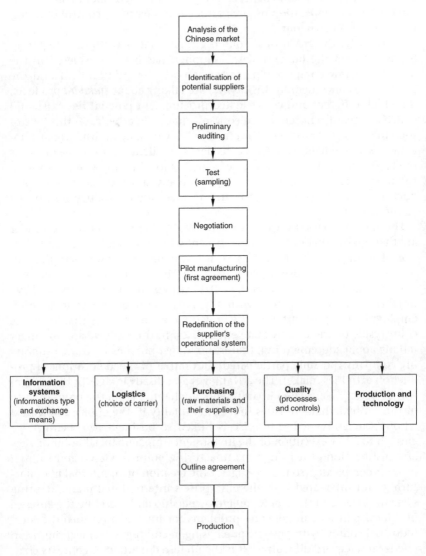

Figure 5.3   The steps for the creation of a purchasing channel in China

Analysis of the Chinese market

The analysis of the offer existing in the foreign market, which is crucial for each international sourcing path, shows some peculiarities in the case of China, a country which, more than others, is different from the cultural and industrial point of view. The sub-steps described below are part of this main step.

Analysis of the characteristics of the supply industry

The elements to be considered are as follows:

- *the current and potential competitive advantages of the Chinese supply.* The evaluation of the Chinese reality can be executed using benchmarking tools that compare the opportunities existing in different countries. It is also useful to identify the choice criteria adopted by the competitors concerning international sourcing. A cost advantage represented by labour alone, being the factor generally considered as the most attractive in this market, cannot ensure the success of the sourcing activity. It is necessary to evaluate the quality/price relationship guaranteed by the Chinese suppliers, that is to consider the total purchasing cost, and the difficulties linked to the procurement of the ingoing materials used in the transformation process. Some of the investigated enterprises have identified a sort of 'saving threshold' below which sourcing from China is considered as not convenient. This threshold varies from industry to industry and must take into consideration different factors, among which are the market situation, the supplier's growth opportunities, the commercial opportunities that a production location in China can have;
- *expertise profile of the local producers.* The investigated cases highlight unique sourcing opportunities, particularly in some industries. We have already mentioned the case of the sports shoes, that could exploit the production relocation and the knowledge transfer executed by many important western companies that have created a state-of-the-art production network in some areas. Similarly, the clothing industry in the low-level segment has developed a productive ability and flexibility that cannot be compared to that of other regions of the world. Other interesting cases are those offered by some electronic and ICT sectors generated by Korean and Taiwanese companies that transferred some production to China a long time ago. These industries have less problematic 'environmental' characteristics (that is, those linked to production, relationship, management, etc.);
- *the presence of possible customs barriers or constraints both on the Chinese side (duties and quotas) and the European side (imposition of quotas).* The forms of protectionism put into effect by the Chinese state authorities (and symmetrically by the European Union, even though generally in a less important way) are strongly moderating and, in obedience to the

agreements for China's entry into the WTO, they should be further moderated in the future; but in some industries they are still present;
• *the risks of infringement of intellectual property (trademark and patent copy).* Counterfeit examples are numerous and are often displayed in a completey unscrupulous way in western countries. Thanks to a series of recent legislative actions, legal protection in China has nonetheless improved with the consciousness that to respect intellectual property will favour foreign investments and consolidate trade relationships with foreign countries. In addition, the Chinese premier, during a recent visit to Europe, pronounced on a course of greater protection of intellectual property. Today there is (and it is improving) a legislative discipline to be used in case of disputes, while in the past negotiations were carried out with an almost complete lack of regulation. Moreover experience taught the Western operators which are the company forms and the organizational solutions that mostly protect these rights or at least limit infringement risks. The experiences analysed in this study show how equity agreements, and in particular the creation of a joint venture with a local partner, can limit the risks of intellectual expropriation. They support a higher control of the activities of the unit located in China, and therefore a higher vigilance of the Chinese party. Where infringements come from outside, a company with a shareholding ensures that the possible legal action is carried out by a legally Chinese subject. This solution is also useful if considered as a preventive measure, since a Chinese counter party proves itself to be more efficient in discouraging potential infringements. Obviously the intellectual property (trademark or patent) must be previously registered in China.

Identification of the purchasing areas

Regional differences are evident, mainly between the internal rural and underdeveloped areas, and the coastal areas. Economic growth has determined the development or the consolidation of industrial geographical clusters with different manufacturing specializations. These 'districts' represent privileged purchasing areas, since they offer manufacturing and logistic advantages. The geographical proximity simplifies exchanges and industrial relationships, favours the procurement of raw materials and components, and facilitates transports. Some of these industrial concentrations have been built by companies coming from neighbouring countries, in particular Taiwan or Hong Kong (today part of the People's Republic of China), that were the first to invest in this context and still today hold top-level positions in the classification of the main investors. Production delocalization has favoured the creation of a local industrial network, which in the past was mainly constituted by large state enterprises. Public control has since left its place to privatization. Moreover it must be said that the companies which are part of the Special Economic Zones (SEZs) better satisfy the needs of western companies by virtue of their larger experience in foreign trade, and of the availability of infrastructures and ad-hoc developed services.

The suitability of a manufacturing area depends on a series of factors, such as:

- the distance from the suppliers;
- the efficiency of the transport and communication infrastructures (rail, road, and water network) and the closeness to ports. From the research, no particular transport problems have emerged, mainly thanks to the fact that the sources used are located along the coast, where the communication structures are considered adequate. The Chinese government is leading a huge infrastructural investment programme. To support the rapid volume growth, ports have been particularly strengthened (the ship is largely the most used carrier for international exchanges) and customs formalities have been streamlined;
- the presence of incentives offered by the regional authorities. The different regions, in particular the coastal ones, are already competing to attract foreign investments, by promising reductions in the duties, advantages at fiscal level and in the building of production plants.

Finally, the choice of China as a purchasing market is often influenced by the sales opportunities that 1.3 billion potential consumers can offer. It is an attractive market mainly in the future perspective, even though it is estimated that currently about 150 million Chinese consumers have a purchasing capacity that can be compared to that in the West. These estimate are based on rather disputable statistical averages, but there is no doubt that the purchasing power is progressively growing. At the same time, if in the past the product distribution and sales met many difficulties, today the situation has improved. Recently important distribution agreements have been signed between Chinese and western operators; at the same time the reduction of the information barriers (for example the spread of the internet) allows the Chinese consumer to know the foreign products better. On a par with sourcing, the creation of a commercial base can develop according to different societal forms (from the simple contractual relationship to joint ventures up to the wholly foreign-owned enterprises (WFOEs)), each with its own characteristics, advantages and disadvantages. Chapter 7 will examine these points in further detail.

Identification of potential suppliers

Obviously, the supply offer depends on the industry, but generally speaking it is broad and the Chinese suppliers tend to do anything satisfy the customer's requests to obtain the order. This is due to the negotiation habits, but also to the manufacturing over-capacity of some industries.

However, Chinese suppliers do not always have the technology and the know-how necessary to answer suitably the specifications required. It is therefore necessary to identify which are the really suitable sources.

Information channels

According to the experiences collected and the literature analysed, the information channels used and their relative efficiency are briefly described below.

- *Trade fairs.* This is the privileged channel for many industries. Extensive exhibition events (the China Export Commodity Fairs – CEFCs) are organized every year and they represent important occasions to make contact with potential suppliers. They allow that personal communication, which is a necessary prerequisite to enter into business relationships, and to ask for quotations.
- *Foreign trade companies.* Until some years ago these companies were the only (state) subjects, which possessed export rights (foreign trade rights.) Today the situation is more complex and continuously evolving. More and more Chinese companies interface directly with the western customers, while the local foreign trade companies often seem to be ineffective. According to some experiences we collected, they can represent a good information reference, that is, the means through which it is possible to know efficient suppliers, with whom it is possible subsequently to create a direct relationship. It must be said that they still represent the only international trade link for a large part of the small businesses. Together with the Chinese we have Taiwanese or Korean intermediation companies, which are generally considered more efficient and reliable.
- *The internet.* The internet network, whose diffusion was hampered in the past by the government, is now undergoing a rapid development. The number of enterprises (usually large ones) which have developed their own web-sites is still limited, but often the regional government bodies put their own domain at the disposal of the enterprises. The development of e-commerce solutions is even more limited; it is, however, hindered by negotiation and interaction habits which, as we already underlined, favour personal contacts. In any case, it is reasonable to think that in the future the internet can prove to be an additional information channel.
- *Other enterprises.* Another important source of information is that represented by other purchasing companies that have already explored the Chinese market and have identified suitable suppliers. In the same way, the Chinese businesses, with which supply relationships have been established, can represent an important reference in order to select new purchasing opportunities. In this case the Chinese relational 'guanxi' of the Chinese partners themselves is exploited. It is not by accident that it

is easier to identify other reliable suppliers for the companies which invest in a cooperation relationship.

- *Specialized institutions*. The MOFTEC (Ministry of Foreign Trade and Economic Cooperation), the various regional ministers and the industry government bodies represent a point of reference for the Chinese small and medium-sized manufacturing companies, which often rely on these structures to start their contacts with foreign countries. On the purchaser's side, institutes for International Trade can represent an important reference, together with the Chambers of Commerce or other bodies specialized in international trade.

Check of the foreign trade rights

The Chinese government has gradually abolished the State monopoly of foreign trade and liberalized its foreign trading system. According to the amended Foreign Trade Law which came into effect from July 2004, all types of enterprises, including private enterprises, can register for the trading right. Individual Chinese are also allowed to conduct foreign trade under the amended Foreign Trade Law. In some industries, however, the sales to foreign countries are still ruled by the so called foreign trade rights and/or by license and quota systems. Beginning from January 2005, the categories of export products subjected to licensing controls were cut to 47. If the product is within the list of restricted goods, that is the list of the restricted goods prepared and periodically updated by the MOFTEC, it is also necessary to obtain the relevant license. Where the goods are also subject to impositions of quotas, the Chinese supplier must obtain some quotas for the export, the level of which is annually planned by the central authority.

Supplier's preliminary valuation

Before the inspection visit that will allow a better knowledge of the general profile of the enterprise, a recommended practice is to collect general information about potential suppliers: their size (turnover, people employed, export volume), their capacity and production profile, the nature of the ownership (public or private). This information may be accompanied by product samples manufactured for current or past customers. An element that the investigated enterprises considered as particularly important is the existence of an already-consolidated relationship with western customers, and this element is linked to an ability to create efficient relationships, to give an adequate response to the specifications and to offer a reliable quality. The information collected in this way can allow the identification of a reduced number of suppliers, to which an indicative quotation can be asked based on a product sample or general specifications. These research/valuation activities concerning the potential suppliers and the request for samples can be also delegated to intermediation companies at relatively low cost (see the ZenAsia case).

Auditing

The collection of general information about the suppliers represents a first screening. A deeper and more selective analysis should follow it and it must be carried out through a supplier auditing. First of all, it checks the information previously transmitted by the vendor concerning his company's size and its daily and aggregated production capacity. Recurrent valuation elements are those concerning the state-of-the-art level and the layout of the machines, the personnel's working conditions, the plant's cleanness, the showroom (this is a parameter which is attentively considered by some of the interviewed companies). The valuation is then extended to the single process steps and, for highly labour-intensive productions (some sectors of the textile and clothing industry and of the toy and shoe industry) to the personnel's manual dexterity. A practice, which is efficiently used by the sampled intermediation company, is to collect photographic documentation about the supplier's profile, so as to make it 'visible' for the customer, too.

An important valuation method is represented by the quality of the materials used by the vendor. The case studies reported in the second part of this text prove that the buyer quite frequently redefines the raw materials and the relevant purchasing sources.

The auditing phase is delegated to third companies in case of resort to the intermediate sourcing. If the buying firm has an IPO, it generally deals with this phase.

Test sampling

Once the supplier's capacities and profile have been evaluated, the next step is the test the product sample. The customer sends the product's technical specifications, which can also include technical drawings, samples of similar articles, information concerning the production process, and the technologies to be used. The technical sheet containing instructions for each manufacturing phase, materials to be used, product characteristics and details (colours, shapes, etc.) possibly together with photographic documentation, is transmitted to the supplier. The technical description and the level of communication during this phase depend on the type of product to be manufactured; however, generally speaking the examined experiences show that the main reference of the Chinese supplier is the sample that the buyer sends to him. As a matter of fact, graphical conventions are different and the level of familiarity with CAD systems still seems to be inadequate, even though it is growing.

The supplier manufactures one or more samples of the required code and sends them to the customer. Before sending these samples, two of the investigated companies send a 'counter document', in which the product is described, and with which digital pictures of the details are enclosed. In this way it is possible to stop samples in good time which are clearly non-compliant with the specifications.

The samples sent by the vendor are then accurately analysed, the non-conformities are identified, if any, and communicated to the vendor himself. There is interaction between the parties until a sample that complies with the required standards is obtained.

Beyond the technical capacities, a point to be considered is the supplier's collaborative attitude, that is, his real intention, particularly if the products require a transfer of *know-how* and technology, to accept the continuous presence of external operators, and to follow a development path that can determine investments in production assets, and training. The supplier's acceptance of the constant presence of external technicians or of the IPO quality controllers can be included (and agreed upon) precisely during this phase.

Negotiation

Negotiation is an activity which is carried out at various times, involving different phases of the creation of the purchasing channel. Some of the interviewed buyers have complained about the difficulty the Chinese interlocutors have in creating a precise and detailed offer, which can also be used as a reference afterwards. There are different reasons for this: lack of technical preparation by some Chinese export managers; insufficient decision-making power delegated to them; or unwillingness to avoid binding commitments during the first phases of the negotiation in order to allow room for subsequent negotiations or price redefinitions. Essentially there is a cultural diversity that is translated into a real negotiation style based on reciprocal understanding and trust more than on clarity and realization of the technical and economic elements. The extension of the negotiations, which is sometimes considered as painstaking, must not therefore be considered (only) as an effort to obtain better conditions, but as a sort of interpersonal and inter-organizational path for reciprocal knowledge. As a matter of fact it frequently happens that the transactions subsequent to the initial one are concluded rapidly. The cultural critical aspects related to negotiations will be discussed in further detail in the next chapter.

Many of the investigated cases agree on the fact that the Chinese suppliers demonstrate a readiness to accept important price restraints, but that this inevitably represents a disadvantage in terms of quality. Moreover, they agree in indicating that the greatest difficulty for the buyer is to communicate to the customer his intention to found a solid and reliable relationship, and that important volumes and repeated transactions will be the natural consequence. On the other hand, the demand for orders with high quantities is impelling.

Negotiation, which is an activity that cannot be confined to a single step, but which crosses the creation phases of the purchasing channel, reaches an initial agreement – the preliminary contract – within which the intellectual property must be regulated, if necessary, and the penalties in the case of non-observance of the agreements. Moreover, the specifications relating to the next pilot production must be defined in it, and in particular these concern:

- quantity;
- price of the production lot (the price concerning full production will be defined later on);
- technical characteristics of the product to be realized;
- packaging;
- types of inspections to be carried out (online or pre-shipment) and identification of the controller. In fact a control can be defined by the personnel of the supplying company (in this case the supplier will have to send the relevant documentation), by the customer's employees and/or by a third company;
- delivery terms;
- terms of payment (usage of letters of credit or other forms);
- export documents;
- transport type;
- final destination.

These elements will be renegotiated during the final agreement phase, which will take into consideration the exchanged volumes (on which obviously the product unit price will depend) and the changes, if any, made following the valuation of the pilot production.

Pilot production

Once the supplier's capabilities have been been tested and an agreement about the first batch has been reached, then the pilot production can start. Its realization requires an attention to quality, to details, and to process solutions higher than that dedicated to the manufacturing of the test sample.

The experience of the logistic service *provider* examined by this research suggests, in this case too, the preliminary transmission of a chosen sample of the pilot batch, so that it is possible to identify possible defects and to carry out the necessary corrections at the proper time. Moreover it suggests anticipating in digital format (through e-mail) the results of the outgoing inspection control, possibly together with digital images. From an organizational point of view, the quality control carried out on the pilot production is different from that carried out on the continuing production, mainly because the latter will require solid organizational structures and will be located at the supplier's plants. The most efficient control type highlighted by our sample is that provided by the quality controllers working at the IPO, but operating in suppliers' units.

As far as the shipment is concerned, sales contracts define the FOB (free on board) term: this means that the goods are delivered to the harbour authorities by the suppliers themselves. The customer must then manage the shipment and customs formalities. It is possible for the western enterprise also to manage directly transport from the factory to the port, but during this phase at least, this doesn't seem to be convenient. Recently custom formalities have been streamlined and made faster; nevertheless in recent months we have been registering situations of congestion of the port infrastructures due to the sharp volume growth.

Redefinition of the supplier's operational system

If the evaluation of the pilot production is successful, and the most suitable sourcing typology for the considered code is (direct) collaborative sourcing, it may be necessary to adjust the supplier's operative system to the buyer's needs, in order to make it able to support those interactions that are implicit in this sourcing type.

The examined experiences describe the Chinese suppliers as inadequate mainly as far as organization and management are concerned, but generally well disposed towards the Western partner considered as a growth and development opportunity. As far as the production profile is concerned, the situation is more heterogeneous: besides still underdeveloped enterprises or whole industries we can find enterprises provided with the most advanced process technologies. As far as the various areas in which substantial organizational and managerial interventions can be required, we set out below some considerations emerging both from our research (and therefore from the purchaser's point of view) and from that carried out by the Chinese partner (that considers the suppliers' point of view).

Logistics

This is probably the area in which the profile of the Chinese offer, mainly of the small one, is more underdeveloped. There is little integration, limited forms of computerization, and often a confused organizational subdivision of the tasks among the incoming logistics (activities concerning transmission of the order, expediting rush orders, transport, reception, control, and storage of the material), production planning and control (production scheduling and definition of material requirements, stock management, and internal movements) and the outbound logistics (management of the finished product stock, transport and product delivery to the end customer through the distribution channel). As far as these elements are concerned, many of the sampled enterprises have suggested important interventions to their suppliers. It is worth repeating that this poor profile is destined to improve rapidly following strong pressure from foreign customers, the competition dynamics that have been created among the Chinese producers, training projects and projects for the transfer of technological and managerial know-how that the State has undertaken.

As far as distribution is concerned, the offer of local providers is spreading. They offer transport and shipment services by exploiting their local relationship network. Once again we have observed the presence of instances of collaboration among the Italian purchasing companies in order to obtain scale advantages against the international carriers.

Sourcing

Unlike other developing Asian countries, China has the advantage of having some raw materials at its disposal. The search for sources poses the same problems as those previously described, in particular the difficulty in identifying really reliable enterprises. In some of the investigated cases the raw material has been initially supplied to the Chinese producer by the customer himself, once the inadequacy of the materials available in China has been verified. Once suitable local sources have been developed, the 'subcontracting' has been substituted by internal procurement.

The choice of the raw material (and the correspondent suppliers) is one area in which the buyer's intervention is more vigilant. His control often extends to the whole supply chain. The search for raw material suppliers is an activity that is frequently assigned to an IPO. However, in source selection the social network represents a privileged information channel. The other channels used by Western companies identify raw material sources are the same as those previously described.

Information systems

The supplier's computerization level of the analysed companies is growing, but it still seems to be modest, both on the internal side, and on that of the inter-company connections. The research carried out on a sample of Chinese enterprises by the NCSTE partner in Beijing indicates a limited usage of management software. On the inter-organizational side, the tools used for the exchange of information are e-mail, telephone, fax and, sometimes, teleconference. For several years e-mail has been the main communication tool by virtue of its speed, low cost and user-friendly usage. The telephone is used to give rapid answers for urgent problems; the time zone and its cost limit a greater use.

Some of the investigated buyers have developed a company web-site that can be accessed by suppliers by means of a password, on which information about the production plans and the material requirements is available. Also the Chinese suppliers have become familiar with this tool.

Quality system

The case studies highlight quality controls carried out on one or more of these levels: by the vendor himself, by the customer's (or third party's) quality controllers located at the supplier's plants, by the customer company itself in its plants. A control only involving the first level (supplier) is considered risky and justified only for standard products with limited complexity, and in any case it is activated once the source reliability has been checked. The control at the second level is the one that offers higher safety and better results.

We can distinguish between online quality control and pre-shipment inspection. The former often requires a previous transfer of know-how, and therefore the involvement of the technicians coming from the customer's central departments. It can include a definition of tests to identify reasons for defects, the choice and the calibration of the tools, as well as the process control methods.

Pre-shipment quality control, namely the control concerning outbound quality, is very important in order to avoid shipment costs for defective batches. A suggested practice, already introduced as far as test sampling is concerned, is that of the transmission of the report test (with digital images of the required details, if any), and of a pre-sampling. Once the customer has checked the documentation received, he confirms or rejects the shipment, notifies possible changes or completely deletes the order. The pre-shipment inspection can be carried out at the supplier's plant or immediately before embarkation, by the same personnel who is in charge of online quality control, by a third company or, on the occasion of targeted visits, by the foreign purchasers of the customer company. These visits allow the buyer to check the productions which haven't been completed yet and to make arrangements about future supplies.

Production and technology

The production and technology restructuring carried out by the supplier generally requires a transfer of know-how, that is, it requires that an intangible property is shared (and if necessary it can be subject to an evaluation and become part of the partner's share). Nevertheless, the know-how transfer is generally an ambivalent process. On the one hand it can be necessary to improve supply standards in order to reach required values. On the other hand, it exposes the buyer to the risk of a supplier's opportunistic behaviour, exploiting any knowledge acquired by violating the contract or company agreement. In any case the creation of a wholly foreign-owned enterprise, that is an enterprise totally owned by foreign capital, also determines the fertilization of an industrial context that could compete with the buyer himself in the future. The problem of the expropriation of intellectual property will be briefly reconsidered in the next chapter.

The analysed experiences agree that the use of an IPO with personnel always located at the suppliers' premises allows greater local control and reduces the risks of the loss or copying of knowledge.

Frame agreement

Once a trust relationship has been established, the agreement for continuing production doesn't pose problems, so that some of the interviewees have defined it as 'nothing more than a formality'. Besides the price, which is obviously linked to quality and quantity, other elements to be defined are the sampling cost, possible support for the supplier's initial investments, production methods and their scheduling, and possible penalties linked to delays in the production and to non-compliancy.

The most comman form of payment is the letter of credit: this costs more than other solutions, but it also offers higher guarantees for both parties. In the cases analysed payment is carried out 60–120 days after delivery according to the customer's contractual power. Particular attention to the contractual elements must be given in case of an imposed sourcing and in cases where intellectual property must be safeguarded (trademarks, patents and licenses). Imposed international sourcing poses complex problems, and is subject to a constantly evolving juridical discipline; it therefore needs an in-depth knowledge of the constraints, of the industrial legislation, and of the industry-specific issues. A separate agreement will be then signed with the logistic carriers, who are responsible for the shipment.

Continuous production

Once an agreement has been reached, and not only at contractual level, but also at production and organization level, then continuous production can start. At this point it is important to protect quality, to control the whole production process and to intensify cooperation, as well as the information exchange with the supplier. When the sourcing in China concerns quite important volumes, then the creation of an IPO in China can be considered. This topic will be explained in the next section.

The creation of an IPO (International Purchasing Office)

A sequence of steps and activities can be defined for the creation of a Purchasing Office, as shown in Figure 5.4.

The decision to create an IPO can be taken only where adequate volumes and certain sourcing types justify it. All the interviewed companies that have chosen a direct collaborative sourcing have created a Chinese office.

Such creation follows an adequate exploration of the local market. Sending to China personnel who have mature experience and familiarity with the Chinese reality is necessary to probe the opportunities and the difficulties implied in the process of an IPO creation. The first element to be assessed is the choice of location. Some parameters to be considered include the following:

- the distance from current or potential suppliers;

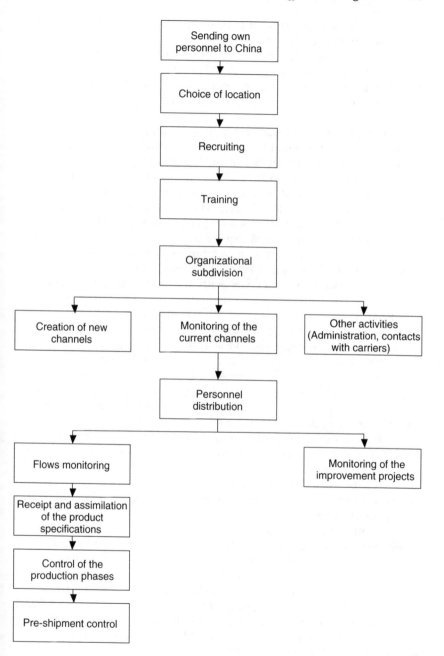

Figure 5.4 Phases for the creation of an IPO

- the proximity to ports and airports (from which goods are dispatched);
- the presence of suitable communication infrastructures;
- the places in which the industry-relevant trade exhibitions are held;
- the cost of creating, and maintaining an office;
- possible opportunities at commercial and/or fiscal level offered by SEZs (Special Economic Zones).

The number and the characteristics of the employed personnel obviously depend on the nature and the volume of the activities that the IPO has to manage. Western personnel can be assisted (and progressively substituted) by Chinese personnel. Recruiting and training of personnal, critical activities for good office operation, are processes carried out by the IPO itself in cooperation with the central bodies. The investigated cases demonstrate that it is not difficult to recruit well-trained personnel, sometimes also with a reasonable level of technical experience. The offer of English-speaking personnel, and personnel used to relationships with the Western world, comes from the State-owned companies, which are being broken up or from foreign trade companies. Generally speaking, emplayment at an IPO of a foreign company is really sought-after, because it offers pay levels significantly higher than average. The recruitment of local personnel reduces the trips and the transfers of the western personnel. Moreover the knowledge of the language and of the local culture makes the communication with suppliers' managers and workers easier, results in lower costs, allows a greater willingness to take a job that requires frequent trips or transfers to the supplying units, and finally allows the use of the social network of this personnel to identify and manage better the relationships with the new suppliers or the government authorities.

As far as the distribution of work within the office is concerned, we can identify three main tasks that identify three correspondent organizational units: the creation of new purchasing channels; the monitoring of the current channels; and the management of administrative activities. Further duties concern the link and the coordination between the central departments and the office itself.

The monitoring of the current suppliers includes activities, such as the quality control and the transfer of know-how, that require allocation of personnel at the vendors' plant. On one hand these activities concern the control of the agreed productions (through the flow monitoring, the reception and the assimilation of the product specifications, the control of the production phases and pre-shipment control) and, on the other hand, the development of new productions (and therefore the monitoring of the improvement projects). The creation of new channels concerns the identification and the selection of new suppliers.

Table 5.1 lists the main activities of an IPO and the relevant needs and motivating factors. The quality control carried out by the employees

Table 5.1   The activities carried out by the IPO and the 'critical' needs satisfied by it

Quality control	Adjustment of the products to European market regulations and standards. Timely identification of manufacturing defects and search for technical and organizational solutions. Supplier's training to carry out self-control on quality according to the relevant product and process requirements. Maintenance of a suitable and uniform quality level.
Know-how and technology transfer	Constant monitoring of the production elements, mainly when there are suppliers who are unable to autonomously adopt the product specifications. Ability to understand the suppliers' doubts and difficulties and respond rapidly and punctually. Check on site of the suppliers' progress. Direct control of the supplier's activity in order to limit 'copy' danger. Development and consolidation of a collaborative and trust relationship.
Search for new suppliers	Identification of the supply local market. Visits to and auditing of the new supplier. Direct control of the quality of material. Know how transfer to the supplier.
Recruiting and training of the Chinese personnel	Development of a techno-structure that can be more easily interfaced with local operators. Direct supervision of the new employees' activity. Training 'on site' (that is, during the visits to the suppliers' plants). Possibility of transfering know-how in more punctual and functional way.
Negotiation	Availability of technically-educated personnel, culturally similar to the local suppliers. Definition of the contractual terms.
Information exchange	Need for faster, more punctual and precise communication.
Other activities (management, legal, organization, and administrative)	Base for the travels of European employees. Presence of a legal protection in case of counterfeiting or breaking-up of the contractual agreements. Coordination of the controller's activities located at the suppliers' premises. Definition of the contract with the logistic carriers. Coordination of the different transport types, if necessary.

located at the Chinese suppliers' plants represents, as indicated, the main responsibility of the office. It answers the following needs:

- adjustment of the products to regulations (for instance regarding safety), and to the European market standards;
- timely identification of manufacturing defects and search for technical and organizational solutions;
- training of supplier to carry out self-control on quality according to the required product and process requirements;
- maintenance of a suitable and uniform quality level.

The transfer of know-how and technology is another of the activities that may be necessary for the supplier's growth. The need for a direct control of his activities is linked to the complexity and the uniqueness of the processes that determine the manufacture of a product, and it is motivated by a series of needs:

- constant control of the production elements, particularly if there are suppliers who are unable to implement the product specifications autonomously;
- the ability to understand the suppliers' doubts and difficulties in a rapid and punctual way;
- checking on site of the progress to date;
- direct control of the activity in order to limit the danger of copying;
- development and consolidation of a collaborative and trusting relationship;
- importance of direct communication in the Chinese culture.

The search for new suppliers is prompted by volume growth, the objective of higher exploitation of the potentialities and opportunities offered by this market, and the search for more favourable conditions. It must be considered that sometimes the presence of export constraints (quotas, licenses or customs duties) obliges customers to look for more profitable opportunities in neighbouring countries (for example Vietnam) using the Chinese IPO as a support base.

According to the above-mentioned reasons, the exploration of supply markets quite often also concerns the suppliers of raw materials. Direct contact with these suppliers extends the monitoring along the supply chain and offers cost and quality advantages.

The Chinese office can represent a base for the business trips of the central bodies' personnel, for example in case of trade fairs or during the perfection of agreements with suppliers. The creation of a juridical Chinese office simplifies legal protection in case of counterfeiting or breaking-off of contractual agreements.

The IPO also carries out management, organizational, and administrative tasks: the coordination of the controller's activities located at the suppliers' plants, contact with the logistic carriers and the coordination of the different transport types, if necessary. The Chinese office can represent an important point of contact for the transfer of the central departments' information to suppliers and vice versa.

6
Aspects and Critical Issues of IS in China

Introduction

In this chapter, some topics – introduced in the previous chapters and corresponding to critical issues relating to sourcing in China – will be reconsidered. In the first section, the importance of intermediation and the corresponding changes are pointed out. In the second section, some critical issues linked to the creation of organizational infrastructures in China are underlined. The third section proposes some discussions on cultural aspects characterizing the relationship between the western buyer and the Chinese supplier; these aspects are often important for companies dealing with the eastern reality. Finally, the fourth section proposes some considerations on know-how and technology transfer.

Intermediation

The opening of new markets and the improvements of tools and communication networks stimulate the industrial system to reorganize manufacturing at international level. Therefore, the subject of international sourcing – as with that of international manufacturing – has become a central issue for company strategic decisions.

Recent research carried out by the TeDis Observatory on 182 leading Italian companies in 20 industrial sectors (working in the fashion, house-furnishing, and mechanics industries) points out that 90 per cent of the analysed companies outsource one or more activities, 41 per cent have a value chain distributed internationally, 14.2 per cent have plants abroad, 25.1 per cent have strategic suppliers abroad and 8.7 per cent use foreign subcontractors. International distribution of the activities will remarkably increase in the future (TeDis, 2003).

This internationalization process automatically generates a higher logistics service demand, which is much more frequently assigned to procurement (or logistic) service providers (PSP). Their increasing relevance is pointed out by a recent study carried out by Accenture and based on 219 interviews with European and American companies. The study shows that by 2006 the percentage of the companies turning to services offered by PSP will increase from 22 per cent to 47 per cent. In particular, 42 per cent of the interviewed companies are considering turning to PSP by 2006 (Accenture, '2003 Procurement Survey'). The use of external experts is particularly important in the Chinese market which is more articulated and complex than others from a social and industrial point of view. With reference to this market, many western companies assign not only logistics tasks but also cultural intermediation tasks to service providers.

The change process of the Chinese industrial system has also determined strong changes within the intermediation realities. Until few years ago, only public foreign trade companies (FTC) had a foreign trade right, namely the right to deal with foreign countries. With the opening to international markets and the progressive privatization of the industrial system, FTCs lost their monopoly over foreign trade and their power started to decrease. Therefore, possible contact enterprises available to western companies increased and accordingly so did sourcing opportunities. An example is the Campagnolo Commercio company whose experience in China will be described in detail in the section about business cases. Once it was no longer necessary to refer to FTCs, the company could establish direct relationships with Chinese suppliers, therefore reducing costs – the intermediary cost was eliminated – and achieving production flexibility; however, relationships with more heterogeneous businesses became more complex. In this situation, the company decided to create a foreign office in China in order to monitor its suppliers and to assure them technical support.

Once again, it is necessary to stress that there are relevant differences between geographical areas and industries in China which generate different cultural and technical intermediation requirements. From a technological and production point of view, some favoured areas (real industrial clusters), long since used to dealing with western customers, have developed thanks to a consolidated foreign presence. Also, within a geographical area or an industry there are differences between manufacturers, mainly linked to company size. Generally, large enterprises are more qualified to deal with western buyers, while small enterprises generally have an outdated profile. Therefore, FTCs often play an almost irreplaceable role in the relationships with these small enterprises. NCSTE of Beijing – partner of the international project – has recently carried out research on a sample of Chinese SMEs in order to point out their average technological, organizational, and managerial profile and to understand why companies refer to intermediaries. These reasons can be summarized as follows:

- the possibility of exploiting FTC contacts, capabilities and experiences in the foreign trade;

- the difficulties of dealing with a world – international trade – which is considered difficult to understand: cultural and language differences are often considered as an insuperable obstacle;
- payment terms defined by the foreign buyer that stress the imminent risk of liquidity crisis. FTCs, using economies of scale and a higher capital availability, can sustain longer payment terms and obtain more favourable conditions thanks to a higher contractual power and international market knowledge. Once an enterprise reaches a certain size – valued by interviewed Chinese managers at around two million dollars – it often frees itself from FTCs and creates direct links with foreign customers;
- notwithstanding the improvements during recent years, law-enforcement still limits international trade development, particularly with regard to small enterprises. Impedimental elements relating to (international) trade may be related to custom duties, problems linked to foreign currency, and untimely fiscal reimbursements that are often responsible for liquidity crises;
- the organizational and management structure of most of the small enterprises comprising the sample seems to be outdated. The implementation of supply chain management practices is still a long way off, first of all because of a cultural delay and a lack of proper IT systems. Another reason pointed out by some interviewees is the weak interest in real partnerships with the eastern supplier shown by western companies.

It is therefore possible to understand why FTCs continue to be an important trade interface for many small enterprises by taking the responsibility for:

- market analyses and the search for foreign customers;
- contacts with western buyers;
- negotiations concerning agreement conditions (deliveries, payment terms, etc.) and prices;
- order transfer to supplier;
- international transport and deliveries;
- warehousing;
- customs declarations and agreements concerning the international exchange rate (foreign exchange settlement); this bureaucratic aspect is very difficult for Chinese suppliers that do not have a proper administrative structure.

According to experiences considered in this study and to the analysed literature, these public FTCs are seldom able to meet western buyers' requirements properly . Actually, most of them are ineffective, even if they keep a favoured contact with most of the local suppliers. As already shown, FTCs can, however, provide information used to gain knowledge local producers with whom companies could establish a direct relationship in the future. The ZenAsia case described below in case studies shows how it is possible to use relationship networks and information (about characteristics of the product manufactured by suppliers, about supplier localization, etc.) provided by FTCs to discover interesting sourcing opportunities.

In addition to FTCs, other (sino)korean and (sino)taiwan intermediation companies have been developed. These units, familiar at the same time with western and Chinese cultures, offer a valid intermediation mainly during the most critical steps of the buyer-supplier relationship: negotiation and specification transfer. They can also work in close contact with several local manufacturers by ensuring western buyer advantages linked to the availability of many sources and by representing the only contact subject; in this way, sourcing management is simplified.

Another intermediary type includes western companies which have gained experience and developed organizational infrastructures in China. The western purchaser assigns to them outsourcing activities requiring a presence in China: the search for supplier and raw material, transfer of specifications, know-how and technology, quality control, post-purchasing assistance. Moreover, legal support, a faster information exchange, and better logistics support are offered. Compared to Chinese FTCs and (sino)korean and (sino)taiwan intermediation companies, they offer advantages linked to the geographical and cultural proximity to the customer who they substitute during the management of the above-mentioned activities. As far as the supply side is concerned, the quality of the offered service depends on the relationship network and on infrastructures they have developed in China. In any event, an intermediary having two interfaces – a western one in contact with the customer and an eastern one in contact with suppliers, each of them managed by local personnel – seems to be the most efficient structure to manage supply transactions in the Chinese market.

Organizational decentralization

International sourcing, and more generally the transfer of value chain parts abroad, introduces many complexity factors: cultural heterogeneities, the presence of several actors, relationships with different and distant contacts, introduction to an environment with different regulations and behaviours. As a result, relevant organizational and coordination efforts have to be made, suggesting the creation of an IPO controlling the local supplying area.

Table 6.1 summarizes the main requirements, costs, and critical issues linked to the creation of an IPO in China.

Table 6.1 Main requirements, costs, and critical issues linked to the creation of an IPO in China

---

Requirements
- dependence on the adopted sourcing type
- sourcing volumes

Costs
- approval by local authorities
- investments to create and maintain IPO

Critical issues
- distribution of activities and responsibilities among IPO, central units and suppliers
- IPO coordination and control
- local personnel recruiting

The advantage (and the requirement) of a Chinese office mainly depends on the adopted sourcing method: the experiences analysed show how collaborative direct sourcing and the imposed sourcing require creation of an IPO. On the other hand, traditional direct sourcing has a limited complexity and therefore it does not require a stable presence in China. In a collaborative intermediated sourcing, the intermediation company carries out the IPO function as it has to ensure a regular and skilled control on the local area. In the same way, in case of equity agreements, activities carried out by IPO can be assigned to joint ventures or to subsidiaries. In the case of imposed sourcing, a more extended public control and the peculiarity of the involved ('strategic' or 'encouraged') industries suggest the creation of an IPO in order to manage legal aspects (that are more binding compared to other sourcing types) and to enable a more effective coordination of the imposed suppliers.

In order to create an IPO, it is also necessary to observe that considerations concerning sourcing types are combined with those concerning purchasing volumes.

Data shows how the requirement of a local control arises when volumes and the number of local suppliers increase. In other words, the creation of an IPO meets not only qualitative requirements (*sourcing* type) but also quantitative requirements. Only proper volumes justify investments required to create an IPO and costs relative to its maintenance (personnel and structure). Moreover, it is important to consider times and procedures required for the approval by the local authorities. It is also important to observe that the creation of an office in China can be the cause, not just the result, of an increase in purchasing volumes: organizational infrastructure is created only when advantages offered by this market have been examined.

In addition to these economic aspects, it is also necessary to consider some possible organizational issues. It is important to define exactly task distribution among IPO, central (purchasing) departments, and suppliers, for example with reference to quality control. In other words it is important to understand *the activity of each single subject* by defining the (in)dependency link between IPO and central purchasing office, identifying responsibilities and the required control measures. An excessive IPO decisional autonomy cannot be accepted by central departments (this problem was faced by Trudi which had to reorganize task distribution among the central and the peripheral purchasing offices). Therefore, centralization/decentralization requirements must be balanced: on the one hand, it is necessary to assign some responsibilities to decentralized purchasers, on the other hand, it is necessary that the central purchasing office manages the overall sourcing policies, connects the IPO and other operating units by justifying its decisions. The technical role of the IPO must also be aligned to the centrally-decided general sourcing strategy according to the opportunities offered by other international markets. Periodical visits of western managers, together with the triangulation of some information flows (central planning–IPO–suppliers), represent an important requirement for effective coordination.

The analysed experiences show how western personnel responsible for IPO creation and start-up are then supported by Chinese personnel for the reasons already mentioned in the previous chapter. Recruiting is carried out by the IPO itself and represents a very important activity for a successful organizational decentralization. Almost all interviewees recognized qualities and work skills of these personnel who were properly trained also through training periods at central departments.

Relationship logics and negotiation

Cultural differences between eastern and western countries often represent an important obstacle to entering the Chinese market. This section proposes some considerations of relationship dynamics with Chinese contacts, describing the main aspects characterizing the interpersonal relationships (*guanxi*, reputation, and *renqing*) and the negotiation steps, namely when western operators, face and meet Chinese culture and relationship style for the first time.

Guanxi

This word refers to an interpersonal relationship type characterized by mutual aid and favour-granting. Two people linked by this kind of relationship are aware of the mutual commitment it involves (Pye, 1982). It deeply penetrates Chinese society representing an essential element: Chen (2004) maintains that in different historical periods, *guanxi* was able to fill gaps in the legislative and political system by providing a kind of social protection and by fixing behaviour rules.

Mutual favour-granting is an important element of *guanxi*: it is not generated by feelings of friendship but, first of all, by a valuation of the offered advantages. This logic can be summarized as follows: 'the social network to which my contact belongs can be useful and in return I will put my social network at his/her disposal together with all advantages, connections, and opportunities it implies'. Therefore its nature is more utilitarian than emotional. Another important aspect is the reciprocity: if the attitude of a person is not 'right' he/she does not return the favour, his/her behaviour is considered disgraceful and *he/she loses face*.

The status of a person in China also depends on the extension and level of his/her *guanxixue*, that means on his/her relationship (social) network. The relationship network expansion is a very important element in the Chinese society and it has a relevant impact on all environments: from politics to economy. Above all, it penetrates business relationships. Generally, the meeting with the western businessmen goes through a study step aimed at valuating his/her reliability and the possibility of entering the mutual *guanxixue*. This results in an understanding and offers opportunities that sometimes are more binding than those formally defined in the agreement.

This dynamic also has a relevant impact on inter-organizational relationships: Chinese companies are part of multiple connection networks (called *guanxiwang*) that deeply influence their business. Within a mutual inter-organizational network, relationships do not follow pure market rules but meet the reciprocity commitment defined by *guanxi*. For this reason, it is important to evaluate 'suggestions' carefully about business opportunities that Chinese contact people propose to western buyers.

Reputation

Confucianism pursues the achievement of social harmony which depends not only on keeping right relationships between people, but also on the protection of the individual reputation, dignity, and prestige. Social relationships (and therefore business relationships) must meet harmony requirements and individual respect.

Reputation is divided into two sub-dimensions: *lian* and *mianzi*. The former is linked to individual behaviour; the latter considers what a person has done and the results he/she has achieved. A Chinese person is blamed at a social level if he/she does not have a *lian*, while he/she is judged a loser or is hardly considered if he/she does not have *mianzi*. The latter can be considered as a sort of social credit (Hu, 1944; Redding and Ng, 1982) and it represents a very important element in *guanxi* dynamics: the easy development and maintenance of relationship networks depends on it. Generally, social and economic status is proportional to the *mianzi* level. Each person can improve his/her *mianzi* by developing relationships with more important people and by exploiting their relationship networks.

Renqing

Within the scope of *guanxi* development, *renqing* plays a very important role. It can be translated as 'commitment towards a person' and it refers to the previously described reciprocity principle. This principle includes mutual favour-granting (which strengthens the interpersonal link) but also the respect for some social customs: 'offering, congratulations, condolences' (Chen, 2004) which are important for a right and 'balanced' attitude between subjects. It is clear that the *guanxiwang* creation (relationship network) proceeds alongside the *renqingwang* one ('commitment network'). The *renqing* level between two people defines the strength (and therefore also the *guanxi* strength) of their connection.

Each person must know regulations governing *renqing:* if this person does not know this regulations, he/she is considered unable to manage personal relationships and to maintain 'behavioural dignity'.

To understand these relationship dynamics better, it may be useful to observe the scheme proposed by Huang (1989) and shown in Figure 6.1. The chart defines two groups of people: the first is composed of people asking a favour of the person to whom they are linked; the second is composed of people who can offer this kind of favour (namely resources).

Consider a certain Mr Fang belonging to the second category. He can have one of the following relationships with a person belonging to the first category:

- an interpersonal relationship ruled by an objective attitude suggesting the best decision for that situation;
- an 'emotional' relationship ruled by the need or the tendency to favour relatives and friends;
- a mixed relationship. In this case decisions are more complex. Actually, if the 'price' to be paid to grant a favour is lower than the expected return, Mr Fang will be willing to help his friend; conversely, if the 'price' will be higher than the expected return, he will not grant the favour. Finally, if it is not easy to define the favour/return ratio, it is possible that Mr Fang will postpone the decision. Any decision taken by Mr Fang will have a direct impact on his reputation and on keeping the relationship. Actually, if Mr Fang grants the favour, he gains a good reputation and his friend will help him in the future. But, if his friend does not return the favour, he 'could lose face' and would be morally blamed. If Mr Fang does not grant the favour, he will lose the reliance given by the person who asked him the favour. In order to obtain favours in the future, he will have to regain the esteem of his friend by giving him something special.

This is only an example of the logic ruling relationships in China; relationships that depend on many other factors. However, it simplifies the

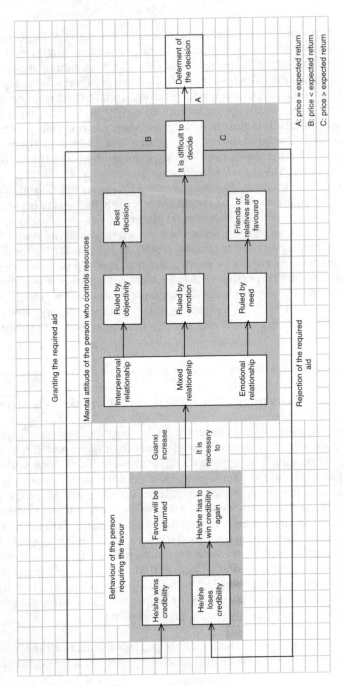

Figure 6.1 Interaction model between *guanxi* and reputation
Source: Huang, 1989

cultural context in which relationships develop. It is worth stressing that *guanxi* plays a very important role in the business world. Chinese entrepreneurs are linked to the relationship network they created: a Chinese businessman respects his commitments, he hangs on to his friends, grants favours and tries to keep his reputation by honest behaviour. Obviously he wants that his partners behave in the same way. In this way, he can gain advantages not available by using 'formal' tools.

It was observed that dynamics relating to *guanxi*, reputation, and *renqing* can interfere with the economic modernization process of the Chinese society. These relationship practices are blamed by many Chinese who are obliged to follow a favour exchange system which does not allow transparency and free and selective competition. In any event, *guanxi* is a phenomenon deeply rooted in Chinese society and culture, and even if it has been weakened – compared to the past – thanks to the economic process and the introduction of other relationship practices, it will continue to pervade in the political, economic and cultural life of Chinese society.

Negotiation

It is clear that an effective introduction to the Chinese market can depend on the quality, but also on the 'quantity' of personal relationships. Confucianism, which created this kind of relationship style, favoured individual capability and shrewdness instead of the dependency on a formal rule system. For this reason, 'Chinese have had few competitors in the negotiation activity for centuries' (Pye, 1982), and therefore the Chinese contact is more interested in a long-term relationship and (verbal) agreement rather than in its detailed formal coding. Many surveyed experiences show how Chinese suppliers tend to study in detail single agreement conditions once they agree in principle on production (and therefore on the quantities, on the quality of raw materials and process, on manufacturing solutions, etc.). This behaviour is often misunderstood but has deep cultural roots.

Signature of the contract often defines only the first step of a more articulated relationship: it defines the introduction of the partner to its *guanxixue*. To achieve this kind of understanding, a negotiation process often considered exhausting is necessary. Actually, as already observed, it must not be considered (only) as an effort to obtain better conditions, but as a kind of interpersonal and inter-organizational path of mutual knowledge. It aims at valuating the real potentials and purposes of the counterpart: it would be wrong to consider this approach as a method to confuse or exhaust the counterpart.

According to these considerations, the approach used by some western companies seems to be out of place: that is, the hurried search for a manufacturer ensuring the lowest price, unwillingness to get to know Chinese companies properly, and the worry to code all possible contingencies during the contractual step. To visit the possible supplier, to understand his real potential and the technical-cultural environment in which he/she works, require time and resources. However, it is a required investment to define conditions for a profitable and lasting agreement. The intermediation agency examined in this study maintains that exploration of the sourcing opportunities in China is '*not so much by a matter of product, rather than of people*'.

In short, the examined gathered experiences and the examined literature suggest some rules or at least some strategies useful in the negotiation stages:

- Negotiation requires time, and therefore it is necessary to be patient. It is unlikely that Asian companies will force one's hand or give an ultimatum. On the one hand, patience and self-control are important characteristics for the Asian culture; on the other hand, time favours eastern companies: a long negotiation is stressing and, above all, expensive for the western countries.
- It is necessary to gather proper information about the Chinese supplier/partner. It is especially important to identify the decisional hierarchy and the elements of the relationship network of the counterpart which can have an impact on decisions. In this case, contacts with other Chinese suppliers or with Chinese customers can be useful.
- It is important to reach an agreement in which each part meets the other part. Unlike the western view of an agreement, in China the 'middle' agreement generally represents the preferred solution (please, consider again the harmony concept) that can support, not only the economic interests, but also the dignity and the prestige of each party. Actually, a mistake often made by the western party is represented by the excessive rigidity of requests from which limited negotiation possibilities result.
- Anxiety and irritation are behaviours banned from negotiations. Not only are they pointless, but they can jeopardize one's reputation both towards the current contact, and towards the whole relationship network. *Guanxi* enables a fast diffusion of information.
- If negotiations are not successful, it is important to leave the possibility open for future negotiations. The entry into the relationship network of the Chinese counterpart does not depend only on the current negotiation success. When new occasions occur, the western company can start from a pole position compared with other companies.

Technology transfer and industrial property rights

One of the greatest problems faced by foreign investors in China is the protection of technology transfer and industrial property rights. In particular, they complain about insufficient transparency and limited enforcement of rules defending intellectual property.

Since China has entered the World Trade Organization, it has improved its legal structure and promulgated laws and regulations in order to be aligned to WTO principles. In spite of these efforts, measures used to limit a phenomenon so diffused in the country are not yet sufficient.

Among the main reasons weakening the enforcement of the laws, it is possible to underline the limited use of (unsuitable) penalties in case of plagiarism (usually there are only fiscal penalties), corruption, local protectionism (D'Agnolo, Dal Colle, 2001; Moga, 2002).

The subject described in this section is the matter of many publications (D'Agnolo, Dal Colle, 2001; Weber, 2001; Moga, 2002; Davies, 2003; Pattlock, 2003; Shuang, 2003; Tang, 2003; Birindelli, 2004; Browning, Wang, 2004; Canigiani, 2004; Zhang, 2004). Useful information can also be gathered from many institutions (such as Embassies, Chambers of Commerce, the National Institute for Foreign Trade)

In this section we want to offer an overview of these subjects. Please, refer to the literature for deeper analysis.

Technology transfer

One kind of import that requires special attention in China is technology transfer. The need for proper vigilance is mainly linked to the need to protect information in a complex system aimed mainly at defending the interests of Chinese society.

The law regulating technology transfer in China is today very extensive and articulated. Since 2002, *Regulations on the Administration of Technology Import and Export ('New Regulations')* have been in force and they changed previous laws.

The contracts subjected to this regulation are for example:

- patent licenses:
- know-how transfer with reference to production processes;
- technical support or advice in activities where the supplier uses his/her own technology;
- supply of production line or machinery involving patent transfer.

The law provides that technology can be transferred in two ways: through a simple agreement between the foreign company and an independent Chinese society (in this case there are no special interdependence relationships between the two subjects); or through a license given to a Chinese subsidiary (e.g. in case of joint ventures or wholly-foreign-owned enterprises). In the latter case, a technology licence can also represent a contribution of capital by the foreign shareholder.

Technology is divided into three categories:

- free transfer
- limited transfer (subject to restrictions)
- non-transfer

For instance, the import of technology threatening public security or that may inhibit the creation of a particular industrial sector can be prohibited.

For the first time, the *'New Regulations'* specifically rule the principle of free technology import (even if for some product categories import is forbidden or limited). It is important to observe the simplification process adopted thanks to this new normative scenario: in the past, all technology import agreements took effect after approval by MOFCOM (Ministry of Commerce). The approval process often took a long time and it was very complex at bureaucratic level. Today, even if the agreement has still to be registered, approval is no longer a prerequisite for its effectiveness. The only technologies requiring approval and the subsequent agreement registration are therefore the limited ones.

The *'New Regulations'* also solved a problem linked to the old meaning of the Chinese word 'licence': until few years ago, according to a local rule, this word meant a kind of buying by 'instalment'. At the contract expiration date, the Chinese licensee was free to use the received technology. Royalties paid every year were considered as payment by instalments with the result that the license was definitively transferred to the Chinese company on the contract expiration date.

These rules have been eliminated thanks to the *'New Regulations'*. Now it is possible to enter into usage license agreements for period longer than 10 years and to prevent the licensee from keeping use of the transferred technology after the contract expiration date (Birindelli, 2004; Italian Embassy in China, 2004).

Even if this problem, which created considerable difficulties for many western companies in the past, has been solved in the Chinese normative scenario, many others have to be settled. For example, Chinese law provides that western companies have to guarantee that transferred technology is able to give the performance results defined in the agreement. This is very risky, because a malfunction of equipment may be attributed to the technology supplier when the problem is linked to other factors.

Trademarks

Each sign that can be graphically represented can be registered as a trademark in China: letters, ideograms, numbers, three-dimensional symbols, drawings, and each combination of them. In China, companies can register the following trademark types:

- product trademarks
- service trademarks
- collective trademarks
- certification trademarks

A graphic symbol or sign is liable for registration if meets the following characteristics:

- it is distinctive
- it is recognizable
- it is lawful (these are signs and symbols that have not been previously registered or that have not been forbidden by Chinese Trademark Law).

Moreover, the law defines terms and symbols that cannot be registered as trademarks.[1]

It is generally agreed that before carrying out any business transaction in China, it is necessary to register one's own trademark directly in the People's Republic of China (D'Agnolo, Dal Colle, 2001; USA Embassy in China, 2004; Birindelli, 2004; Italian Embassy in China, 2004). Prompt registration in China is important for two reasons: first of all, it represents the only protection tool in case of violation (granted by the Chinese Trademark Law); secondly, it prevents the registration of one's own trademark by other subjects. Actually, in China the registration priority principle is in force: this principle considers that the owner of the rights is the first subject to register a trademark. If this happens, the 'real' owner not only suffers the damage deriving from the use of the trademark by a third person, but he/she cannot commercialize his/her products in China because he/she will infringe the law. In this regard, it is important to observe that, in the past, third parties registered trademarks for extortion: once they had the ownership of a trademark, they offered it to the real owner at a high price.

As far as registration is concerned, there are special regulations for 'well-known brands': only in this case, the law also defines a penalty when there isn't a registration (D'agnolo, Dal Colle, 2001; USA Embassy in China, 2004; Birindelli, 2004; Italian Embassy in China, 2004).

'Chinese version' of the trademark

The expression 'Chinese version' of the trademark means the translation of the trademark into the local language: this practice isn't required by the People's Republic of China but it is suggested from both a legal and a business point of view. From a legal point of view, the non-registration of the Chinese version of the trademark can cause the same problems resulting from the non-registration of the original trademark: in this case too, legal protection is missing. Moreover, if the foreign company does not propose a

Chinese version of its trademark to the market, the consumers themselves will do it (on the basis of a phonetic likeness), but the resulting assonance is often far from the product meaning or can give it a negative meaning.

It is important to remember that the Chinese language is composed of ideograms that are not only words but also a graphic representation of an idea or a concept. Even more than the alphabet, they can have a parallel communication function. They transmit an explicit message given by the word and an implicit one given by the meanings suggested by the signs. The translation of a trademark into Chinese is not only important to maintain an idea, but it is also necessary to create expressions which are able to suggest mental connections relating to sales and product distribution (Canigiani, 2001).

Another important element of languages is phonetics. It is possible to select the trademark name favouring the sound instead of the content. As an alternative, it is possible to find a compromise between sound and content by choosing – even if it is not always possible – ideograms enabling the sound and semantic affinity with the original name to be kept.

In order that the trademark name can be best translated into Chinese, it is important to take the advice of agencies creating trademarks and their relevant linguistic adjustment to the Chinese environment. These agencies also manage bureaucratic aspects required for trademark registration (see the discussion in the next section).

Trademark registration procedure in China

The company that wants to register its own trademark in China has two choices:

1. to submit the application to the Trademark Office of the People's Republic of China; or
2. to extend its own international registration to China.

In both cases, it is necessary to submit an application for every product class for which registration is requested. (The product classification system is the one defined by the 1994 Nice Convention for the international classification of products and services.)

Generally, the registration procedure lasts between 12 and 18 months from the application submission date. If there are no subsequent objections to the initial approval, the registration certificate is released.

The registration procedure following the Madrid Convention (extension of the international registration to China), is usually less expensive and takes less time; however, it is necessary to emphasize that trademarks registered using this method are treated as trademarks registered in the country of origin; therefore deletion of the trademark in the country of origin also involves its deletion in China (D'agnolo, Dal colle, 2001; Birindelli, 2004; Italian Embassy in China, 2004).

Patents

A patent is an exclusive right granted to a new invention. According to patent law, to register inventions, usefulness and *design* models, it is necessary to meet the following requirements:

- *Novelty*: the patent object must not have been previously distributed or submitted to be patented;
- *Originality*: the patent object has distinctive aspects and represents (at the submission of the application) a clear progress compared to the state-of-the-art technology;
- *Industry applicability*: the patent object can be applied.

Patent registration procedure is the same as the trademark registration procedure. The patent is issued by the State Intellectual Property Office, or the foreign company can ask the Patent Cooperation Treaty to extend the current patent rights – already existing in other international markets – to China.

As the People's Republic of China joined the Paris Convention (1995), the *priority date* is also valid as regards China: if a company submits a patent application for an invention previously submitted in one of the nations joining the convention, this patent is rejected.

As far as inventions are concerned, the patent lasts 20 years; patents concerning usefulness or design models last only 10 years. The patent owner must pay an annual patent tax or, otherwise the patent is cancelled.

Consideration concerning trademarks can be also applied to patents. For instance, in the case of violation of the right, it is possible to choose from administrative petitions, civil suits, legal complaints or to appeal to customs authorities.

Notes

1. Symbols like or similar to the name of the Chinese Nation, or to the national flag, to the national symbol, to military flags or to military decorations of the People's Republic of China, to inter-governmental or international organizations of other nations (unless authorization is given by these governments or organizations); symbols like or similar to special names of places in which the Chinese government offices have headquarters, or to names or pictures of symbolic buildings; symbols like or similar to official symbols, or to inspection abbreviations indicating control executions or giving guarantees (unless authorized); names or symbols like or similar to Red Cross or to Red Crescent; symbols that are unfair at racial level; symbols that have excessive requests or that are fraudulent; symbols offending the socialist morality or having other undesired effects.

7
Foreign Investments in China: Methods and Legislative Constraints

Introduction

Following the opening of the People's Republic of China to foreign direct investments in 1979, it has been necessary to define a set of rules (which was completely missing) that could regulate and at the same time attract these investments. The increase of inflow of foreign capital into the country registered in recent years and the adjustment required by the recent entry of the People's Republic of China into the WTO[1] have determined a further acceleration in the promulgation of laws and in their modernization, mainly in the fields in which the historical set of rules was more inadequate: foreign investments and international trade.

Starting from the first law on joint ventures (1979), that in only 15 articles stated the principles for the constitution of the first type of foreign investment in the People's Republic of China, now we have a rich legislation, able to give direction to the economic activities in the whole territory (*Foreign Investment Industrial Catalogue*, 1995).

A foreign company interested in investing in China therefore now has many ways to act, an articulated and quickly evolving set of rules.[2] There are various alternatives and each of them has specific characteristics and binding requirements that must be evaluated according to the size, the objectives, and the structure of the foreign company.

The issue described in this chapter is discussed in various publications (Setter, 2000; Weber, 2001; D'Agnolo, Dal Colle 2001; Romiti, 2002; Davies, 2003; Geld, 2003; Goldstein, 2003; Shuang, 2003; Tang, 2003; Birindelli, 2005). Institutional public bodies (Italian Embassy in China, Chamber of Commerce, Industry and Handicraft, National Institute for Foreign Commerce) offer further information on this matter. For further details please refer to this literature. In the following paragraphs we will offer an overview of the main elements and we will supply some ideas upon which to reflect.

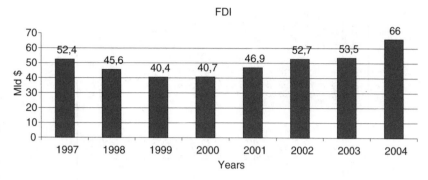

Figure 7.1   Trend of foreign investments in the period 1997–2004
Source: China Statistical Yearbook, 1999–2003; China Monthly Statistics, 2004

Historical trend of the investments from foreign countries

After the decline registered in 1998–99 and the stagnation of 2000, foreign investments in China have started to grow again significantly, registering a growth rate of 24.3 per cent in 2004 (Figure 7.1).

In the three-year period 2002–04 the mean value of the investments amounted to 57.4 billion USD; this value is also higher than the record of 1997, the year before the Asian crisis.

These data indicate that the international community is trusting China; this trust has also been obtained thanks to events such as the entry of the country into the WTO, the assignment to Beijing of the Olympic Games in 2008 (it is estimated that the city alone can determine an annual increase of 0.3%, 0.4% of the GDP) and of the Shangai World Expo in 2010.

Hong Kong[3] is by far the major investor in China (as it is indicated in Table 7.1). One third of the investments still arrive from there, even though their percentage value has registered a strong drop since 1997, the year in which the British colony became again a part of China.

From an investigation of the last five years a progressive substitution of the investment origin emerges: the relative importance of the regions which are geographically closer to China (Hong Kong, Taiwan and Singapore) has decreased, while the capital flow from western countries has strongly increased. This data probably represents a sign of maturation of the economy, and of the Chinese industrial system that seems to be becoming more and more open to international markets.

Finally, in Table 7.1 you can also see that among the European countries, in the first four places of the classification we find the United Kingdom, Germany, France, and the Netherlands; these are the same countries that are now also leading the classification of the trade exchange.

Table 7.1   Classification of the main investors in China – billion USD

	1997	1998	1999	2000	2001	2002	2003	% 1997	% 2003
Total	**52.4**	**45.6**	**40.4**	**40.7**	**46.8**	**52.7**	**53.5**	**100%**	**100%**
1 Hong Kong	21.5	18.5	16.4	15.5	16.7	17.8	17.7	41.03%	33.08%
2 Virgin Islands	1.7	4.0	2.7	3.8	5.0	6.1	5.78	3.24%	10.80%
3 South Korea	2.2	1.8	1.3	1.5	2.15	2.7	4.49	4.20%	8.39%
4 Japan	4.4	3.4	3	2.9	4.3	4.1	5.05	8.40%	0.40%
5 USA	3.5	3.9	4.2	4.4	4.4	5.4	4.2	6.68%	7.85%
6 Taiwan	3.3	2.9	2.6	2.3	2.9	3.9	3.38	6.30%	6.32%
7 Cayman Islands	0.2	0.3	0.4	0.6	1.06	1.1	0.87	0.38%	1.63%
8 Singapore	2.6	3.4	2.6	2.2	2.14	2.3	5.05	4.96%	9.44%
9 West Samoa	0.2	0.1	0.2	0.3	0.5	0.87	0.99	0.38%	1.85%
10 Netherlands	0.4	0.7	0.5	0.79	0.78	0.57	0.73	0.76%	1.36%
11 Germany	1.0	0.7	1.4	1.0	1.2	0.92	0.86	1.91%	1.61%
12 United Kingdom	1.8	1.2	1.1	1.2	1.05	0.89	0.74	3.44%	1.38%
13 Australia	0.3	0.3	0.3	0.3	0.3	0.38	0.59	0.57%	1.10%
14 Canada	0.3	0.3	0.3	0.3	0.4	0.58	0.56	0.57%	1.05%
15 Mauritius	0.1	0.1	0.2	0.26	0.3	0.48	0.52	0.19%	0.97%
16 Macao	0.4	0.4	0.3	0.35	0.3	0.46	0.42	0.76%	0.79%
17 France	0.5	0.3	0.9	0.9	0.5	0.575	0.60	0.95%	1.12%
18 Malaysia	0.4	0.3	0.2	0.2	0.26	0.36	0.25	0.76%	0.47%
19 Italy	0.2	0.3	0.2	0.2	0.21	0.17	0.32	0.38%	0.60%

Source: China's Ministry of Foreign Trade & Economics Cooperation (www.moftec.gov.cn.)

The main investment sources

In China there are essentially three investment sources which are most used by foreign parties:

1) the equity joint venture (EJV);
2) the cooperative joint venture (CJV);
3) the wholly foreign-owned enterprise (WFOE).

These investment forms (with the exception of a particular CJV typology) require the creation of limited companies, in which the foreign party owns a part (EJV) or the whole of the capital stock (WFOE).

Starting from the second half of the 1990s, together with the above-mentioned investment forms, new company typologies have become available: foreign invested companies limited by shares, holding companies, etc. However, these alternative solutions that will be described at the end of this chapter are still rarely used.

The *equity joint venture* (EJV)

The JV is a stock company whose corporate purpose can be wide and can include manufacturing and trade activities or services. There are two JV typologies: equity joint venture and cooperative joint venture (also called contractual joint venture).

The EJV is a limited Chinese *de jure* corporation with mixed capital, in which one or more foreign partners own a capital share (usually at least 25%). The shareholders can contribute to the formation of the capital stock with money, technology, machinery, and properties. The Chinese enterprise usually contributes the land, the buildings and the human resources for the production; the foreign partners contribute capital and technology. The EJV usually lasts between 10 and 20 years; this duration can also be extended upon agreement between the parties.

Since the law on EJC *'Law of the People's Republic of China on Chinese Foreign Equity Joint Ventures'* (approved on 1 July 1979), which was the first company law regulation aimed at allowing (and encouraging) the formation of mixed-capital enterprises, important amendments have been made to it, so that today the law seems to be clearly more open (allowing, for example, the creation of a JV as a company limited by shares).

The JV is established on the basis of an agreement (memorandum of association) defined between a Chinese party (legal person) and a/some foreign party/parties (natural person or legal person). The articles of association containing the company's management rules are drawn up together with the contract. The memorandum and articles of association, both subject to the Chinese law, must be approved (the JV formation is not a 'right' of the parties).

Procedure for the formation of a JV in China

From the experiences reported by the companies analysed within the research project and from some studies (Weber, 2001; D'Agnolo, Dal Colle, 2001, Birindelli, 2004) it has emerged that the main steps for the formation of a joint venture in China are as set out below and in Figure 7.2:

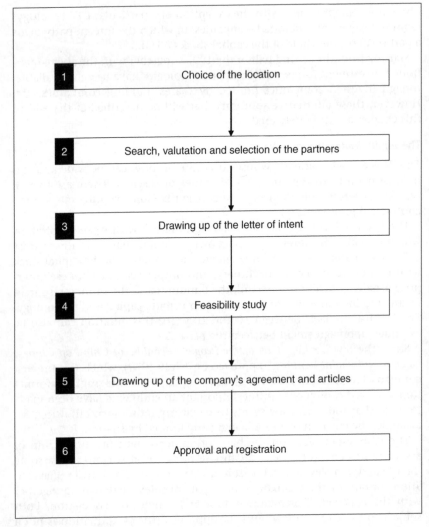

Figure 7.2 Main steps for the formation of a joint venture

1) Choice of location

First of all, an enterprise which decides to form a joint venture in the People's Republic of China will have to choose a reference area. China is a huge country, and it has regions with heterogeneous characteristics as far as climate (if you travel the country from north to south you go from the almost Siberian frigid climate of the northern areas to the tropical one of the southern areas, from the mild climate of the western areas to that hot and wet of the coastal area), economic development (from the strongly underdeveloped areas of the north-west of the country you go to the advanced realities of the coastal area), population density (very high only along the coast), resources available to the territory, manufacturing specializations (they are different according to region), and fiscal systems are concerned. It is therefore important to identify which are the areas offering the most relevant strategic opportunities.

2) Search, valuation and selection of partners

It is important to identify a shortlist of possible partners by carrying out an accurate research and a subsequent classification. For this purpose the sectorial fairs can be very useful, as well as the precious information obtained by the Chinese partners, who can be themselves interested in these types of agreements.

An in-depth evaluation phase follows this first research and classification phase, during which the Western enterprise carries out an analysis of the potential Chinese partner and of the assets he is willing to contribute for the JV formation.

Very important information in the evaluation of possible partner are those relative to the characteristics of the management, to the quality of the labour force, to the existence of a commercial network, to the technological level they own. It is noticeable that at the moment reliable sources of information on a potential partner's financial and patrimonial position do not exist. Auditing is a practice still limited to some public companies, to few privately-owned companies, and to quoted companies.

This information must therefore be found through unofficial channels.

From the experiences examined, it can be seen that in this evaluation phase it could be useful to start two or three parallel negotiations in order to be protected from possible last-minute withdrawals that are anything but uncommon.

3) Drawing up the letter of intent

Once the partner has been identified, the parties start drawing up a letter of intent that defines time scheduling and ways for the realization of the common project. The law defines that this document must clearly express the purpose of the JV, the value of the capital and of the estimated investments, the distribution of property and of the investments among the parties, and the future organization chart.

In this document it is useful to indicate the requests to the competent authorities for tax exemption or for a specific status (such as export-oriented or technologically-advanced) but without indicating too many specific definitions that may later be binding.

The conditions contained in the letter of intent can be changed in the contract upon agreement among the parties. Nevertheless, the western companies must not underestimate the importance the Chinese give to this document. If the western company wants to change, even partially, the content of the letter of intent, once it has been signed, it will be obliged to make important concessions to the Chinese partner.

Once it has the letter (and a preliminary feasibility study) the Chinese partner can go to the competent authorities in order to obtain the *'Approval of Project Proposal'*, that allows negotiations to continue between the parties.

4) The feasibility study

This is a sort of business plan that describes in a detailed way the estimated development of the JV. It quotes the main technical data about the cooperation project (information such as the future company form, the management structure, the investment amount, the financial resources used, the machine technology, the production site, the possible use of patents and trademarks and sometimes also a preliminary production plan).

This is a very important document in the formation process of an EJV: the Chinese authorities consider the contents of the feasibility study as real obligations undertaken by the parties, that will therefore have to be reproduced within the JV agreement.

5) Drawing up of the company's agreement and articles

Once the feasibility study has been approved, the partners can draw up the agreement and the articles of the new company.

Usually the Chinese partners propose to the western enterprises a 'typical agreement', which is supplied to them by MOFCOM (Ministry of Commerce). It is important to know that this agreement proposal contains various regulations, which favour the Chinese party: some of them are strictly fixed by law, others are subjected to possible negotiations. First of all the western enterprise must identify the negotiable clauses and then redefine the clauses which mainly favour the Chinese party.

Once the agreements and the articles have been established, they must be approved by the competent authority. According to local legislation, the Chinese authority has three months to approve the the request, but it seldom approves the submitted document as a whole; most of the time it 'suggests' changes on which the Chinese and western partners will have to negotiate again.

The agreement must contain indications about the corporate purpose (that the foreign investor should try to define in the widest possible way in order to avoid subsequent limitations), the composition of the board of directors, the partner's rights and obligations, their contributions, the shares, the duration of the JV and the reasons for its possible breaking up, and the responsibilities. Moreover the agreement must define contents, time scheduling and methods of the total investment. The parties can contribute to the creation of stock by supplying technology, machines, buildings and money.

6) Approval and registration

The demand for approval of the EJV must be submitted to the competent authority (MOFCOM). Any possible subsequent changes (for example to the internal structure, to the subdivision of capital and shares) must be notified (in order to obtain approval) and be registered by SAIC.

Approval is also necessary for share transfers to third parties, provided that the other shareholders, who have a purchase option on the shares, have expressed their agreement to the transfer.

The capital stock

In Chinese terminology the total investment (which must be indicated in the agreement) includes both the owners' equity (or 'registred capital') and the debt capital.

The law defines a proportion (Table 7.2) between the total investment and the shareholders' equity (and therefore between the shareholders' equity and the debt capital) in order to avoid the establishment of companies with an unreasonable debt in comparison to the capital stock. The minimum capital for EJVs must be, as the law indicates, 'adequate to the company's characteristics.' It has been observed that approval of companies with a capital lower than 100,000 USD is uncommon.

In the agreement it is necessary to indicate the time scheduling and to define the ways in which the parties decide to carry out their contributions.

Table 7.2 Proportion between total investment and registered capital

Total investment	Minimum registered capital
Less than 3 million USD	70%
Between 3 and 10 million USD	50%
Between 10 and 30 million USD	40%
More than 30 million USD	33%

Source: Birindelli 2005

Table 7.3 Time limit to deposit the capital according to the amount of registered capital

Registered capital	Maximum time for the capital payment
Less than or equal to 500,000 USD	12 months
Between 500,000 and 1 million USD (included)	18 months
Between 1 million and 3 million USD (included)	24 months
Between 3 and 10 million USD (included)	36 months
More than 10 million USD	Decided by the competent authority

Source: Birindelli 2005

The partners can choose to deposit the capital in a single payment, within six months from the granting of the business licence, or to deposit it in multiple payments. However, in this case the shareholders are obliged to deposit at least 15 per cent of the capital within 90 days from the granting of the licence, and in any case to finish their contribution according to a schedule that depends on the entity of the registered capital (Table 7.3).

The Chinese government, and in particular the SAIC, carries out frequent and strict controls on companies with foreign stocks to check the real observance of these deadlines. It is enough for one of the shareholders to fail to observe the deadlines defined by the law, for the business licence to be revoked and the joint venture dissolved.

As indicated above, the parties can contribute to the capital of the EJV by contributing money, movables and immovables, industrial property rights, technology, know-how, right of use of their land. In the case of JVs, the Chinese shareholder usually contributes machines, buildings and right of use of his land, while the western partner contributes money, trademarks, patents or know-how.

Industrial property rights and know-how can considered as a valid contribution if they satisfy at least one of the following requirements:

1) they must improve the product quality and the plant productivity;
2) they must allow to significant savings to be achieved in the use of the resources necessary for production.

The technological contribution must be supported by a precise documentation, and although it cannot usually exceed 20 per cent of the registered capital, it can exceptionally reach 35 per cent, if it is 'advanced technology' (see the classification defined by the State Science Commission).

As far as the valuation of the foreign investment in the JV capital is concerned, it has been defined that the value of each machine (given by foreign companies as a contribution) must be estimated by the competent state office that will issue a specific certificate, once the valuation has been carried out.

The value of the machines will be checked when they are in China. This situation can lead to a clear problem when the value defined by the assessment is lower than that defined by the parties to the agreement. In this case the law defines that negotiations with the partners in order to reach an agreement concerning the compensation can start. Otherwise the foreign company has to increase capital with a sum of money corresponding to the difference in value.

The rights to use the land

Chinese law establishes that the land can be state-owned or collectively-owned (when it belongs to local urban communities), but it is never owned by private citizens or enterprises, which can only obtain the right to use a land, and to create buildings on it once the necessary authorizations have been obtained.

There are two main categories of right to use land: allocated rights and granted rights (Table 7.4). Due to the characteristics typical of granted rights, it is necessary that the JV is signed with this type of agreement.

When a JV is formed, the three following situations can occur:

1. The Chinese partner has granted rights: the right of use represents a contribution by the Chinese partner to the capital stock; from this moment on the new company becomes the owner of this right for the whole duration of the right itself;
2. The Chinese partner has neither granted rights nor allocated rights; the JV can acquire a right of use for a 50-year maximum duration from the Republic (the company will have the opportunity to make use of this right or it can sell it off against compensation) or it can acquire the rights granted by a subject, who owns them.
3. The Chinese partner has allocated rights: in this case the western partner must check that the Chinese company has requested the conversion of

Table 7.4 Allocated rights and granted rights: main characteristics

	Allocated Rights	**Granted Rights**
Rent	Null or reduced	Considerable
Agreement expiration	Endless	Determined
Expropriation	Not uncommon (without any penalty)	Rare (with penalty)
Limits	They cannot be transferred or rented	No limits

these rights into granted rights; if not they cannot be used. This check is even more important when the Chinese partner uses these rights as a contribution to the capital stock.

The ownership of the real estate is strictly linked to the possessory title of the right to use the land on which the facilities are built.

Management and administration of the equity joint ventures

The most important body of the JV is the board of directors, which makes the most relevant decisions. It consists of three or more directors (with a four-year and renewable mandate) chosen by the shareholders according to the capital share they own.

The law defines that some decisions (increase of the capital share, share transfers, incorporations) must be taken unanimously within the board of directors, while other decisions need other types of majority to be approved. Moreover, we wish to point out that in China many internal decisions (for example the modification of the statute) must be approved by the government too. This provision represents a disadvantage for the western shareholders, since it quite often happens that the government approval is influenced by the interests of the Chinese party.

Finally the law defines that each JV must appoint a chairman, that is, the legal representative of the company, who has the power to call the board of directors, and a vice-chairman. The company management is assigned to a general manager, assisted by one or more deputy general managers, all of them chosen using criteria similar to those used for the nomination of board of directors.

The cooperative joint venture (CJV)

Chinese law defines two types of CJV (contractual or cooperative joint venture):

1. a 'pure' CJV, in which a simple 'partnership' is created without forming a new company;
2. a 'combined' CJV in which a new company is formed. In this case we have something similar to an EJV, and it is not by accident that this type of company is subjected to a regulation which is very similar to that ruling EJVs.

The CJV is therefore a company form which is similar to the EJV. The main differences are:

- in this case the foreign participation share is not limited;
- the minimum duration is not established by any regulations;
- shareholders' rights and obligations are defined during the negotiations and are not linked to the capital share owned;

- the profits deriving from the joint activity are not distributed according to the share capital owned, but according to the arrangements reached and indicated in the agreement itself.

This last point is particularly relevant since it offers important opportunities to the western enterprise: a company which wants to recover its investment in the shortest possible time in order to leave the JV has, in this way, an opportunity to do it.

The CJV is also formed on the basis of an agreement between the Chinese and the foreign party, approved by the MOC (or by the local authority) with a very similar procedure to that used for the EJVs.

As far as the management and administration bodies are concerned, there are few differences in comparison to what has already been explained for the EJVs. The main differences can be summarized as follows:

1) the directors' mandate does not have a fixed duration;
2) in case of a pure CJV, there is a joint management committee and not a board of directors, since a new company has not been created;
3) the types of decision that be must be taken unanimously by the joint management committee or the board of directors of a CJV are more numerous than those taken for the EJVs;
4) the types of decision that must be approved by the government are fewer than those necessary for the EJVs.

The wholly foreign-owned enterprise (WFOE)

The WFOE is a wholly foreign-owned company.

The '*Law of the People's Republic of China on Foreign Capital Enterprises*' that disciplines this form of investment dates back to 1986, and its executive regulation was published in 1990. Although the WFOE represents a quite recent solution, it has nevertheless become in a few years the alternative preferred by the foreign investor

The formation procedure

The procedure for the formation of a WFOE is speedier than that used for an EJV, because the phases concerning the partner selection, the negotiations, and the drawing up of the agreements that rule the partnership are absent in this case. The activity is limited to the following phases:

1) submission to the competent authority of the 'Project Proposal' (containing several data about the company you wish to form, such as the business purpose, the production line, the energy needs, etc.);
2) submission to the MOFCOM of the request for the formation of the WFOE (during this phase various documents must be attached, including the articles of association);

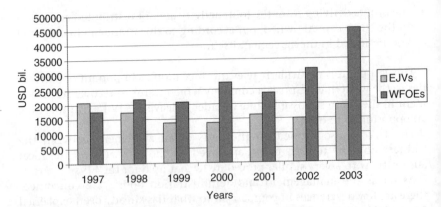

Figure 7.3   Trend of the investment equivalent value in the period 1997–2003: EJV vs WFOE
Source: China's Ministry of Foreign Trade & Economics Cooperation

3) submission to the SAIC (State Administration for Industry and Commerce) of a request to obtain the business licence, whose date of issue is the formation date of the WFOE.

The capital stock

The juridical system of the WFOEs is very similar to that of the EJVs; there are only some slight differences.

First of all it must be noticed that for the WFOEs no minimum threshold for the capital stock is defined. There is only a quite generic rule indicating that it must be suitable to the activity the enterprise is going to carry out.

The investor can contribute to the WFOE capital with foreign currency, machines, and plants, industrial property rights, technology, and know-how. The contributions with rights and know-how cannot, however, exceed 20 per cent of the capital stock.

The law doesn't require the presence of Chinese administrators within the company.

The advantages of the WFOE against the EJV

In recent years the WFOEs have rapidly grown, so that in 1998 they exceeded EJVs (considering the investment equivalent value) (Figure 7.3).

The choice of the way in which to enter the Chinese market is strategic. Growing preference for the WFOE can be explained by the major advantages that this model offers (Table 7.5).

1) *More autonomy and speed of decision-making*: since there isn't a Chinese counterpart with which an agreement must be reached for each decision (please remember that the Chinese law states that many decisions must

Table 7.5 Reasons for a more and more widespread use of WFOEs

EJVs vs WFOEs	
Advantage of the EJV • Quicker introduction into the Chinese industrial context	Advantages of the WFOE • More autonomy and speed of decision-making • Greater control of know-how and technology transferred to China

be taken unanimously), the western company is able to make decisions rapidly. This represents an obvious limit of the EJVs, in which partners with different business objectives and approaches are necessarily obliged to reach an agreement and, in doing so, they waste time.

If the problem with the JVs described above is true in general, it is particularly true in the Chinese context, in which the local partner usually has a short-term motive (that is obtaining technology, capitals, and experience), while the foreign enterprise has a longer-term horizon (and thinks about long-term co operation).

2. *Greater control of know-how and technology transferred to China*: many companies with a JV agreement have experienced the transfer of their technology to other companies.
3. *The changes to government policies against WFOEs*: as a matter of fact since 2000 many constraints, which in the past limited WFOEs in comparison to EJVs, have been eliminated: as an example let's consider the regulations that required that the majority of products had to be exported or those concerning the purchase of raw materials, which had to be necessarily carried out on the Chinese territory. Moreover in the past the law required that WFOEs had to be characterized by technologically advanced productions. Today many of these limiting regulations are no longer valid.

An identified advantage of JVs is the presence of local partners that can guarantee a better introduction into the local industrial context (realization of trade relationships). For JVs there are also some (limited) fiscal advantages (and more generally government rebates), which are still not valid for WFOEs. Moreover, nowadays in some industrial sectors only the establishment of JVs is allowed.

Constraints to the creation of joint ventures and wholly foreign-owned enterprises

Chinese law defines some constraints to the creation of JVs and WFOEs, which are linked to the industrial sectors in which these companies intend to operate. As a matter of fact, in the Dragon's country there are four categories of industrial sectors (as indicated by the *Foreign Industrial Investment Guidance Catalogue*):

1 *'supported sectors'*: these are characterized by technologies that China is interested in importing. The Chinese government has activated some facilitations aimed at obtaining an expansion of foreign investments in these sectors (for example the companies established in China, and which produce goods belonging to these sectors can import the machines that represent the contribution to the capital stock with customs and tax exemptions);
2 *'allowed sectors'*: these offer neither facilitations nor limitations to foreign investments;
3 *'limited sectors'*: these are subject to some limitations. The most important of these are the restrictions on foreign participation to the capital stock. In some 'limited sectors' a western company cannot create a WFOE; in others, the regulatory system states that not only is the foreign partner unable to possess the whole capital stock, but that he must hold the minority within the JV;
4 *'forbidden sectors'*: these are sectors in which foreign capital cannot be used.

The classification of the sectors into these four categories is continuously evolving. The *Foreign Industrial Investment Guidance Catalogue*, and the measures delivered by the ministries change these classification frequently.

Further investment forms

The representative office

The representative office is an office created by a foreign enterprise in the People's Republic of China. It represents the simplest form by which a foreign company can work in China. It is created because of the need to monitor the local market, to create and to maintain good relationships with the eastern customers without necessarily investing large amounts of money. Moreover, for many western companies the representative office represents a sort of first 'exploration' step before creating a JV.

The representative office may not only be a choice, but also an obligation. As a matter of fact, Chinese law states that it is mandatory to open such a structure for those foreign companies which have been running economic activities in China for more than six months.

The activities that the representative office can carry out in Chinese territory are important, but limited: promotions, search for trade information, market analyses, negotiations and intermediations (on behalf of the company to which they belong). Moreover, these offices can also control the activities of the parent company operating in the People's Republic of China.

On the other hand, the representative office cannot carry out sales or production activities. As a consequence it can neither invoice nor sign agreements in its own name.

The procedures for opening a representative office are quite simple: it is enough to send a registration request to the competent authority through a foreign or Chinese authorized company. Once the authorization has been obtained, it must be subsequently registered by a local authority.

Holding companies

The first regulation about *holding companies* (HCs) dates back to 1995, when the MOC issued the *'Provisional Regulations Concerning the Establishment of Investment Companies with Foreign Investment'*. This regulation has been modified (first in 1999 and then in 2001) so that today the actual version has less heavy constraints than the original.

The regulation has been created in order to answer requests coming from the most important Chinese industrial groups that have experienced some problems in managing various activities simultaneously.

Although HCs can take the form of a JV or a WFOE, they are generally created as a WFOE according to the reasons which have been explained above.

In the beginning, the corporate purpose of the holding companies was very limited (in the past they could only finance investment projects, supply services to joint ventures and carry out few other activities), but it has been widening year by year. Since 2001 the holding companies have been allowed to market the products manufactured by their controlled companies and carry out research, transport and storage activities.

Many advantages derive from the creation of a holding company: think, for example, of the possibility of creating economies thanks to a central management structure or of adopting group strategies.

From the fiscal point of view, HCs enjoy tax reliefs if the foreign investor's share is at least 25 per cent of the capital stock.

In order to obtain approval from the MOFTEC, the enterprises which wish to create an HC must demonstrate that they possess a solid financial situation, and a real need to manage multiple projects in China. Since the regulation is quite rigid and selective, as far as these elements are concerned, the possibility of creating an HC is only granted to the companies that have a very high level of foreign direct investments in China; this is the reason why this form of company is very rare.

Foreign invested companies limited by shares (FICLS)

A foreign invested company limited by shares has notable advantages in comparison to the creation of a JV, a WFOE or an HC, but also some limits.

The main advantages are:

1) this form of company doesn't need unanimity within the board of directors for its resolutions; this allows decisions to be made more rapidly than in other investment typologies;
2) the transfer of shares is not subject to the other shareholders' consent;
3) the FICLS can be quoted on the Chinese stock exchange and on foreign stock exchanges;
4) They can issue new shares or bonds: this allows to find easier financial resources.

The main disadvantages are:

1) the creation of an FICSL is a choice reserved to important investors (the minimum capital must be 30 million reminbi);
2) the creation procedures are complex: the FICLS can be created through the 'system of the promoters' (which in this case must underwrite all the company shares) or through a public subscription (in this case at least 35% of the shares must be underwritten by the promoters). In both cases the promoting parties must number at least five people, of whom at least 50 per cent must reside in China and at least one must be a foreigner;
3) the promoters cannot transfer their shares to third parties until three years after the formation of the company (or, alternatively, until the moment they have completely paid their contributions). Also in this case, the foreign investors must have paid up at least 25 per cent of the capital in order to obtain tax reliefs.

Notes

1 The entrance of China to the WTO (2001) has had numerous implications, among which the main ones are the reduction of the customs duties, progressive elimination (2005) of the quotas system, the progressive liberalization of the foreign investments, thanks to the review of the 'Foreign Investment Industrial Guidance Catalogue' (1995)
2 E.g. some restrictions in insurance, real estate, constructions and transports sectors have been recently eliminated; others (like the mobile communications limitations) have been introduced.
   Also 'a particularly controlled' aspect as the international commerce has been recently reviewed in depth to make it more open.
3 Even though Hong Kong is a part of China, it is still a separate region from the rest of the country from a cultural, geographical, and economic point of view. This explains why today the studies carried out by the

China's Ministry of Foreign Trade & Economics Cooperation classifying the foreign investments in China still consider Hong Kong together with the other foreign countries.

8
Transport Infrastructures

Introduction

Transport represents a complexity factor for sourcing in general, and for sourcing from China in particular. This chapter offers a brief overview of the current transport situation in China. Starting with a brief description of the infrastructural evolution of the last decade, the main transport types (rail, air, road and ship) are examined, and their specific characteristics and issues outlined.

Transport evolution

In the early 1990s the Chinese government started to understand the need for important infrastructural investments in order to support the country's economic development project. The capillarity and the quality of the transport network was clearly inadequate (particularly the roads) both from a quantity (actual network length) and a quality (percentage of asphalted roads) point of view. Besides the structural limits, there was the problem of the transport companies, which were mainly state-owned (for example COSCO – China Ocean Shipping Company – and Sinotrans – China National Foreign Trade Transportation Group). They were outdated and inefficient, unable to supply clients with a satisfactory service. The agricultural industry alone reported a loss of almost 30 per cent of fresh products along the internal supply chain. The high costs and the constant delays in the deliveries were two of the factors limiting foreign investments.

Being conscious of this situation, the government started an important project to strengthen the rail and road network. In the early stages these investments revealed the limits of planning that didn't accurately consider traffic volumes. The result was some areas more and more subject to continuous traffic congestion, and others which operated below capacity. An example is the motorway which links Beijing to Tianijin Port: it was designed in 1992 for an average of 50,000 vehicles per day, but just a few thousand vehicles use it (Weber, 2001; www.ice.it; www.dhl.it).

These planning errors have since been extensively corrected and today the situation of transport in China has largely improved. Two problems, however, still remain almost completely unsolved: the strong lack of infrastructure in the internal areas of the country, and the high fragmentation of the logistic sector. As far as the first element is concerned, the great inequality of industrial development between internal territories and the coastal area has been described many times. Foreign investment concentrated along the coastal area for geographical reasons and therefore the first great infrastructural interventions also concentrated there. On the other hand, current investment projects tend to favour the development of the internal areas or at least to reduce the differences between the internal and the most advanced areas.

As far as the second point is concerned, the carrying trade high fragmentation of the transport sectors means that companies need to delegate their logistic flows to many (small) operators, each of which is characterized by a limited range of competences and geographical coverage. In this way transport becomes more complex and onerous. Some state intervention has tried to favour the aggregation of these enterprises into groups. Together with this state action, further action is being carried out by private enterprises and foreign operators. In recent years important new entries in this sector have been recorded thanks to some important manufacturers, who have broken their logistic activities away from their core business, making them autonomous and purchasable. At the same time many important international operators have entered the Chinese market by investing substantial resources and increasing the quantity and level of the logistic offer available in China increasing the quantity and level of offer (www.dhl.it, www.China-Italy-Trade.net; www.it.danzas.com).

Rail transport

In the early 1980s the rail infrastructure had a total length of almost 50,000 kilometres; over the years it has registered a constant growth (about 1 per cent on an annual base), and a progressive improvement of rolling-stock and of the whole system. Many single-track lines have been 'doubled' and the most important of them have been electrified.

The electrified network, which in the early 1980s represented only 2 per cent of the total network, stands now at 50 per cent. Similar data concern the evolution of the double-track network in comparison with the single-track (Figure 8.1).

This development of the rail network has not, however, blocked a progressive reduction in use of rail transport. Until the 1970s the railroad represented the most frequently used means of transport in China. In 1970

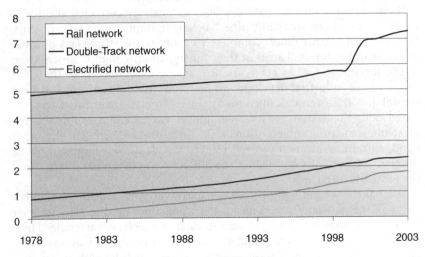

Figure 8.1 Evolution of the rail network (1978–2003)
Source: www.china.org

freight traffic amounted to 1,503 million tons per year and about 681 tons (more than 45 per cent) were transported by rail. Over time this percentage has gradually reduced, so that today rail transport is used for a load of 2,042 million tons, which represents only 14 per cent of the total traffic (Figure 8.2).

The costs determined by this type of transport are extremely competitive (about one-third of those for road transport). The progressive reduction of rail use is therefore not justified in terms of cost, but in terms of capacity, flexibility and time, which are still unsuitable notwithstanding the improvements which have been carried out.

The fact that some lines are not available (or that some of them have inadequate capacity) obliges operators to book their services well in advance (even a month in advance for the Xinjiang). According to a decision by central government, a large part of the available space is reserved for coal and steel, which are crucial goods for the country's economy. Moreover, the availability of means of transport is subject to strong seasonal variations: during harvest time priority is given to foodstuffs which occupy a large volume.

Finally, slow engine speed, container standardization, insufficient infrastructures for special transports, and inadequate level of the inter-modal exchange areas and of the information systems are additional factors pushing towards the non-use of rail transport.

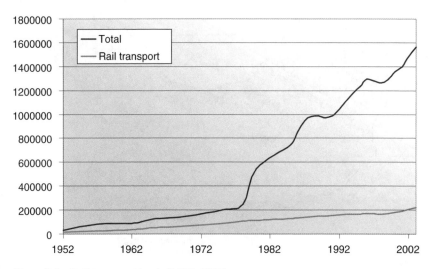

Load of rail transport (10,000 tons)

Figure 8.2 Rail transport loads (1952–2003)
Source: www.china.org

As far as the capillarity of the network existing today in China as a whole is concerned, the average density is 0.007 km per square kilometre – about ten times lower than that of European countries such as France and Great Britain. However, the most sensational data is the high lack of homogeneity in China between the eastern areas (characterized by a network very similar to the European one) and the western areas (where there are areas with a density 1,000 times lower than the European standards) (www.china.org) (Figure 8.3).

In the future an increase of the rail network is estimated. The network will increase to almost 150 per cent of the structure currently working: by 2010 an extension of 100,000 kilometres should be reached in order to allow more comfortable connections both from north to south, and from east to west (Figure 8.4).

Air transport

This is the type of transport that registers the highest growth rate (Figure 8.5): nearly 16 per cent per year in terms of tons and 17 per cent in terms of tons/kilometres (survey carried out from 1990 to 2002), with a substantial balance between national and international flights.

The constant growth of air cargo allowed five Chinese airports to come in the top 50 positions of world classification, as far as goods handling is concerned.

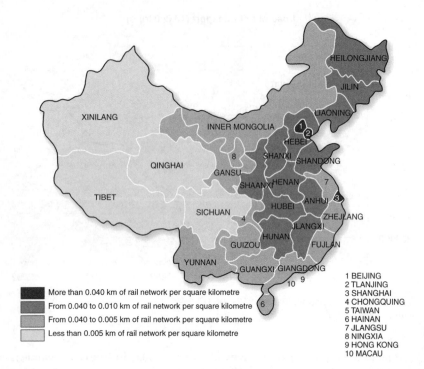

Figure 8.3 Distribution of the rail network in China
Source: www.chinadatacenter.com; *China Statistical Yearbook*

At the moment the infrastructures used for air transport are distributed so that they can ensure a good coverage of the Chinese territory: in each province there are airports with availability of national flights (more than 200). The density of airports with international lines is lower, but nevertheless sufficient.

Capital Airport in Beijing is the busiest in the country (Table 8.1): it allows travel to 60 Chinese cities (therefore ensuring an almost total coverage of the country), and to 40 foreign regions and countries. Moreover, the city government has already planned a further expansion of the airport with new strips and terminals, in consideration of the Olympic Games in 2008.

With the Olympic Games always in mind, Binhai Airport in Tianjin will be also enlarged: the objective is to increase the frequency of flights on the existing routes to the main national and international destinations.

The air traffic of the south-east coast depends on two large cities: Shanghai and Canton. Hongqiao, in the Shanghai municipality, is the second airport in the country, and it has many international lines and routes which cover all the main internal stations. In 1999, with the

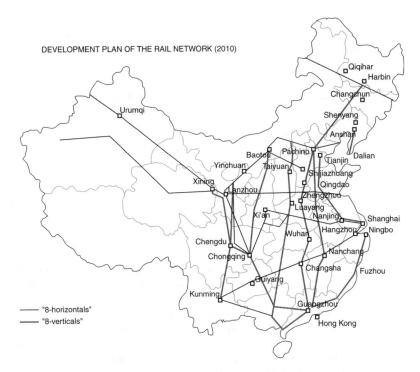

Figure 8.4   Long-term projects for the development of the rail network
Source: www.dhl.it

Loads of the air transport (10,000 tons)

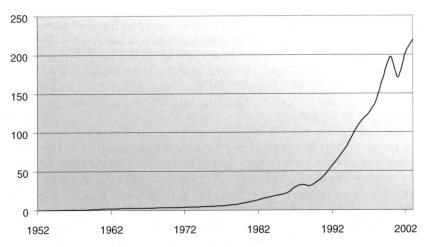

Figure 8.5   Air transport loads (1952–2003)
Source: www.China.org

Table 8.1   Goods handled by the main airports

Rank	Airport	Goods transported (in tons)
1	Beijing Capital Int'l Airport	774.205
2	Shanghai Hongqiao Int'l Airport	612.220
3	Guangzhou Baiyun Int'l Airport	491.868
4	Shanghai Pudong Int'l Airport	266.682
5	Shenzhen Huangtian Int'l Airport	202.743
6	Chengdu Shuangliu Airport	158.635
7	Kunming Wujiaba Airport	125.034
8	Xiamen Gaoqi Int'l Airport	99.484
9	Xi'an Xianyang Airport	76.445
10	Dalian Zhousuizhi Int'l Airport	76.283

Source: CAAC Airport Annual report

opening of the new and modern Pudong airport, Shanghai became the only Chinese city with two international airports. The total freight traffic amounts to 1.1 million tons, and this means that the city ranks first in the country as far as volume of transported freight is concerned.

Many flight routes connect Canton with the other main Chinese cities and with many capitals of south-east Asia, such as Kuala Lumpur, Singapore, Bangkok, Rangoon, and Vientiane. The new airport will also allow direct connections with European countries. Besides Baiyun Airport in Canton (third Chinese airport in terms of traffic volume) in Guangdong, there are Shenzhen airport (fifth Chinese airport), and the airports of Zhuhai, Shantou, Zhanijang, and Meixian.

As far as the central part of the country is concerned two main airports are located there. Xi'an (capital city of Shaanxi) airport manages nearly 100 national and international flights. The main international routes include Hong Kong, Macao, Japan, South Korea, and Saudi Arabia.

Chengdu Shuangliu Airport, in Sichuan, is the main airport in the south-west of China. At the moment international flights for Hong Kong, Bangkok, Singapore, Japan, and the Korean Republic are available (www.ice.it, www.dhl.it).

In China there are 31 different carriers. Government policy regarding the air cargo industry is aimed at improving the concentration of the most important companies: Air China, China Eastern, and China Southern represent a market share of 61 per cent of the national total as far as cargo handling is concerned. Air China, based in Beijing, also controls Air Dragon, the second air company in Hong Kong. Today China Southern, the company that controls the Guangdong area, has flights along six hundred national and continental lines thanks to an aggressive acquisition strategy.

There are no particular functional inefficiencies as far as air transport is concerned; nevertheless other transport modes are often favoured due to cost reasons, both for transfers within the nation, and for international lines.

Road transport

In recent times the road network has been subjected to rapid development (Figure 8.6) thus registering a high average annual growth (5 per cent in the last decade). Nevertheless this growth started from an initial situation of serious infrastructural shortage; this is the reason why road coverage is still quite limited: the national average is about 0.17 kilometres of road per square kilometre – nearly a fifth of that existing in the United States and about a twelfth of that in Germany. Motorways connecting the biggest cities represent only 10 per cent of the total road network, notwithstanding the massive investments of recent years.

Large differences exist between the different provinces as far as network density is concerned (Figure 8.7): we have up to 0.80 km/square kilometre in some provinces of the coastal area and as little as 0.02 km/square kilometre in the west. The north-western provinces, mainly mountainous, are experiencing the greatest difficulties. The current five-year government plan provides for the realization of new important national main roads for a global extension of the road network of an additional 200,000 kilometres.

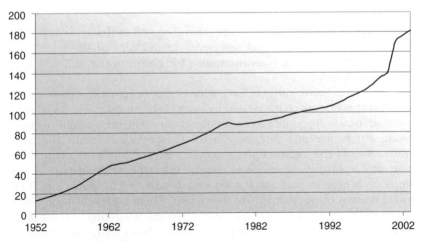

Evolution of the road network (10,000 km)

Figure 8.6 Evolution of the road network (1952–2003)
Source: wwww.chinadatacenter.com, *China Statistical Yearbook*

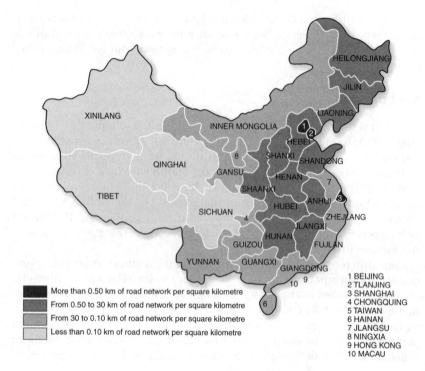

Figure 8.7   Distribution of the road network in China
Source: wwww.chinadatacenter.com, *China Statistical Yearbook*

This type of transport is very important (Figure 8.8) (today the quantity of goods transported by road represents 75 per cent of the total loads handled in the country), notwithstanding the problems that still exist with this type of handling.

For example, the territory offers a wide choice in terms of logistic operators, but this offer is characterized by high costs, an excessive fragmentation and, on average, quite a low service quality. The tax burdens imposed by current regulations determine high transport costs, while the fairly limited size of the logistic operators makes it necessary to resort to more than one company in order to satisfy interregional transport needs. Moreover it must be said that the available means are not satisfactory at all, and this often causes damages to the freight. There are frequent problems linked to the presence of non-specialized personnel working in these logistic companies. If it is true that freight suffers from frequent damage, it suffers particularly from the increase of the necessary number of shipments as a consequence of the unsuccessful optimization of the load capacity.

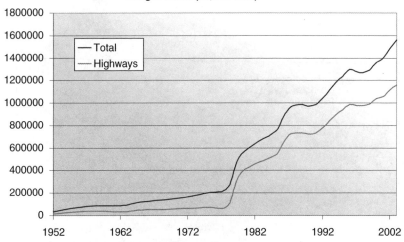

Figure 8.8 Road transport loads (1952–2003)
Source: www.china.org

Moreover, road transport is strongly penalized by bans and regulations at local level; local administration often imposes licences or bans, or carries out special controls with serious consequences on delivery times.

Other malfunctions strictly linked to functional elements can be summed up as bureaucratic problems. Anything but irrelevant for a cost analysis is the high frequency of failure of the means of transport due to low road quality.

Nevertheless, the choice of road transport, in spite of the faults just described, is very common, since it represents the only alternative (in particular for time-sensitive goods) to rail, which often cannot be used.

Companies usually prefer road transport for short transfers, while for longer ones they prefer to transport by ship (when their geographical location makes this possible) or by air (for time-sensitive products and those with a high value/volume ratio).

Generally speaking, enterprises use road transport for the greatest percentage of loads (Weber, 2001; www.china.org; www.dhl.it; www.China-Italy-Trade.net).

Transport by ship

The ports in China

The geographical characteristics of the country have highly favoured the development of transport by ship: in addition to a wide coastal area that

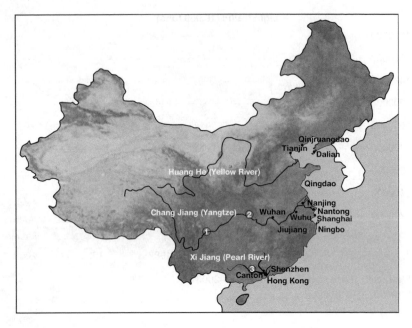

Figure 8.9   Chinese ports
Source: Omnia Atlante

runs from the port of Dalian (to the north) to the city of Beihai (to the south), China is provided with an important internal river network, which represents the real backbone of the transport system. Unfortunately the natural flow of the rivers, besides not ensuring a complete coverage of the territory, does not favour any type of north–south connection.

The main internal navigable routes (two-thirds of the total network) are positioned in the southern regions, where the basins of the Yangtze and the Xi Jiang (Pearl River) are located (Figure 8.9).

The Yangtze, the major river of the continent, rises in the Tibetan highlands in Tsinghai, then goes to Yunnan and to the east in Sichuan; it passes through almost all central regions of the Chinese territory to flow into the Eastern Chinese Sea with a wide delta located immediately to the north of the port of Shanghai (to which it is directly connected by the river Huangpu). It is navigable from Sichuan (to be precise, from Yibin), and from Yichang by small–medium capacity commercial ships. Among the various river ports located on the banks of the Yangtze, we should mention Nanjing, Wuhan Wuhu and Nantong, which are strategic nodes for goods distribution to the inland provinces.

If we proceed to the southern area, to Guangdong, we find the second fluvial route of the country, the Xi. It rises in the Guangxi Province from the confluence of two watercourses. It goes to the south-east, flows through Wuzhou (where it becomes navigable) and then it runs into the Guangdong Province (where it flows to Canton) and at the end it flows into the Southern Chinese Sea with a wide delta.

The northern territories are washed by the waters of the Yellow River, often muddy because of the enormous quantity of loess carried to the surface. For decades, important interventions have been carried out in order to smooth its route, but still today the river is not navigable.

The eastern coast is the most active area for sea freight, both as far as international routes and internal river connections are concerned. The crucial point of this system is Shanghai. It is situated at the intersection between the 'gold coast' and the 'golden waterway' (the Yangtze) with an area of 3,600 square kilometres. It represents the most important port in China. Also, thanks to the realization of many facilities that have favoured intermodal transport with the rail networks, and thanks to the reconstruction of part of the old docks along the Huangpu river, it is destined to become one of the most important places for international container handling. It has been estimated that the annual traffic will soon reach 250 million tons, getting close to Singapore levels (the first port as far as traffic volumes are concerned).

The most used routes are those to Hong Kong, Taiwan, the Korean Republic, Japan, Australia and the whole of South-East Asia, in addition to the transoceanic routes that allow connections with the Mediterranean Area, Northern Europe, South Africa, South America and the two coasts of the United States. The coastal routes connect Shanghai with the main national ports, while the internal river routes allow access to the port stations along the Yangzte river. The inland area covered by the port of Shanghai is huge and includes all the neighbouring provinces besides Hunan, Hubei, and Sichuan.

The services for container ships are efficiently managed by SCT (Shanghai Container Terminals), a joint venture created by the Shanghai harbour authorities and Hutchison Whampoa Ltd. The main weakness of this facility is its accessibility: in spite of numerous dredgings, the water depth is insufficient, and it represents a problem for the entry of ships with a tonnage greater than 6,000 teus. In the short term, the adjacent port station of Ningbo represents an additional port for the docking of these ships, though the future creation of a deep-water port in the south of Shanghai is being studied. This port will be able to receive bigger container ships.

The modern, multifunctional Ningbo port station, jewel of the Zhejiang Province, is located to the south of Shanghai (less than 150 kilometres as the crow flies). The basic structure of the port is over 1,000 years old, but the decisive developments have been carried out only in the last 50 years:

in 1949 the port capacity scarcely came close to 40,000 tons. By the end of 2005, the loads handled by Ningbo should be more than 150 million tons. This facility is connected to the United States, Europe, the Mediterranean area and the main Asian cities through countless commercial routes. All the Chinese ports can be reached by coastal navigation, while through river transport the cargos reach the internal cities located on the banks of the Yanghtze. The national lines activated by the adjacent airport and the massive presence of rail infrastructures are an essential warranty for the development of inter-modal traffic. The strong point of Ningbo is the access channel: 24 of the 60 available quays are located in deep water and are able to receive high-tonnage ships. Moreover, the favourable geographic location of this port also represents an advantage.

In the southern part of the country, besides the famous international port of Hong Kong, there is the port of Canton (third for tons handled), one of the most ancient sea ports. It has been the starting point of the Silk Route for centuries. The last decade has been decisive for the development of facilities suitable for international trade, such as an inter-modal terminal for the transfer of containers with specific products. The port is situated at the centre of the Xi valley, surrounded by many roads, motorways, railways and navigable channels which favour communication with the adjacent inland provinces.

On the northern coast, Dalian and Tianjin are the most important ports. The first is located on the tip of the Liaodong peninsula. It manages more than three quarters of ingoing and outgoing traffic of north-eastern China. The Harbin–Dalian railway line connects the harbour facility with the main network. The routes to Russia, Japan, and South Korea have become particularly important thanks to the geographic closeness to these countries.

The port of Tianjin is located less than 300 kilometres from Dalian (as the crow flies). Its location (hardly more than 150 km from Beijing) has contributed decisively to its development. Almost all loads destined for the capital and for the majority of the neighbouring provinces pass through Tianjin.

The port is equipped with more than 60 berths, the majority of which are well-suited to receive ships with a tonnage higher than 10,000 tons. At the moment there are six quays in deep waters (four for cargos and two for the products of the oil-chemical industry). Works for the realization of a basin able to receive 250,000-ton oil tankers are now starting. Between Tianjin and Shanghai there are Qingdao and Qinhuangdao ports, which have a particular importance as far as the ore, coal, and oil trades are concerned (Weber, 2001; Omnia atlante; www.china.org; www.ice.it).

Water transport is very important in China, mainly for goods with a low price/volume ratio. It has grown proportionally to the total freight traffic and still represents 50 per cent in terms of ton–km (Figure 8.10).

Freight Ton–Kilometers (100 million ton–km)

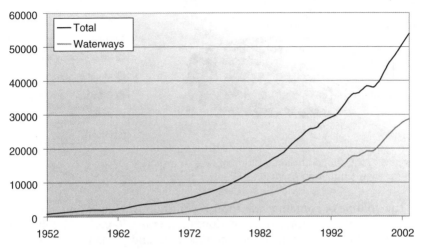

Figure 8.10   Freight traffic with ship transport
Source: www.china.org

The data shown in Table 8.2 indicate that in 2003 the Chinese ports handled more than 2,000 million tons with a growth of 20.7 per cent with respect to the previous year. Shanghai alone covers about 15.7 per cent of the total goods handling; then the ports of Ningbo and Canton follow, with slightly less than 10 per cent. Please consider that the two most important ports of the Yangtze delta, that is, Shanghai and Ningbo, are enough to cover more than a quarter of the national total.

Table 8.2   Goods transport in the main Chinese ports

Volume of freight handled in major coastal ports (1,000 000 tons)						
Seaport	**1980**	**1990**	**1995**	**20000**	**2001**	**2002**	**2003**
Total	217.31	483.21	801.66	1256.03	1426.34	1666.28	2011.26
Shanghai	84.83	139.59	165.67	204.40	220.99	263.84	316.21
Ningbo	3.26	25.54	68.53	115.47	128.52	153.98	185.43
Guangzhou	12.10	41.63	72.99	111.28	128.23	153.24	171.87
Tianjin	11.92	20.63	57.87	95.66	113.69	129.06	161.82
Qingdao	17.08	30.34	51.03	86.36	103.98	122.13	140.90
Dalian	32.63	49.52	64.17	90.84	100.47	108.51	126.02
Qinhuangdao	26.41	69.45	83.82	97.43	113.02	111.67	125.62

Source: www.china.org

Main items of the cargo transport

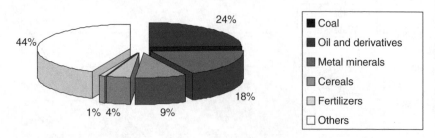

Figure 8.11   Commodity composition of cargo transport
Source: www.China-Italy-Trade.it

The volume of container transport is continuously increasing: the containers mainly have foreign destinations (more than 70 per cent), followed by internal routes through coastal connections, and partially, river routes. It has been estimated that during 2005 total handling will reach 50 million teus. The average travelling distance of sea loads is more than 1,600 km, while the travelling distance of the river loads is just above 200 km.

Figure 8.11 shows the main items of cargo transport, which consists of various products, but mainly of goods with a low value/volume ratio.

Almost half of the cargo traffic is managed by national shipping companies. In particular, the companies which hold the most considerable industry market shares are: China Ocean Shipping (Cosco), and China Shipping (Sinotrans), both of a size that can compare with those of the most important international operators. Cosco, ranked the fifth shipping company in the world (in terms of gross tonnage), dominates the international traffic, while China Shipping is the main operator in internal transport by ship .

Eleven medium-sized companies operate internationally, while there is a large number of small ship-owners that work locally (www.china.org; www.dhl.it; www.China-Italy-Trade.net).

9
Conclusions

China has been at the centre of the economic debate for a long time. We usually use terms such as 'Chinese miracle' when we refer to the extraordinary development that the country has registered during the last 20 years, witnessed by a GDP increase always higher than 7 per cent (and often with two-figure increases), and by a trade exchange that has increased fourfold in ten years.

A recent study published by the *International Finance Corporation* (2004) shows that 8 per cent of the world manufacturing is currently located in China; this percentage is going to grow to 14 per cent in the next three years and therefore exceed the production rate of western Europe. Some other studies indicate that the Dragon's Country is going to become the first world economic power in the third decade of the 2000s.

This development originates from many factors; the first is the low cost of labour. To quantify the gap existing between China and the other countries it is enough to recall that the average wage in the United States and in Europe is about 15–17 euro/hour, in Korea it is about seven euro/hour, in Mexico two euro/hour, while the Chinese average wage per hour is only 0.4 euro. Cost advantages can then be coupled with regulations (if existing) which are far less restrictive in terms of safety and hygiene at work, environmental and social protection (security and health service).

Nonetheless, the cost advantage alone cannot explain the extraordinary growth the country is experiencing. Similar advantages exist in the whole Asian area. In order to understand the genesis of this growth it is useful to retrace the recent history of this country and the sequence of reforms that have accompanied its economic transformation, as well as the progressive international opening according to far-sighted vision. As already explained in Chapter 2, the Chinese state has passed a series of reforms, which have gradually prepared the ground for development. It has granted special conditions and incentives for foreign investment, nevertheless establishing mutual terms in order to favour local industrial production, and technology transfer from western countries. It has created logistic platforms in order to simplify the inter-continental transport. For a long time it has ignored international complaints about the widespread counterfeiting phenomenon, as well as about production processes with strong environmental impact, in order not to hinder the first industrialization phase. It has anchored the currency to the dollar to ensure higher monetary stability, and secured privileged conditions when it entered into the WTO. It definitely wanted to host the Olympic Games in 2008 and the Expo in 2010 to give a further impulse to the infrastructural development and above all to affirm a new image of 'made in China' in the whole world. It has heavily invested in research, which has been defined as a national priority to which 63 billion dollars are dedicated each year (only the USA and Japan invest more resources). The results of the considerable research investments are now beginning to be tangible in the technological profiles of the companies, which are the most advanced in the world, as far as some specific productions are concerned.

Many reforms have been previously tested in limited areas: the Special Economic Zones (Guangdong, Beijing, Shanghai, Zhejiang, which are today the richest regions in the country), where a consumer segment is developing, whose income can be compared with that of some Western standards.

This new class represents a further reason for the enormous flow of ingoing foreign investments. The demand is increasing at a fast pace, so that production is sometimes completely absorbed by the internal market. As a confirmation of the importance of this phenomenon, let's consider the figures about Chinese imports: if it is true that Chinese exports have grown by 77 per cent during the five years 1998–2002, imports have registered an even higher growth (110%). Although an important percentage of these is represented by semi-finished products which are processed in China to be exported again to their countries of origin, data concerning the imports shows the importance of this country as an outlet market too.

Many problems must be solved: from unemployment to a heterogeneous development from a territorial point of view, from the inadequacy of the legal system to the exposure of the credit system, from the insufficiency of the infrastructures to environmental pollution. The main query is represented by the social sustainability of the transformation, and the stability of the political system of China, that is a nation that, after having known enterprise freedom and private property, could ask for more democracy and participation in the future.

One common question is how long the varying advantages offered by China can last. The experience lived in countries such as South Korea, Taiwan and Singapore shows that the wage growth has followed the industrial development without substantial delays. But China's profile, not only geographic or demographic, cannot be compared with that of the countries mentioned.

Thus a country risk exists, but despite it, China represents an area of the international chessboard that cannot be ignored. More than 500,000 companies operating today in China prove it.

The Chinese–foreign joint ventures, and (in particular in recent years) the wholly foreign-owned enterprises have deeply changed the Chinese industrial structure, whose backbone was represented in the past by the inefficient state-owned enterprises. The foreign trade companies (state-owned intermediation companies), which in the past were the sole interlocutors for the foreign companies venturing into the Chinese market, are now progressively losing their monopoly of the international trade.

Of the 500,000 companies only a limited number are Italian. In Italy China has been 'discovered' later than in other countries. More generally, the Italian industrial system seems to be slower than others in the processes concerning international growth, in particular from a production point of view.

Notwithstanding the rash growth, the Far East is still considered as a distant reality, which can be hardly understood. The knowledge of this context is made even more difficult by the ongoing transformation process that makes it a moving target. Not only the East is considered as an uncertainty, but also as a great threat. The exploits of the Dragon's Country have also caused strong repercussions on the western industrial system. China is often seen as a 'far and mysterious disturbing enemy' (Romiti, 2004).

The reasons for which China is considered a threat are visible; less visible is the fact that the same reasons make it a great opportunity. By taking part in that process of economic development, by transferring production to China, and by aiming to attack a market of 1.3 billion consumers from the inside, it is possible to win a challenge from which many entrepreneurs inevitably cannot escape. Riding the dragon is possible and the companies investigated in this research prove it: it is possible to enter the Chinese market successfully, choosing the most suitable sourcing method and conveniently deciding on some critical aspects, in particular the organizational decentralization, the negotiation and relational approach, and the know-how and technology transfer. Some of the investigated companies have been able to lead the Chinese manufacturers through a development path that made them qualified and favourable partners. Moreover the cases analysed show that China is not only an opportunity for the large entities, but also for small and medium-sized enterprises, for example through suitable intermediation forms.

Therefore various solutions are available to western enterprises, which wish to enter the Dragon's Country. A Chinese motto says that even a 'thousand-mile journey begins with a single step'. We hope this book will represent a valid reference for a more conscious valuation and planning of this single step.

Case Studies

1: Black&Decker Italia

The worldwide reconfiguration of manufacturing and
the Global Purchasing Asia unit

General information

The Black&Decker group, world-wide leader in the electrical and gardening tools industry, has approximately 32,000 employees and a turnover of more than 4,500 million dollars. The group trades in all the main markets and stands out for the numerous factories, every one of which realizes a limited range of products that are distributed world-wide.

Black&Decker Italy S.p.a. is part of the group. It has a sales centre, located in Monza (that manages product distribution in Italy) and it has a manufacturing unit in Perugia.

The plant at Perugia was founded in 1953, when two local entrepreneurs started the production of machines for wood working. The firm aimed to widen its own range of products; in 1969 Black&Decker acquired the company, widening and, subsequently, replacing the original brand with its own.

The company increased production volumes, so much that in 2003 the company staff of the Perugian plant numbered 300 employees, realizing a production value of over 40 million euro.

The unit at Perugia specializes in the manufacturing of stationary machines for wood working: the product target is mostly a professional user.

Black&Decker commercializes this kind of product using the DeWalt brand, already well known in America and Europe and brought to success thanks to an aggressive marketing operation in the mid-1990s. It is distinguished, therefore, from the brand Black&Decker, mostly focused on consumer products.

The launch of DeWalt was such a big success that now, in the field of professional tools, it is the market leader in America, whilst in Europe (where it has been present since 1997) it contends with Bosch for first place for market share.

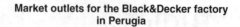

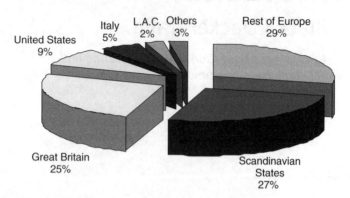

Figure CS1.1   Market outlets for the Black&Decker factory in Perugia

The products, realized at the plant of Perugia, are mainly destined for European countries (85% of the total) see Figure CS1.1. If the Black&Decker policy is to commercialize the same type of tool in all the markets worldwide, it will also be necessary to consider that the position of the factories is not totally separate from the main market outlet.

With this purpose, the product mix Black&Decker is subdivided in two categories:

1. standard products that need a few adaptations to be used in single geographic markets;
2. products that are designed to be used solely in a defined geographic area.

The evolution of the group's manufacturing strategy

Until 1993, Black&Decker's production of electrical tools was realized almost entirely in the United States and in Europe. In particular, in the old continent five factories were available: Molteno and Perugia (Italy), Limburg (Germany), Delemont (Switzerland), Spennymoor (England). The presence in countries characterized by a low cost of the labour factor was still limited.

From 1993, the manufacturing strategy of the multinational firm began to be defined in two main directions:

1. a greater presence in countries characterized by a low labour cost;
2. the closing or reorganization of some western plants.

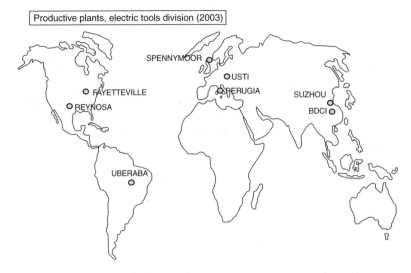

Figure CS1.2 Location of Black&Decker production plants in 2003

The activities of the European factories of Limburg (1994), Delemont (1996) and Molteno (1999) stopped. Subsequently this process included various North American plants and touched the English factory at Spennymoor too, that was heavily reorganized. Following the progressive productive disengagement in western Europe and in the United States, the productive locations in Mexico and Brazil were developed. Further changes were the creation of the new low-cost plants of Suzhou, in China (2001) and Usti, in the Czech Republic (2002).

The plant at Usti, approximately 70 kilometres from Praha, was in near disuse before being merged with Black&Decker. The restructure and reactivation of the plant – that now has over a thousand employees – was finished in little more than one year: in approximately 15 months the greatest part of the production previously realized in England was completely taken over by this new site.

However, the biggest part of the production relocation involved China. In 1993, Black&Decker appeared for the first time in China with BDCI. It was not a plant under sole control, but a joint venture with local entrepreneurs (this was the only way granted to the foreign investor at that time). As a result of the changes to the social and fiscal norms, the plant went through a phase of slowing down of its development. Currently, the volumes realized there are rather moderate.

Black&Decker has recently found two different directions of interest:

- The development of the units used in *core production* (it can be realized exclusively with a direct and total control of the production and therefore with the constitution of a wholly foreign-owned enterprise);
- The entrusting to third companies of the productions characterized by a smaller volume and a low technological and innovation content (enterprises already operating in China, that are used both by the main concurrent, European and American societies, and by the big distribution chains).

In this context, joint venture turned out to be an intermediate solution, on which the group did not want to invest further resources.

The Suzhou plant was therefore created, belonging totally to Black&Decker, situated less than 70 kilometres from the international port of Shanghai. In 2001, Suzhou had little more than 600 employees; now the number has doubled (see Fig. CS1.2).

The constitution of plants in Eastern Europe and Asia turned out to be a necessary route: in the Black&Decker industry the labour cost represents one of the main cost elements. The value of this parameter, extended to the totality of the manufacturing chain, records meaningful differences corresponding to the various geographic areas where the group is present: from the 15–16 euro/hour in the western countries, to the 3–4 euro/hour in the Czech Republic, right down to 0.5–0.6 euro/hour in China.

This analysis acquires greater weight if the concept of 'cost of labour' is extended to the whole value chain involved in the realization of the goods. Considering these aspects, it is obvious that the relocation to China has allowed the selection of local suppliers who, in turn, can count on a low cost of human resources.

Most of all, for the simpler products, the differential of cost turns out to be enormous. In fact, the main competitors of Black&Decker, like Bosch and Makita, are also transferring manufacturings activities to own bases localized in Far East.

Global Purchasing Asia (GPA) Black&Decker

The constitution of GPA

Black&Decker began exploring the Chinese market in 1985. The objective was to understand and estimate the real potential of the country, whether for the purchase of components and finished goods, or for the transfer of productive systems.

With this purpose, Global Purchasing Asia (GPA) was founded, in 1987 in Hong Kong, a branch of Black&Decker enterprises aimed at monitoring the

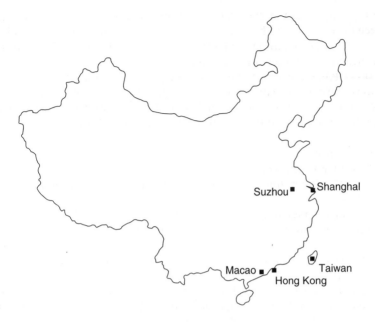

Figure CS1.3 Location of GPA offices in China

Chinese market, finding new opportunities and garrisoning those already activated.

The firm understood the strategic role covered by GPA and therefore in the second half of the 1990s, new offices near to Shanghai and Taiwan were inaugurated (also to support the joint venture BDCI).

In 2000 a division of GPA, called CEG (Component Export Group), was constituted, specialized in the sourcing of components for western plants.

GPA is currently present in China with offices in Shanghai, Suzhou, Hong Kong, Macao and Taiwan (as shown on Figure CS1.3), with a total of approximately 50 employees. The staff to who the management of the several centres is entrusted is constituted mostly from local people.

The work distribution within this structure is based on a labour specialization according to the different product types. Moreover ulterior specializations relate to the geographic context, where the offices operate. For example, the supply management for the DeWalt product mix is assigned to the office in Taiwan, an area endowed by the most advanced technological competences.

Today GPA has a fundamental importance, thanks to the abilities of this organization effectively to support the purchasing process in the Far East of all the productive units of the group.

The GPA organization can count on employees who assure a constant presence near to the suppliers. In addition, there are some supporting units with various tasks: planning the logistic activities, quality control, administrative attendance, project management, etc.

In 2003 GPA acquired goods for a value equal to 230 million dollars; the CEG division produced components for approximately 11 million dollars.

The evaluation of the activity carried out by GPA and CEG is made on the purchase volume and through some performance indicators:

- quality indices
- level of guaranteed service
- savings by re-sourcing (difference of cost between western and eastern suppliers)
- savings of leverage (advantages of cost obtained through the competition between the western and eastern suppliers).

For all western divisions, GPA represents the unique contact with the Asiatic manufacturers. The Chinese companies are experiencing a phase of extraordinary increase, above all thanks to the strong demands of multinationals clients. In order to manage and control these continuous changes a precise methodological approach is useful.

The activity of GPA, aimed to guarantee adequate levels of quality and timing, follows a series of steps (Figure CS1.4).

The objective of the first stage is to identify a solid supply base. The search for new suppliers is ongoing: the dynamics of the Chinese industrial system change so fast that this continuity becomes necessary.

After a potential supplier is selected, a qualification report is written up containing general information: technological characteristics, ISO certifications, type and level of organization, equipment available, main customers, manufacturing capability, trend of sales, core competences, etc. Based on these aspects, an appraisal is assigned and that is continuously brought up to date through periodic programmed inspection visits from GPA.

The second step is the beginning of the supply relationship. An essential part of this phase is the initial quality control: besides the samples and the demand for quotations, the supplier receives the 'component-card', an adopted module with data and measurements. Samples and documentations are examined by GPA members that prepare an approval report.

This report (*First Piece Control Report*) (Figure CS1.5) is made up of four sections containing general information about the inspection, information relative to the reasons the control activity was made, the type of control realized and the result of the inspection.

With reference to the control of the samples, the cards attached to the report describe in detail the activity carried out. Dimensional verifications

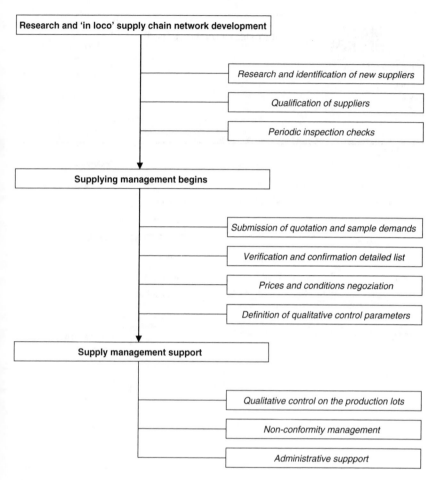

Figure CS1.4 Activities of GPA

can be realized, as well as controls on the materials used, on the functionality, and on the aesthetic features of the purchasing code. A comparison between the agreed measures (with respective tolerances) and the values actually reported is the performed, followed by a written appraisal (see 'Process of appraisal of sample' illustrated in Figure CS1.6). The sample can be judged acceptable/not corresponding but acceptable with modification of the design/not corresponding but usable/not acceptable.

Only at this point, generally with a test batch, the supply relationship begins. The Black&Decker productive plants agree with the GPA responsible the qualitative standards for the requested components. Meanwhile the negotiaton on prices and other conditions takes place.

BLACK&DECKER	**FIRST PIECE CONTROL REPORT**	Mo. 01.01 Rev. B Pag. 1 do ___ Date :

(1) GENERALITIES   DATE   N°

PART. N° .... Rev ....   DESCRIPTION
SUPPLIER ....   BUYER ....   OFFICE ....   DATE ....
TOOL ....   SERIES ....   E.C.N.N° ....
N° SAMPLES ....   N° CAVITIES ....   RC.P.P REC N° ....

ENCLOSED DIMENSIONS [ ]   STUDY OF CAPACITY [ ]   OTHER [ ]

(2) REASON

NEW PART	MODIFICATION OF PROCESS [ ]	**DISTRIBUZIONE**	
PART MODIFIED [ ]	NEW TOOLING [ ]	PURCHASING	[ ]
NEW SUPPLIER [ ]	MODIFICATION OF TOOLING [ ]	QUALITY	[ ]
NEW PROCESS [ ]	_____ [ ]	TECHNICAL DEVELOPMENT OFFICE	[ ]

(3) TYPE OF CONTROL   TECHNICAL PRODUCTION OFFICE [ ]

DIMENSIONAL [ ]	FUNCTIONALITY [ ]	SUPPLIER	[ ]
MATERIAL [ ]	OUTPUT [ ]	PRODUCTION	[ ]
FINISHED ASPECT [ ]	_____ [ ]	INCOMING GOODS DEPARTMENT	[ ]
		_____	[ ]

(4) FINAL APPROVAL 1	SAMPLE APPROVAL NOT ACCEPTED	3	APPROVED IN DEROGATION
QUALITY _____ DATE : _____		UTP _____ DATE : _____ QUALITY _____ DATE : _____ UTS _____ DATE : _____	
2	APPROVED - MODIFICATION OF DRAWINGS	4	APPROVED
UTP _____ DATE : _____ QUALITY _____ DATE : _____ UTS _____ DATE : _____ ECN N°		UTP _____ DATE : _____ QUALITY _____ DATE : _____ UTS _____ DATE : _____	

Figure CS1.5 First Piece Control Report: approval of sample report used by Black&Decker Perugia

The last stage comprises the activities carried out for the shipment. The GPA technical staff write an 'Inspection Report' that accompanies every batch sent. Attached to the details of the supply relationship (purchase centre, supplier, inspector GPA, etc.), this document contains the measurements carried out on the critical parameters, that had been previously agreed, the modalities used for the control and eventual non-conformity (Figure CS1.7).

GPA also carries out different operational and administrative actions: management of the non-conformities, invoicing, eventual objections, etc.

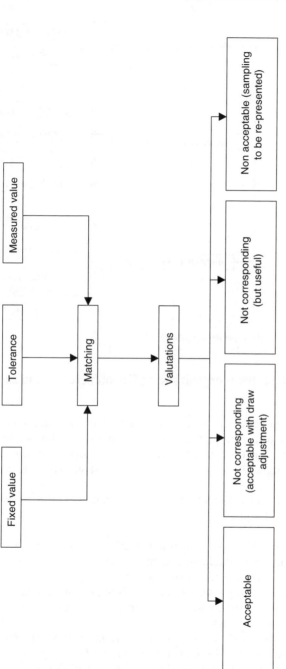

Figure CS1.6 Process of appraisal of sample

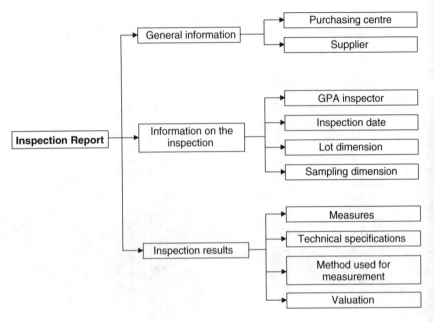

Figure CS1.7   Inspection report schematization

The Perugia plant: the reorganization of manufacturing and supply activities

When the delocalization process was launched, the Perugia plant was the first productive unit candidate to close because of the low performances recorded. Today, it is the only plant in western Europe (with the exception of the one in England, strongly reorganized) that survived the delocalization process.

Three fundamental aspects have probably guaranteed the survival of the Perugian unit up to now:

1. *The type of product realized*: a technologically rich and complex tool, from the design and manufacturing points of view (therefore a difficult production to transfer in *low cost* countries);
2. *The dimensions of the productive unit*: the Perugia plant is relatively small, if compared to the recent sites at Usti and Suzhou. Delocalization would bring limited advantages;
3. *The high performances*: in recent years the plant has realized the best performances in the whole group, in terms of quality, flexibility and time. The optimum service level (near 100%) and the stock of finished products reduced to the minimum (approximately equivalent to one

half of daily requirements) were performances that have made Perugia a model for the other Black&Decker productive units.

The key for the drastic improvement of the productive performances derives from the precise managerial choices that have allowed the entire productive apparatus to be reshaped according to the lean production principles.

In 1993 the Perugia unit started a process of internal reorganization that in a couple of years brought an evident improvement of the performances. The new system permitted a considerable increase of productivity of the system: the volumes have practically tripled in 10 years (from 70,000 pieces in 1993, to 220,000 units in 2003), while the working hours have been maintained the same.

The results achieved are due to three main fundamental activities:

1. kanban systems for the management of shop floor activities;
2. drastic reduction of set-up times (reduced to ten minutes in a whole year);
3. continuous training: the employees, used to operating with traditional modalities, needed adequate education to implement the new productive organization.

The requirements of complex components is planned with a traditional Material Requirement Planning system. For components characterized by a low unitary volume (screws, bolts, etc.) the 'double cassette' is used, a system of variable cadence replacement, with a predefined amount of reorder and minimal supply. This procedure has involved a remarkable saving, both in terms of cost of the material stored and in terms of space occupied.

Along the production line an amount of closely sufficient components is available to realize a one-day production for every demanded item. The choice to assume a supply lead time equal to 24 hours was determined after deeper appraisals on the productive ability of the lines. Both the internal units and the external sources can guarantee this operating performance.

Procurement activities at the Perugia plant

The local suppliers

To support the requirements of a lean manufacturing system it is necessary to reorganize the supply chain. Although mechanical industry in Umbria was not particularly developed with respect to other closer regions, the first choice was to give preference to local suppliers (within one hundred kilometres), geographic distance being a critical factor for operation in kanban systems.

However it was possible to maintain relations even with the more distant suppliers using alternative logistic solutions. An identified system was the 'collecting at turn': the general strategy consists of creating districts of supply with the aim of optimizing the collection activities and transport. Another solution was to resort to a logistic provider. The supplier, in order to reduce transport costs, can deliver to the provider weekly (rather than daily), using a deposit account. The Perugian plant is supplied daily by the logistic operator.

The Chinese suppliers

Currently, the Perugia unit purchases approximately 130 types component from China. In November 2002 only ten were acquired. The number increased in little more than a year.

This development of the Chinese sourcing channel began towards the end of 2002 when a programme called 'China Sourcing' started, finalizing the purchase of low cost components from China. The challenge was to conciliate the high level of service and flexibility guaranteed by the productive system created in Perugia with a supply chain geographically further than the traditional one.

The China Sourcing project presents the following guidelines (and see Figure CS1.8).

The approach was as follows: through a detailed analysis of the product bills, the different components (with the exclusion of a part of elevated technological complexity) were subdivided into various classes. Searches and appraisals in the Chinese territory, were carried out by GPA staff on these categories, and brought about the selection of some suppliers.

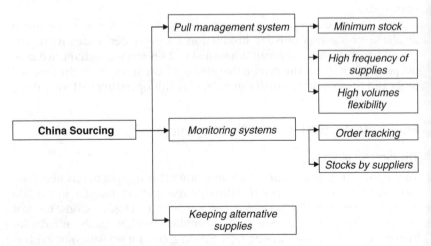

Figure CS1.8   Guidelines of the China Sourcing project 2002

From the logistic point of view, the elevated lead time 'door to door' of the supply from the Far East represented a critical aspect. The objective was to carry out weekly deliveries in order to minimize stock. The solution identified was to aggregate various orders so as reach the critical volume for the shipment. This way it was possible to intensify the frequency of shipments.

Specific agreements with some carriers were moreover stipulated to guarantee safety and traceability of the deliveries. On the basis of these agreements, it is possible to monitor, at any moment, both the shipments in course, and the stock with which Chinese supplier works (the estimated minimum stock of two weeks).

The presence 'in situ' of GPA was determinant in order to activate an efficient sourcing channel. The GPA staff, taking care of the quality controls required by the customer, verify the information on the quantity of components available in the supplier's warehouse. This is a fundamental aspect in order to guarantee complete respect of the predicted timing.

Recently, the fast growth of the price of raw materials (copper, steel and aluminium) has determined breathtaking increases in the prices of some components, rendering still more critical the use of resourcing activity.

In spite of these improvements in the management of the Chinese supply chain, in the Perugian plant a local supplier is maintained for every component acquired from China. This choice may be expensive, but is still necessary to face eventual delivery problems (defects, delays, etc.).

Case Studies

2: Campagnolo Commercio

From seller to product developer: the 'Chinese factory' gives rise to a new business idea

General information

Campagnolo Commercio is a company with headquarters at S. Romano degli Ezzelini (Italy). Its market products belong to different product typologies and market segments in the textile sector: clothes for men, women and children, domestic textiles, night-wear, furniture. Born as a wholesaler, the company has succeeded in taking advantage of the opportunities available in the international context (and in the Chinese one in particular). It demonstrates the ability to use foreign manufacturing to produce its collections. The enterprise records, over the passage of time, substantial internal changes at organizational and structural level. The reconfiguration of the offer allows Campagnolo fast growth, (sales have gone up exponentially in recent years).

In order to understand the firm's evolution, we start by illustrating with some data.

The company has 250 employees. Sales in recent years have recorded a continuous increase, attesting in 2003 to a value of approximately 100 million euros. Italy is the main outlet market (90 per cent of sales are made here). The company is, however, entering (even if still cautiously) some international markets, preferring those culturally and geographically closest to Italy (Germany, Austria, Slovenia and Croatia).

The customers are subdivided into three categories: large-scale retail trades, department stores and retail shops. Sixty-five per cent of sales are purchases made by retailers (this type of commerce constitutes therefore the Campagnolo core business).

Campagnolo's sourcing activities from the Far East, started up approximately ten years ago, are mainly developed in China. The company, nowadays, imports from China approximately 400 containers a year (for a sourcing value of more than 12 million euros). Campagnolo Commercio foresees a 40–50 per cent annual increase in its transactions with China. The increase rate may increase even more rapidly thanks to the elimination (in January 2005) of the quotas that currently limit the imports of some products.

The organizational structure

Campagnolo's organizational structure, until ten years, ago had the typical characteristics of a wholesaler. Supply management was delegated to the division manager (clothing, domestic textiles, night-wear, furniture) that bought in the international markets goods belonging to their own division. The organization of the purchases therefore was divided not considering the geographic sourcing areas, but the product typology.

The rapid increase of sales (and the connected increase of the purchased volumes) imposed year by year more strongly an organizational change: initially the manager of every division was supported by a 'foreign purchasing office' and then this office became the only unit undertaking international sourcing because of the importance it had assumed year by year. The staff belonging to this office succeed in creating in the various markets (in particular the Chinese one), a sourcing net able to allow the company to consolidate relationships with the suppliers and to increase constantly the volume and quality of the purchased goods.

The purchase managers have relationships on the one hand with all the heads of the divisions (and in this way their requirements are known), and on the other hand with the suppliers; they have, besides relational and commercial abilities, also technical/productive competences essential if the supplier does not know how to make the required products.

In order to take the best from the productive capabilities of the Chinese companies, combining them with creative and graphical abilities of Italian designers, Campagnolo Commercio introduce into the company some professionals atypical for a 'traditional' wholesaler: in the 'foreign purchasing office' it inserted designers and draftsman, who developed new models and collections, both independently and in synergy with the most important customers. In this way Campagnolo has succeeded in creating models in line with the requirements of its customers (taking advantage of the typical ability of the Italian designers) and at the same time it has benefitted from the competitive advantages obtainable through the production of high quality goods made economically thanks to the access to the Chinese low cost productive factors.

Campagnolo's 'foreign purchasing office' today is very different from that of 10 years ago, employing internally several professional: graphic designers, model makers, product developers, pattern book makers, administrators. An office (totally controlled by Campagnolo Commercio) has been opened in Guangzhou (Canton).

The evolution of the organizational structure of the Campagnolo Commercio is illustrated in Figure CS2.1. The company, that initially kept a relationship with its own suppliers through the head of each division, developed initially a 'foreign purchasing office' and then a 'chinese office' finally kept the most important sourcing market for the company: the People's Republic of China.

The Chinese office

Chinese industry has changed immensely in recent years. Until some years ago it was based on large state corporations, that constituted the only lawful interlocutors with western companies. The strong movement to privatize made recently by the Chinese government, has caused a high number of small manufacture enterprises to establish direct contact with western enterprises. If on the one hand the relationships with these small producers can guarantee greater advantages in terms of cost and productive flexibility, on the other hand the management of the relations with a high number of producers (often characterized by different characteristics and abilities) is more complex and difficult. For these reasons, in 2002 Campagnolo Commercio created an office in Guangzhou. In this office, Campagnolo employs a native staff, who know the Chinese textile market well and are able to maintain a direct and constant contact with the suppliers.

The office carries out the following activities: searching for new suppliers, quality control and pre-shipment inspection of the goods. There is an administrative area too.

This office at Guangzhou is an operating base for the Chinese employees, but it also has also the task of supporting the Italian managers of the 'foreign purchasing office'.

Localizatiom of the suppliers and the Chinese office

The purchases carried out by Campagnolo Commercio are divided as follows (and see Fig. CS2.2): 70 per cent in China, 12 per cent in Bangladesh, 12 per cent in Pakistan, 5 per cent in India and the remaining 1 per cent in Turkey and Bulgaria. As time has passed, the Egyptian supplier (because of frequent delays in deliveries) and the Portuguese ones (mainly for cost reasons) have been dropped.

Campagnolo has approximately 50 Chinese suppliers and they are periodically controlled by two inspectors of the Chinese office. This is possible because, for the greater amount of articles bought, the control function does not need of a full-time presence at the suppliers, but just some visits at the critical moments of the production process. The suppliers are all close to each other. There are, in the textile sector, two productive zones where most of the Chinese companies are concentrated (Fig. CS2.3): the most important area is in the zone that includes among Ningbo, Hangzhou, Shanghai and Nanchino, between the regions of the Zhejiang and the Jiangsu. The second area is situated in the Fujian, including the cities of

First step: initial frame

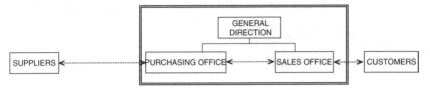

Second step: creation of two units: Foreign Purchasing and Product Developement

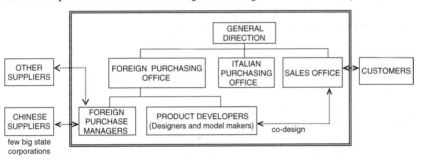

Third step: establishment of a Chinese office

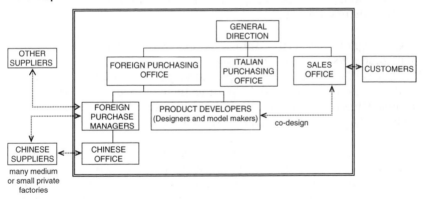

Legend

═══ Enterprise limits

◄┄► Informative flows and interface frame

Figure CS2.1 Evolution of the organizational structure and of interaction between suppliers/customers of Campagnolo Commercio

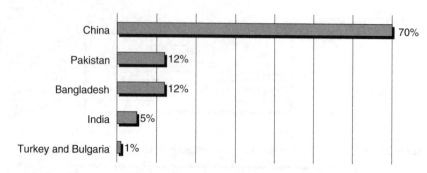

Figure CS2.2   The purchasing markets of Campagnolo Commercio

Fuzhou, Zhangzhou and Xiamen. It is easy to travel between these two zones in a few hours.

Campagnolo chose the city of Guangzhou as its Chinese headquarters, that is, in a zone far from the region where most of its suppliers are located. This choice was supported by the following:

- Guangzhou, like Shanghai, is an international city; but Shanghai has higher costs;
- Guangzhou is the centre of the most important textile fair in China. It is useful to have an operating base near to the fair to manage effectively the activities linked to it.

Campagnolo has relationships in China with private producers, with state producers and with *foreign trade companies*.

Above all, the state producers proved very skilful in understanding the material specifications and in putting them into practice. The Italian company has recorded that this ability has increased in recent years thanks to intensifying contact with the Western world.

A very important characteristic of the Chinese companies is the flexibility with which they adapt themselves to different productions.

Some developing countries have specialized their productions in limited market segments or niches; in these segments they succeed in being generally more attractive than China (for instance India is more competitive in some valuable productions, Pakistan in that of domestic textiles). China guarantees, instead, a real competitive advantage on a wide range of productions and for this reason it can (at least inside the low–middle level segments) lay down the law.

Campagnolo Commercio is satisfied with the service level offered by the Chinese suppliers, in terms of times, timing, quality of deliveries, reliability as regards product specifications and flexibility as regards mix and volumes.

Figure CS2.3 The main purchasing areas of Campagnolo Commercio and the location of the Chinese office

The Chinese suppliers, in the company's opinion, are much more reliable than those of other underdeveloped nations (eg, Egypt).

A negative aspect is that the Chinese producer rarely gives hints that are interesting to the western market (unless it has had a long relationship with the western environments and therefore knows their tastes and requirements).

Campagnolo Commercio also has business relations with two big foreign trade companies located in Hangzhou and Nanchino. Until a few years ago, western companies could only have relationships with these enterprises; nowadays, instead, the greater part of Chinese producers succeed in connecting directly with foreign customers. The decline of the intermediation bodies coincided with the passing of Hong Kong to China: when many Chinese cities opened to the western world, the foreign trade companies whose strong point was their position in Hong Kong, lost this distinguishing element. As far as these trade companies are concerned, the experience of Campagnolo Commercio shows that in by-passing these companies it is possible to obtain remarkable reductions in purchasing costs.

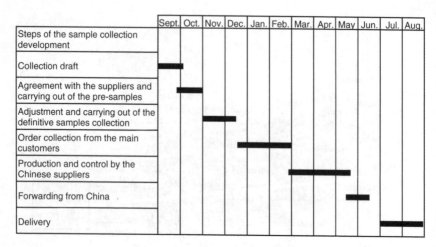

Figure CS2.4 Activity planning for the development of the autumn–winter collections

Production phases

To better understand the characteristics of Campagnolo's sourcing activity, it is useful to describe in synthesis the steps of the production process. We will use as an example the development of the autumn–winter 2004 collection (see Figure CS2.4), (characterized by a purchase volume that exceeded one million articles).

The process begins in September 2003 when the general idea of the collection is elaborated: the kinds of products are individualized, the types of fabric for every article are selected, the first designs are made, the suppliers are quantified and localized (the quantity of the various models are assigned to the producers), etc. This activity, the result of which is a first paper draft of the models and a preliminary definition of the orders, engages approximately 15 people.

At this point the purchasing manager goes to China, contacts the possible suppliers, communicates the requests and the generic specifications (measurements, fabric and inner composition, accessories, trimmings, etc.) for the pre-samples. By the end of October Campagnolo receives the pre-samples, that have to respect the transmitted generic specifications (the draft is therefore a sort of 'raw model').

The pre-samples are inspected and, eventually, corrected. Within the first half of December the collection is ready.

As this point the Italian distribution network can be activated: from January to February, orders are collected from customers. The articles ordered will be delivered from July to August.

Production starts at the end of February. On the basis of the orders collected in the advance sale phase (January–February) and of the forecasts, the number of articles that every Chinese supplier will have to produce is decided. The Chinese dependents of Campagnolo Commercio work mainly in this phase: they support the Chinese supplier in the search for suitable materials, they control the production process (eg if colours and accessories are respected.) and the packaging (eg the batch dimensions, the choice of wrapping, etc.). This procedure ends in April.

From 15 May to the 15 June the articles leave China and reach Italy after approximately 35 days. Thereafter the deliveries start.

The core business of the Italian company is the development and sale of textile articles purchasable by customers from a catalogue. A Campagnolo label is affixed to these articles. There are approximately 25 Campagnolo labels; the choice of label to affix to the article depends on the kind of product and on the distribution channels (European and Italian large-scale retail trade, department store, the retail shop). For the large-scale retail trade a simple collection is made; for the customers who sell in small shops, however, high-quality collections are made always by Chinese companies. In this case the best materials are used (the origin of the fabric is Korea or Taiwan in order to guarantee a higher quality level), the number of accessories is higher, the final touches are painstaking; there is a select label.

There are some collections that are personalized according to customer requirements. The customers who demand this service belong to the large-scale retail trade or are big chains of shops. These articles are made through the collaboration between the Campagnolo Commercio planners and the customer's designers. The labels of the customer are affixed to these products.

The activities carried out by the Chinese employees

The Italian headquarters writes up a product technical card; it sends one copy to the office in China and one to the supplier. On this card, the technical and qualitative product specifications are described. These specifications must be observed both by the Chinese supplier during production and by the Chinese employees that have to control it. For instance the specifications relate to colours, fabric quality, accessories (buttons, hinges, labels...), etc.

In order to avoid a useless loss of time and resources, before beginning the production the supplier has to send to the head office of Campagnolo and to the Chinese office a sample of the raw materials and the accessories it wants to use, so that defective goods are promptly singled out. When the supplier has completed production, he calls the Chinese inspector, who verifies adherence to the specifications, using a control product sample. It can happen that some particulars (labels, some seams, the packing) are not in compliance with the detailed lists. In this case the product can be promptly modified; however rejection of an entire product has never happened.

Synthesizing the main control is carried out by the inspectors after production. However they also carry out periodical visits to the suppliers during production in order to control the production progress and to solve eventual doubts or requirements of the producer.

Contact between the controller and the supplier takes place every three weeks. In any case Campagnolo tries to maintain, besides a continuous exchange of information between the producer and the Chinese office, a frequent informative exchanges between the producer and the Italian headquarters, for instance regarding production scheduling (eg the supplier sends some reports in which it informs the directors of Campagnolo Commercio about the production scheduling of its orders).

The activities carried out by those responsible for foreign purchases

The Chinese employees carry out a decisive role of constant control of the suppliers' production. Moreover they find answers to the supplier's requests and relay the orders from headquarters.

The presence of Italian staff that have gained experience in the search for new suppliers, in the inspection of their productive systems and in the dealing with the Chinese parties, seems to be fundamental. Campagnolo thinks that some strategic activities can be carried out only by Italian staff because they know the rules, tastes and requirements of the western market.

The activities of the Italian employees of the 'Foreign Purchasing office' are as follows:

Auditing and search for new suppliers.   The search for new suppliers is constant and is due, on the one hand, to the necessity of making new products and, on the other hand, to the increase in volume: many of Campagnolo's suppliers are small and they cannot support a demand increasing so rapidly.

The best occasion at which to identify new suppliers is the Canton fair. It is the most important exhibition of the textile sector. The contacts at the fair are unavoidably superficial (they allow an understanding of product quality and price that the supplier is able to guarantee) and must be followed by visits to the premises. Visits to the showroom and the production plants are fundamental, allowing the staff of Campagnolo Commercio to understand how the suppliers work. The first visits are carried out by the Italian heads of department, or managers, because Campagnolo thinks that they can better understand the suppliers' potential.

At the the the beginning of the trade relationship, the company has some difficulties in communicating trade or operational aspects. An example is given by the recurrent problem relating to the quality of packaging cardboard: according to western standards, the cardboard must lie on the pallet without bending in order to allow stacking. Normally in the Chinese companies this does not happen.

Acquisition of raw materials. Generally the Italian managers of Campagnolo Commercio indicate in the specifications the type of materials that must be used (for example, for a plush fabric, the Italian company indicates even whether the fabric must be carded or combed) and the supplier that can furnish it.

Often during the fairs Campagnolo Commercio makes preliminary agreements with the suppliers of fabric and then it invites its Chinese suppliers to buy these materials directly from these companies. In fact the Chinese producers, if not guided, naturally choose supplies of a quality not adapted to western standards.

The transaction. The level of quality of the articles made by the suppliers is not negotiable (it is fixed by Campagnolo), such as the method of payment (letter of credit is the selected choice).

One transaction problem that the company has found in China is the inconsistency between price and quality. In fact, in the Dragon Country, the cost of raw materials (cotton, polyester, etc.) is easy to identify, being strongly linked to the quality (and so indirectly to the origin), whereas labor costs for instance, are highly variable and there is rarely correlation between price and quality.

The choice of sourcing from China

The main reason that induced Campagnolo Commercio to select the Chinese market is cost, which is a decisive factor in a low-level market segment characterized by decreasing retail prices as the one in which Campagnolo operates. The company, that cannot take advantage of a well-known brand, competes essentially on cost.

The decision to search for a cost advantage in China rather than in eastern Europe (destination of many textile companies) derives from the commercial nature of Campagnolo. Textile companies frequently go to countries such as Rumania, Slovakia, Hungary to delocalize their manufacturing activities in an area geographically and culturally close to Italy.

Campagnolo Commercio, did not have a 'productive experience'. So it preferred a sourcing activity, and China offered quite incomparable cost.

Moreover, from a political and economical point of view, China seems to be stable and it does not give particular problems concerning inflation and exchange rates.

The choice to source in China was not motivated from the intention to enter commercially the Chinese market. Campagnolo Commercio thinks that this market is rather far away, difficult to understand and characterized by the complex competition of local companies.

The problem of copies and of the 'Made in China' effect

As far as Campagnolo Commercio's experience is concerned, the suppliers, both public and private, have never caused lagal problems regarding product copy. The suppliers have always preferred to respect the customer who provides them with many orders, rather than to take risks to commercialize copied products. In the textile sector the problem of the copy mainly affects the companies that have famous brands. Campagnolo Commercio, which belongs to the low-level market, seems not to be subjected to this type of violation.

A problem that the company faces, instead, is the 'Made in China' effect. This is directly connected to the (European) law that requires the origin of the product to be stated. (From 1st January 2004, Campagnolo has affixed a 'Made in China' label to the articles produced in this country.) In the European market the 'Made in China' label is still associated with an image of low quality.

This negative effect increased on the outbreak of SARS: in the months when this epidemic spread, there was a strong decrease in the sales of products so labelled because of the fearr of infection. In spite of the rapid solution of the problem by the Chinese authorities, the SARS effects lasted for a long period.

Communication

Communication with the Guangzhou office is mostly by email and it follows a 'triangular course': the supplier sends documents amd reports, both to the office in China and to the headquarters. The Chinese office and the Italian headquarters operate in the same way.

Face-to-face contacts are, however, fundamental; for this reason the management of the foreign purchase office frequently visits the suppliers.

Campagnolo has had no linguistic problems: they use English for all communications.

The Chinese employees have the opportunity to gain access, through the Internet, to the company's information system and to find the information they need. Also, the Chinese suppliers, logging their own user-id and password in an appropriate space in the firm's web page, can obtain general information on their own products (eg shipment and sale dates, trends of demand for their articles, the success obtained by their articles, etc.). This information tool has been implemented by the Italian company as a result of numerous suppliers' requests; it is the most obvious sign of the mutual desire for greater integration.

The shipment and the storage of the goods

The Chinese producers sell goods to the Italians using an FOB (free on board) procedure. The transport from the factory to the port is charged to the supplier. This contract makes the management of the logistic aspects simpler; probably, in Campagnolo Commercio's opinion, if the transport was managed directly, the cost advantages could be higher, but the difficulties and complexities linked to the coordination of several shipments would increase remarkably.

Transport by road generally does not involve problems, being first-rate in coastal areas. Moreover China is like a wide yard in continuous evolution. Here roads always increase and improve.

Intercontinental transport is made by ship from the ports of Shanghai, Ningbo and Xiamen. An agreement, reporting the indicative number of containers that will annually serve Campagnolo, has been signed with an Italian company. This company has signed another agreement with two other Italian companies that send goods from those ports. Altogether the three societies move approximately 2,000 containers a year for Campagnolo.

The shipment by sea seems to be a necessary choice, since air freight (the only alternative) is much more expensive overall for goods such as those of Campagnolo Commercio, that are characterized by a low price/volume ratio. The shipment costs aren't high: 7 per cent of total cost.

The goods currently arrive in the ports of Geneva and La Spezia (Italy), having historically the first warehouses of the company close to them. With the recent construction of a new warehouse near Venice, Campagnolo Commercio will have some products shipped there.

Case Studies

3: Danieli Group

Imposed sourcing in a 'strategic' sector

The Group

Danieli s.p.a. is the world-wide leader in the design and construction of industrial systems for the iron and steel industry and for the non-ferrous metals sector. Founded in 1914, in 1955 Danieli started its engineering plant activity. Thanks to the acquisition of several firms, the company achieve a world-wide leading position in the construction and supply of systems for the production of steel.

The strategy for the future is to maintain the position of leadership in the design and construction of *minimills* for 'long' and 'plan' products and to become the leading firm in furnace production too.

Under the organizational profile, the Group is constituted of a number of divisions located in Italy, Holland, Great Britain, Germany, Sweden and United States. The main centres are:

- Buttrio, Italy (Danieli headquarters),
- Olpe, Germany (Danieli Fröhling),
- Smedjebacken, Sweden (Danieli Morgårdshammar),
- Paris, France (Danieli Rotelec),
- Pittsburgh, USA (Danieli Corporation).

Danieli today exports almost its whole production employing approximately three thousand workers. The sales of the group for the year 2002 were approximately a billion Euros. The high R&D investments allow Danieli to strengthen its competitiveness on the world-wide market.

The sales of Danieli in China represent approximately 20–25 per cent of its turnover (datum 2002). The Chinese market is judged so 'excellent' that the 50 main job orders carried out by Danieli in 2002, 20 were in the Far East.

Danieli started exploring the Chinese industrial context in 1979; the first contract was signed in 1982. For then on, the presence of the group in the

Chinese market has grown without pause: there have been 150 plans carried out by Danieli in less than 20 years. This trend of increase in China is similar to the one recorded by the whole Group in the world. In fact the company, until the 1990s, was engaged almost exclusively in the market of the 'long products'. The differentiation in the segment of the 'plans products' has made Danieli projected at a world-wide level and at the same time it has allowed consolidation of its presence in China.

The supplying markets

In order to guarantee to the final customers an elevated engineering reliability, high quality levels and quick reaction times, the purchasing function is continually searching for qualified suppliers. Danieli buys approximately five hundred million euros a year of raw materials, components, equipments, auxiliary systems and services

The main supplying markets are: Western Europe, East Europe (mainly Czech, Slovakia, Croatia, Slovenia and, now and then, Rumania and Ukraine), the USA, South America, the Middle and Far East.

The enterprise purchases from these countries a wide variety of items: from components to complete system parts. The choice of the international supply markets in this sector is dictated not only by simple cost reasons, but also by possible contractual ties that link the sale of the product to the use of local supplies. Moreover the offer is often more interesting if it's carried out (at least partially) thanks to the support of the local supply net (even if locally explicit ties are absent).

The purchases

If we assume that the whole cost of a system is 100, approximately half derives from the production of machines designed through Danieli know-how. Of this 50 per cent, 70 per cent is made at the facility of the company, and 30 per cent is bought from international suppliers. The remaining 50 per cent of the cost relates to the purchase of technical products, systems and services (eg motors, electric components, security systems, facilities and assemblages). So the purchasing function manages (on average) 80 per cent of the total cost of a system.

The analysis of the purchases of the company is made distinguishing between:

- the so-called 'from China to China' supplies, produced by Chinese suppliers and assigned to the Chinese market; and
- the so-called 'from China to the rest of the world' supplies, carried out in China and finalized to the construction of systems located in other countries.

Purchases 'from China to China'

The first purchases in China started in 1998 and were connected to Danieli's supply of machinery characterized by a low level of technology. It was carried out in China for local customers. Danieli began to take into consideration the Chinese market first of all for cost reasons (the average pay of Chinese skilled workers is lower than the western average, but it can amount to 4,000 dollars per year) and then to test the local productive capabilities.

The Chinese market nowadays is radically changing: in recent years, the strongly bureaucratic state companies, stimulated by the reforms that are transforming the country, have been restored.

The first supplies made to Danieli from China were often disappointing, so that the company had to rework some purchased items in order to adapt them to its standards. Besides the bureaucratic and state characterization of the local economic system, that sometimes brings with it 'infiltrations' of the political system in the management of the companies, another inefficiency factor exists in China: the local market is overfilled by the internal orders linked to imminent events (the 2008 Beijing Olympic Games and Shangai Expò in 2010).

In spite of these limitations, Danieli continues the strategy of valorization of these products, since China constitutes an important market for its actual and future business. This choice is supported by the fact that the Chinese suppliers demonstrate today a progressive improvement from the qualitative point of view, and also because of the beneficial effects of the transfer of know-how made by the European enterprises that have operated here for quite some time.

The transfer of know-how

China imports on average 10–15 per cent (in value) of its industrial systems. That means that Danieli, also being responsible for whole projects (and, therefore, also of the parts made in China by local producers), forms only a small part of the Chinese steel industrial systems. The Italian enterprise develops the construction designs and the engineering details, produces the more technological parts in its headquarters and commits the remainder to the Chinese producers chosen by the customer. These Chinese producers become therefore 'the shops of Danieli in China'. The company executes an intense activity of supervision on them through its own staff (Table CS3.1)

The 'imposed' resort to a local producer is a practice systematically used by the Chinese government in some 'encouraged sectors'. The local constructors benefit therefore from a protected market and from the technology transfer coming from the most advanced western enterprises. At the same time the Chinese government guarantees local employment.

Table CS3.1   Supply chain in China: performance of and responsibility for activities

	Performance	Responsibility
Planning	Danieli	Danieli
Production	Shared	Danieli
Supervision and Control	Shared	Danieli

A rapid increase has been recorded in the Chinese metallurgical sector, with development rates decidedly higher than the average increase of the GDP. Moreover, the gradual privatization of the state companies operating in this sector has multiplied the offer: if until a few years ago the government assigned production on the basis of economic planning, today customers can select local producers and stimulate the competition among them.

The transfer of know-how takes place in two stages: in correspondence of the transmission to the Chinese producers of the designs developed by Danieli and during the project management, an activity for which, even if is shared between Danieli and the local producers, only Danieli is responsible.

In comparison with the 'traditional' production process that is developed according to the typical sequence of product concept → planning → production, know-how transfer follows an inverse course, proceeding backwards from production towards the planning and research and development phase. On the basis of the growth of Chinese industry, there is no innovation technology as trigger and engine of development, rather the learning from imported technologies.

In order to characterize further its own offer, recorded in the technological and qualitative increase of the local production, Danieli today is trying to transfer planning responsibilities to China, becoming, in this way, the main contractor of a series of orders which are not limited to production tasks.

Representative offices (RO)

The entire responsibility of the plan involves Danieli in an intense activity of supervision of the suppliers and in a close monitoring of their processes. This activity is entrusted to Chinese controllers that are in Danieli's service. These are located close to the suppliers and are coordinated by the representative offices. Currently there are two ROs, one established in Beijing in 1983 and the other in Shangai in 2002. This second office was constituted in order to maintain a close and interactive relation with the Chinese producers in the Shangai area that is the Chinese centre of the steel industry. The actual functions of the representative office are:

- sales assistance;
- assistance in the management of orders;
- assistance in post-sales services.

The process of supplying

The supply process of the Company comprises these three main phases:

1. *The determination of requirements.*   In this first phase Danieli's purchase requirements are based on the plan and on the agreement existing with the customers;
2. *The transmission of the technical designs to the customer.*   The project managers send the plans (eventually translated into the local language) to the customers and at the same time to the representative office which will have the task of controlling the works in progress. The customers then send the plans to the local selected producers. This selection was, in the past, substantially restricted because it was entirely bound by state planning. Today, however, the process of privatization allows a greater freedom in the choice of suppliers, and therefore competition among the companies has increased.
3. *The management of the order.* Quality control is carried out by Danieli through Chinese project managers who are sent to the suppliers' premises. Assisting on the job order is made during the entire phase in which the production is carried out (quality control on the purchases, on the quality of the welding, on the assemblage of the product, on possible treatments of the components, checking the production in progress, etc.). After the positive outcome of the intermediate inspections and of the final inspection (often carried out by quality inspectors from Italy), the certificate of machine acceptance is sent out.

Purchases 'from China to the rest of the world'

The International Purchasing Office of Pechino

The company has established various *International Purchasing Offices* throughout the world, to be always present at the most important sourcing areas. These offices are structured so that they are able to adapt themselves to the characteristics of the different local markets. The use of foreign suppliers can be variously motivated: a good price/performance ratio, interesting opportunities concerning contracts, the possibility of improving the quality level of the offer involving local industry, political impositions made by the local Government. It is therefore necessary to have flexible structures able to adapt themselves to the characteristics of the local markets.

The purchases 'from China to the rest of the world', coming from Chinese producers, are sent to customers in other markets. This trade, up to now, has been modest due to the weak qualitative profile of these products. However the Chinese offer is continuously increasing, thanks first of all to the process of privatization in progress. The decision was therefore taken to

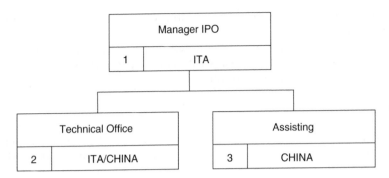

Figure CS3.1   Organizational chart of Danieli's IPO in China

start (even if cautiously) the purchasing activity from China to the rest of the world.

Danieli is strengthening its international purchasing office in Beijing, located close to the representative office. This IPO controls the production in China of machinery for the foreign markets. The IPO employs both Italian and Chinese personnel. The Italian employees are responsible for direction and technical assistance; the Chinese employees have the task of assisting the job orders at the supplier's premises. Currently, this office also manages orders in Vietnam, thanks to the geographic proximity between China and Vietnam. Figure CS3.1 shows the organizational structure of Danieli's IPO in China.

The main activities of the IPO are:

- selection and training of suppliers;
- negotiation with both the suppliers and the Italian head office
- adjustment of the technical designs to the local standards;
- assisting.

Selection of suppliers.   This activity, crucial to guarantee product quality and the reliability of deliveries, is carried out jointly by the Beijing IPO and by the purchasing and quality functions managed at head office. The cataloguing of suppliers follows an audit (carried out by the quality control inspectors) based on a structured questionnaire collecting the following information:

- general information about the company;
- references (regular customers and suppliers);
- organization (organization chart, number of employees, characteristics of the employed staff, data processing systems, engineering used);
- production capability (equipment, machinery and tools, internal lifting and transport systems, characteristics of divisions, of warehouses, even-

tual expansion, previous experience in the use of materials in the production processes);
- feasible processes (welding and non-destructive tests, gauges, equipment for the execution of tests, heat treatments, superficial protective treatments, sand-blasting and painting);
- quality certifications;
- conformity certifications

The purchase office uses the same questionnaire for the characterization both of the Italian suppliers and of those with other nationalities. The selection is therefore independent from geographic localization of the sources, except in the situations previously mentioned. On the basis of the outcome of the questionnaire, the purchase office writes up the 'characterization list', that portrays the profile of every supplier.

Negotiations with the suppliers.   The Beijing IPO has the task of setting up negotiations with the suppliers considering the indications provided by the central purchasing office, which is responsible for closing negotiations. The geographic and cultural proximity to the IPO staff make this agreement easier to reach and more effective. The contracts with the Chinese suppliers have no peculiarities; they are similar to those signed in other nations. This has become the case only since the entrance of China into the WTO, which has contributed to the elimination (or the relaxation) of several clauses that were previously typical in China.

Adjustment of the technical designs to local standards.   The technical office of the Chinese purchasing office has the task of adjusting the designs (drawn in Italy) to Chinese standards. The plan moreover must be adapted to the eventual specific needs of materials or components: it can happen that some components selected by the central technical office are not available in China. It therefore becomes necessary to choose items similar to the Western ones and available locally, eventually partially modifying the original designs.

Expediting.   The term 'expediting' means the assistance of progress carried out during all the production phases. It is carried out by Italian and Chinese employees, belonging to the purchasing office, who have been trained at the workshops at the head office. They have the task of controlling the quality of the purchases and of estimating carefully all workings (e.g. welding, finish, treatments aimed at the assemblage of the machine). The positive outcome of the intermediate and final inspections generates the award of a certificate of machine acceptance.

The collaboration of Chinese inspectors is considered an indispensable element of linguistic and cultural mediation with local interlocutors

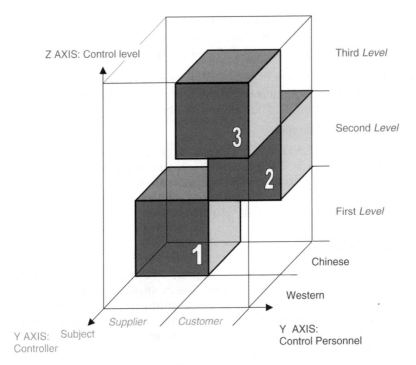

Figure CS3.2 Supply control in China

belonging to businesses where english is known (often) only by the management.

The control carried out by the staff of the IPO is supported by the controls carried out by the suppliers and sometimes also by Danieli's expatriate managers according to the three-level outline illustrated in Figure CS3.2.

The process of supplying. As far as the supply process is concerned, the purchases 'from China to the rest of the world' and 'from China to China' are very similar, with some differences that will be considered in the following paragraphs.

The identification of possible suppliers. The Beijing IPO continuously searches for new suppliers. Their characterization is therefore decided jointly by the purchase office and by quality control. The purchasing office transmits the technical designs to the Beijing IPO, which translates them for the Chinese market.

The classification of suppliers. The producers, previously described, are therefore classified according to the kind of machinery they have to create and their productive capability, which is an essential aspect with respect to delivery times. In this way Danieli has a list of suppliers that can be selected considering the characteristics of the specific demand.

The analysis of the offer. Based on the collected offers, the Chinese purchasing office sets up negotiations that are concluded by the personal of the purchase centre. The allocation of the order to the selected supplier follows this activity.

The management of the orders. The use of Chinese suppliers needs careful supervision during the whole production process in order to guarantee the required standards of quality. The control is therefore carried out by the Chinese staff belonging to the IPO, using systems similar to those used in the case of 'from China to China' purchases.

Other aspects

In past, the progress of Danieli's negotiations in China was often long and difficult, so that it could last for years. The multiplication of the subjects engaged in the negotiations, the lack of a third-party holder of real decisional power, the high costs of the transfers and the timing of the plans, were a famous peculiarly of China unlike other countries of the Far East like Korea, Taiwan, Thailand and Malaysia.

Today the situation is considerably improved: many job orders are currently defined in just a few months. The Olympic Games of Beijing in 2008 and the Shanghai Expo in 2010 are in fact forcing the country to complete in a hurry every kind of infrastructure and this, with the consolidation of the relations and the creation of a fiduciary relationship with the oriental interlocutors, is producing an acceleration in the times of negotiation and realization of the job orders.

In the past, moreover, the performance of the plans was considered inside five-year development plans, generating a longer time for the development of the planned activity. Today the plans are assigned according to bids preceded by a technical pre-negotiation, in which the eventual products, the supplies and other contractual aspects are defined. A recurrent note from Danieli's Chinese customers is the fact that, on base of Danieli's experience, they wish to acquire systems already consolidated in technology and tested in operation. The visiting of systems already built is a prerequisite for the sale, demanded by these Chinese customers.

Danieli does not litigate with its own customers in China. It tries, in fact, to avoid legal disputes, having as its main objective the maintainance of good relationships and remaining open to the opportunity for future interactions and plans. For example, the preamble of a typical agreement recites 'After friendly and mutual agreement'.

With respect to transport, Danieli mainly manages the flows towards China, which are via ship only. Within the country transport is generally by road. In contrast to the infrastructural deficiencies described by many observers, Danieli has never met particular problems in the management of transport flows in China, although the movement of cumbersome and heavy cargos (sometimes up to 350 tons) takes place throughout the whole country.

In relation to communication, China famously opted directly for wireless telephony, according to an outline already implemented in India and in some African countries. The communication infrastructures present in China are therefore judged more than sufficiently adapted. Communication between the representative office and the purchase office frequently takes place by video-conference, whilst that with the suppliers normally takes place by email or telephone. The sales managers located near to the customers are available 24 hours a day. The local staff employed in Danieli's Chinese office have been recruited giving prority to two aspects: knowledge of English and of technical culture. The staff engaged in negotiations must understand the technology and be able to explain it. Moreover, they must also possess those relational abilities so important in this context.

Case Studies
4: Trudi

From West to East: the migration of manufacturing

The company

Established in 1954, today Trudi, with a catalogue of 350 models, is the leader in the Italian market and one of the most important European competitors in the production of soft toys. The group employs approximately 99 people in Italy, Spain, France, Germany and Singapore. Trudi has a yearly turnover of approximately 25 million Euro (42% made in foreign countries (2004)).

Seventy people work in the Tarcento head office in Italy. The most creative activities of the production process are carried out there: product development, prototyping, engineering, quality control, logistics, distribution and post-sales services. The final product, initially localized in Tarcento, is today made in Asia by Chinese and Indonesian producers. The two Spanish and German branches attend to distribution, such as TRUDI&Sevi S.A. (a French subsidiary).

Since 2000 Virgilio, a subsidiary entirely controlled by Trudi with a head office in Singapore, has attended to quality control and the search for new suppliers in Asia.

The organization chart is illustrated in Figure CS4.1.

On the international market there are almost ten competitors (the German *Nici* and *Steiff* are the most important).

In 1999 the company bought Sevi, which is the oldest (1831) European brand in the production of wooden toys and gifts and fancy goods for children.

The sourcing markets

Nowadays Trudi and Sevi purchase only from the Asian market. They spend approximately eight million dollars per year. The suppliers are Chinese (80%), Indonesian (19%) and Vietnamese (1%). In the beginning,

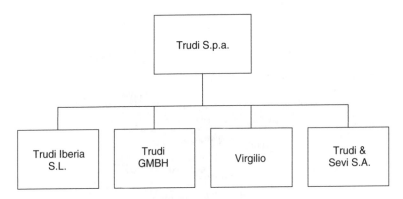

Figure CS4.1 Trudi: corporate chart

the sourcing areas were Sri Lanka, the Philippines, Thailand and Vietnam; later the greater part of the sourcing activity moved to China.

The soft toys Trudi buys are produced in the Shenzen zone by enterprises often characterized by Korean co-ownership. Many of the Trudi suppliers (mainly the spinners) arise from the 'delocalization' of Korean enterprises in China. Some of these companies of Korean origin have maintained Korean management. This is a factor valued favourably by Trudi because Korean management has demonstrated a bigger entrepreneurial attitude and dynamism than Chinese management.

As far as wooden products are concerned, in the past, Sri Lanka and Philippines constituted the main supply markets. Currently Sevi is oversee-ing the last orders made in the Philippines. Ultimately they prefer to buy mainly in the Chinese areas of Ningbo (where their main supplier works) and Tiansong.

The low labour cost was the factor behind the transfer of production to the Far East. The soft toys, in fact, are made almost entirely by hand and, as far as labour costs are concerned, the difference between Italy and China is very big. Trudi is concentrating its sourcing activity in the Shenzen area, in the south-east of the country (see Fig CS4.2). This choice was made essentially for the logistic advantages linked to the proximity of Hong Kong and to the availability of many experienced suppliers. The presence of customs or tax reliefs was not an important factor in Trudi's choice (or at least not a factor that allows China to be distinguished from the other Asian sourcing areas).

Important advantages are offered to the enterprises that decide to produce in China: Sevi's main supplier is a German enterprise that is estab-lishing a factory on a wide productive area near Ningbo. The local adminis-tration donated a residential area to this supplier and has granted a complete exemption from taxes for the first three years following the estab-lishment of its factory.

Figure CS4.2   Location of the main suppliers in China

Supplies in China

In 1954 the company started up the production of soft toys in Friuli. At that time they only bought raw materials abroad (from European suppliers).

In the 1950s and 1960s the soft toys were made using mohair, a fabric popular at the beginning on the twentieth century. They were stuffed with straw, with glass or metal (for the bigger soft toys) eyes. Trudi soft toys were characterized by extreme technical simplicity combined with the high quality of the fabric, often painted in order to obtain a spotted or shading effect. In the second half of the 1960s Trudi started using a long nap material usually used in carpet production (this innovation was very soon imitated by the major competitors). The next change concerned the straw: the traditional stuffing was replaced by padding that made the toy softer and washable.

The search for new materials and the necessity of reducing the costs of supply induced Trudi to search for new supply markets (today the raw materials account for 50% of the total costs). Therefore, towards the end of the 1980s, Trudi started buying from Korean suppliers, who demonstrated that they could reduce the frequent problem of the nap shedding and could guarantee an adequate resistance to the fire through the use of fire-resistant raw materials. The innovation of the materials, often developed in contiguous sectors (such as that of clothing and in particular of artificial fur), became a key factor of success.

These first experiments with Asian suppliers had a good outcome and convinced Trudi, subsequently, to undertake a process of transfer of production to these countries characterized by low labour costs. Trudi signed the first contracts with Korean suppliers of raw materials. In this way they started to understand the Chinese economic context where these Korean enterprises had localized some facilities in order to serve directly the local market. The growing acquaintance with China allowed Trudi to establish direct relationships with some local producers.

Today, out of a total of nine foreign suppliers to which the company is bound, six are Chinese.

Nowadays Trudi's entire production is in the Far East maintaining in Italy activities as marketing, product development (product concept, prototyping engineering), logistics and distribution. Eighty per cent of the product is made in China. Trudi has no direct contacts with the suppliers of raw materials (with the exception of the demand for sample), delegating the purchase of raw materials to its suppliers of finished products. For instance, the soft toy technical specification, sent by Trudi to its suppliers, states the type of raw materials that have to be used. Sometimes the producers have to buy raw materials from suppliers selected by Trudi; otherwise they can choose their suppliers, but respecting what is stated in the technical card.

Trudi now wants to concentrate its production of soft toys in the Shenzen area. This choice derives essentially from the logistic advantages (the closeness to Hong Kong considered above) and by the high concentration of experienced suppliers available in this area. The closeness to Hong Kong makes shipments to Europe and the recruitment of staff easier. Trudi is therefore thinking of transferring Virgilio (that is a body dedicated to the safety and quality control of Asian product) from Singapore to Hong Kong. The aim is to make the movements of their own quality controllers easier thanks to a reduction in transfer costs and times.

Figure CS4.3 shows the path of Trudi's international growth.

Sevi

In 1999 Trudi acquired Sevi, the oldest European brand of wooden toys (its history dates back to 1831). Production, initially in Trentino Alto Adige (Italy), was soon transferred to Asia near to suppliers localized in the Philippines, Sri Lanka, Thailand, China and Indonesia. As for Trudi, the activity of marketing and planning remained in Tarcento (Italy).

In the beginning, product engineering was completely carried out inside the company. Currently, Sevi is involving some suppliers in this activity, giving them a wide autonomy but asking them to respect of the design

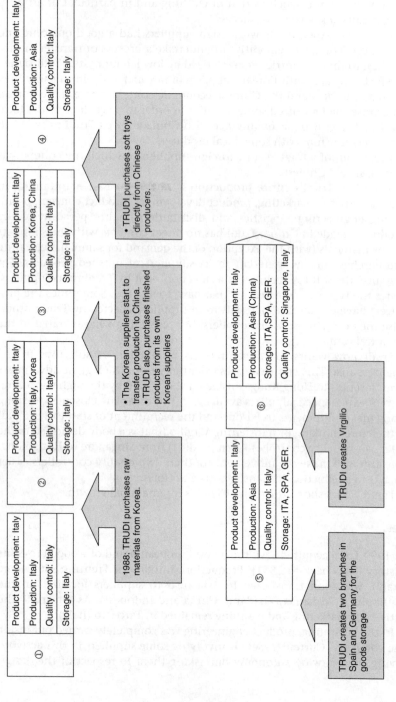

Figure CS4.3   Trudi: path of international growth

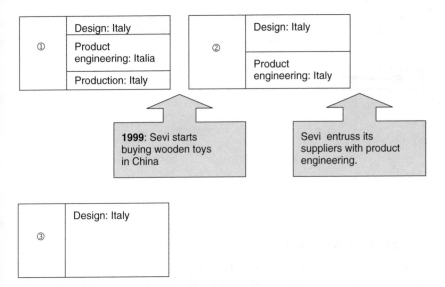

Figure CS4.4 Sevi: path of international growth

characteristics. This choice is caused by the lack of internal know-how that would allow low cost productions in a market segment where the batches are often small (for some items, the annual demand doesn't exceed 250–300 pieces). Outsourcing has allowed Trudi to buy cheap, well-designed, skillfully-made products, and has given rise to a greater involvement of the suppliers through frequent contacts and transfers.

Figure CS4.4 shows Sevi's path of growth internationally.

Sourcing organization

The Trudi brand is famous for its high quality goods. In order to protect this image, despite Asian production, the company has chosen a sourcing strategy based on:

- a transfer of know-how to its suppliers;
- quality control carried out directly at the supplier's facilities.

The suppliers have to pledge that each toy complies with European security regulation EN 71. In addition, the suppliers must sign and apply a code of conduct, the principles of which are: the use of qualified employees paid according to the local norms; the prohibition of child labour or of carrying out political, racial or religious discrimination; the adoption of working hours in accordance with the local norms; the maintenance of a healthy workplace, equipped with modern machinery and fire-fighting equipment.

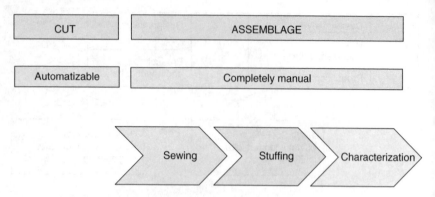

Figure CS4.5   The main steps of soft toy production

The transfer of know-how

The transfer of know-how from Italy has required the intervention of Italian technicians to train the Asian staff. This transfer initially caused communication problems due to the limited knowledge of English (English inside Chinese factories is often spoken only by the management). Trudi therefore had to use interpreters.

Trudi never transfered machinery and equipment to China. The production of soft toys does not call for huge investments in technology and machines. Cutting (an activity that could be automated) is executed by Trudi manually in order to minimize the off-cuts and to obtain greater flexibility (Figure CS4.5). Assembly is made through hand-sewing.

The production process, even if characterized by a very simple process, needs a very highly technical stitching. For this reason the training of the suppliers has occupied Trudi for a long time.

The assemblage phase (that consists in the sewing of the template, in stuffing and in the characterization of the soft toy by the application of moustaches, eyes, nose and accessories) calls for elevated manual labour in order to respect the expressiveness of the subject represented. In toy-making, according to Trudi's experience, it is important to consider not only the technical, but also the aesthetic quality.

Quality control of the suppliers: Virgilio

Initially Trudi entrusted quality control to a group of technicians who periodically had to carry out long visits to China. The high costs of this solution convinced the company to transfer permanently the control activities to the neighbourhood of the Asian suppliers.

So, from 2000, Virgilio (a branch established in Singapore) became responsible for quality control in Asia. Singapore is nowadays becoming less and less the centre of the sourcing area (most of the suppliers now operate in the Shenzen Area), and Trudi is therefore analysing the possibility of transferring Virgilio to Hong Kong.

The main activity of Virgilio is quality control of the Chinese suppliers. It is also engaged in other activities such as the certification of product safety, and the search for new potential suppliers and new materials.

Quality control management

Some employees of Virgilio have been located at the producers with the task of monitoring the process and of guaranteeing quality control of every phase. Virgilio selected quality controllers (QCs) of Chinese nationality with the intention of facilitating communication both with the staff and with the management of Trudi's manufacturers. Another motive for this choice is the low cost of these employees.

Every supplier has quality control functions in its organization chart. The QCs collaborate with them and have the task of approving the batches in three phases: the receipt of the materials, the process of manufacture, and the final inspection. When the containers are closed at the producer's premises, the quality controller writes up a structured form reporting the inspection results. There is also a sample inspection made by the central quality control agency in Italy so the Chinese controllers are therefore subordinated to a periodical verification regarding the congruence between what is reported in the form and what is effectively received. However, the Virgilio supervisor, that is the head of six QCs, visits the suppliers at least once a month.

There are three levels of quality control. The first level is executed by the quality control manager in the supplier's service. The second level of control is made by Virgilio's QCs. The last level of control is carried out by Trudi on reception of the goods in the European warehouses.

Table CS4.1 Levels of quality control

Quality control			
Level	Stage	Controller	Place
1	Production	Producer	China
2	Material acceptance at the supplier; Production; Forwarding.	Quality Controller (Virgilio)	China
3	Acceptance by the buyer	Quality Controller (Trudi)	Italy, Spain, Germany

The management of the certification of product safety

Trudi has to ensure that products comply with European rule EN 71 regarding toy safety before putting them on the market. These controls are carried out by internationally recognized institutes of Hong Kong. The Singapore office coordinates the product certification activities jointly with the Italian safety manager.

The search of new suppliers

Today this activity is assigned to Virgilio. The management of orders, on the other hand, is still carried out in Italy. Trudi think that in this way they will maintain direct contact with their own suppliers. They judge this aspect to be a key factor for the continuation of their activity in China.

Table CS4.2 sets out the criteria (in order of decreasing importance) used by Trudi for the selection of the suppliers. A 5-level Likert scale has been used for this purpose (1 = not important; 5 = very important).

Quality.   The product has elevated technical and aesthetic characteristics; moreover it must comply with European norm EN71 on toy safety. Compliance with this norm has been one of the main problems that Trudi has faced with the transfer of production to China.

Certification from recognized agencies.   The agreements with suppliers certified by recognized agencies would be valued by Trudi as a very important factor. However, today Chinese suppliers are not still certified.

Punctuality and completeness of the deliveries.   The market requires a high ability of programming in order to be ready for most important annual dates (Halloween, Saint Valentine, etc.) for the sale of soft toys. For this reason, Trudi think reliability is a relevant factor in supplier selection.

R&D ability.   Trudi's competitiveness springs from: brand, design and technology of materials. The company therefore thinks that the R&D ability of its suppliers is very important. In various cases it has been a useful support to the innovation activities developed at headquarters.

Geographic position.   Trudi's main Chinese suppliers are localized in the Shenzen area. This choice come essentially from the logistic convenience of this area: Shenzen is close to Hong Kong, that is probably the Chinese area with the best transport infrastructures.

References.   Trudi judges favourably that its own potential suppliers already work for European enterprises. In this case, the suppliers would have to be able to produce goods complying with the safety norms that discipline the toy sector.

Table CS4.2 Criteria used by Trudi for the selection of the Asian suppliers

	Weight
Quality	5
Financial stability	5
Certifications from recognized agencies	5
Punctuality and completeness of the deliveries	5
R&D ability	4
Geographic location	4
References	3
Payment terms	2
Price	2
Well-established business relations	1
Post-sales services	1
Know-how, technology and products original experience	1
Access to advanced technologies	1
Strategic decisions	1
Range of products	1

Terms of payment. Trudi pays its own suppliers 60 days after delivery. So Trudi's financial impact on suppliers is often relevant. As far as soft toys are concerned, Trudi purchases normally account for 80 per cent of the total turnover of its suppliers.

The reorganization of Virgilio

The actual organizational configuration and the responsibility profile of Virgilio is the result of a long gradual path, where the initial configuration has been subsequently improved. Some initial choices, in fact, proved unsatisfactory and they required some changes. It is interesting to analyse briefly the organizational evolution of this unit.

Initially, the responsibilities remitted to Virgilio were as follows:

- the search for new potential suppliers;
- finding new materials;
- negotiating purchase orders;
- planning production.

The choice to transfer to Virgilio (and therefore to Singapore) responsibilities and consequent activities previously carried out in Italy, did not always seem to be working. The main problems met were linked to two factors:

1 the resistance to the organizational change made by the central units, which wanted to hinder the delegation of activities to a peripheral office. For example, the decision to transfer to Virgilio the negotiation

responsibility of purchase orders with the Chinese suppliers was strongly contrasted;

2   the lack of attention paid to recruitment of staff.

The activation of the Chinese office took direct control from the central office, imposing contextually on the head office a heavy task: the transfer to the Chinese office of the customs and methods of the process monitoring. Consequently communication flows between Italy and the Singapore office became heavier. The organizational decentralization was sometimes interpreted from the central units as an unjustified loss of sovereignty and as an addition of work linked to the management of flows of information. This resistance has today decreased, thanks partly to the Chinese staff who, in the meantime, have developed great mastery and familiarity with the qualitative standards required by head office, with process know-how and with the modalities for its monitoring.

The negotiation of Trudi's purchase orders was, however, brought back to Italy. This allows a consistent (up to 10%) cut in prices of the purchased materials. Maintenance of direct relationships between head office and the suppliers is today judged to be an imperative element of the sourcing strategy from China. As far as internal organization is concerned, Virgilio interacts directly with Trudi's Operations manager (Figure CS4.6).

Trudi has been devising monthly purchase plans that are communicated to the suppliers. The visibility of future orders allows the Chinese suppliers to plan better the supply of raw materials and production. It also allows Trudi to reduce the lead time. Trudi is moreover assessing the opportunity of planning and managing jointly with some suppliers the purchase and storage of raw materials. Finally, Trudi is setting up a system of reporting to apply to the main suppliers in order to control the advancement of their production.

At the head of Virgilio there is a supervisor, who coordinates one accounts manager, two product line managers (one for soft toys, and the other for soft toys licensing and articles in wood) and six QCs (Figure CS4.7).

The process

Trudi's core business is the production of soft-toys, whose conception and prototype creation are by Italian designers. In recent years Trudi has signed some contracts for the sale of soft toys and for the production of mascots and promotional articles for some external companies. The processes for the creation of these two product lines are substantially the same, but the time they need on Trudi's production line is decidedly longer.

The time-to-market of a soft-toy collection is approximately one year. The process starts with the marketing function that defines (through a

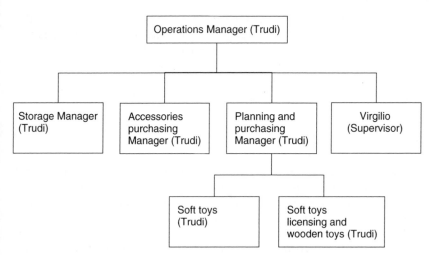

Figure CS4.6   Virgilio in the Trudi organization chart

product plan) the market needs in terms of quantity, types of new models
and distribution dates of the various collections. Trudi has four collections
per year, that is twice the number of the fashion sector (where there are
normally two collections: spring–summer and autumn–winter). Each collection is associated to particular events: Saint Valentine and Easter, back to
school and Hallowe'en, Christmas (which alone accounts for 32% of
turnover) and the 'New January ideas'. Some of these collections, such as

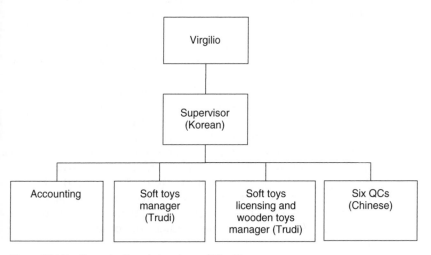

Figure CS4.7   Organizational structure of Virgilio

Saint Valentine or Hallowe'en, are 'one-shot': they are often models with a particular connotation that therefore limits the sale of these goods to a restricted period. Other collections have a longer life cycle.

Trudi has singled out four market segments that are called:

- Nature;
- Happiness;
- Energy; and
- Love.

Based on the indications received from the marketing, the product development department makes a model in clay and, subsequently, creates the prototype with fabric samples and other materials available in the central office. The prototype is subordinate to internal approval.

Having completed the prototypal collection, for every soft toy, Trudi prepares the technical document or card containing the characteristics of the product, the materials used, the assemblage instructions and samples of the materials. At this time the suppliers are selected depending on the product typology and on the supplier production capacity. The physical sample is sent to them, together with the patterns to be used for the cut, the drawings, the assemblage instructions and the technical card. Every supplier then produces a sample composed of at least three pieces. In some cases, the same sample request is sent by Trudi to several suppliers. The three samples made by every supplier are sent to Italy for approval. The product development manager, analysing the received samples, decides whether the agreement for the production can be completed or whether it's important to ask for changes/improvements. The purchase office, on the basis of the sourcing strategies and of the outcome of the negotiations, selects the supplier. One (of the three) approval samples remains in Tarcento (it's a reference used for the control in the final inspection), one is sent back to the supplier as its reference, the last one is given to Virgilio and will be used by the QCs as a control.

At this point the sending out of the order and the carrying out of the first production begins during which Virgilio operates a special check following the process step-by-step. It monitors therefore the shipment from the Asian suppliers to the centres of distribution in Italy, Spain or Germany.

During recent years Trudi has signed some licences for the production and distribution of soft toys of several international groups: Walt Disney (1996–99); Puffi (2000–01); Warner Bros, Harry Potter (2001–02) and Looney Tunes (2002–05), Recently Trudi has created a new internal department called 'New Business Development' oriented to manage promotional articles. This department monitors the product from creation to sale, collaborating with the customers.

Other aspects

The constant renewal of the collections urges Trudi to develop new models every year. For every one of them, once the itemized lists are defined and the supplier's sample are controlled, the negotiations consider, first of all, the price. In the past the target price was the criterion with which Trudi indicated to the suppliers the highest purchase price and the negotiations were conducted using this reference. Trudi's control of the suppliers' costs wasn't very effective, as these companies were not equipped with an effective instrument for management control.

The parties involved in the negotiations are, on the Chinese side the sales manager, who is often also the entrepreneur and, on Trudi's side the chief buyer.

Trudi protects all the items legally, even if the phenomenon of the copy is widespread. The presence of the quality controllers, located near to the sources, limits these risks and allows a constant control of what the suppliers do. Trudi does not ask its partners for an exclusive supply relationship, but it discourages trade relations with its direct competitors, not because it fears the phenomenon of copies, but because it wants to avoid these competitors taking advantage of know-how that Trudi has transferred to the suppliers.

Communication between Trudi and its suppliers is coordinated by Virgilio (in particular by the two managers belonging to the two product lines). Two other employees in Italy, in contact with the production planning and purchasing managers, are in direct communication with Asian suppliers. In this way the company limits the problems linked to differences of time zone, guaranteeing to the supplier the possibility of constant communication either with the headquarters or with Virgilio. For this communication they mainly use telephone, fax and e-mail.

Visits to the producers are planned at particular times of the year. Unscheduled meetings can take place at any time, particularly at the request of the product developers (Table CS4.3).

As mentioned above, the continuous and programmed controls of the production process are made by the Virgilio QCs that are located close to the suppliers. At least once a month, the supervisor inspects the factories for the control of behaviour and of the QC activity. The operations manager goes to China at least three times a year with the aims of planning future activities and of completing quality control. At the same time, the product development managers periodically visit the suppliers of raw materials in order to propose new materials and to attend fairs and shows. Above all during the phase of product development, and often because of problems due to timing, the Italian staff goes to China in order to deliver personally patterns, models and technical cards necessary for producing the

Table CS4.3   Visits to the suppliers

	Planned view		Non-planned view
	Frequency	Objective	Objective
Supervisor	Once at month	Quality control	
Operations Manager	At least 3 times at year	Quality control Planning	
Product development manager		Search for new materials	Reduction of shipping time during product development

samples. They also can assist suppliers (if necessary) during the production period.

Up to 85 per cent of production is now sent to Tarcento; the remainder is sent to the other distribution centres in Spain and Germany. As far as German and Spanish selling activity is concerned, Trudi's future objective is to avoid the intermediate passage in Italy that still affects a part of the goods.

The company mostly uses transport by sea with shipment times of approximately one month. Production lead time is approximately two and half months. So the total time is therefore approximately three and half months. The responsibility for transport belongs to Trudi, which buys free on board (FOB).

As far as the goods destined for the Italian market are concerned, the packaging comprises an inner-box that contains the lowest number of products purchasable by a store. The inner-boxes are contained in a master-carton for shipment. On reaching the warehouse, the material is unpacked and quality controlled. The pallets, made by putting together several inner-boxes, are sent to the gravitational storehouse where the picking is carried out.

Case Studies

5: The ZenAsia Case

The outsourcing of logistics services for SMEs

The company

As is usual with small firms, this company's history is strongly bound to the figure of its founder and developer, an entrepreneur whose destiny is written in his own name: Mario Zen (*'in nomen omen'*). The adventures of the ZenAsia Global Group ('ZenAsia') started in 1986, when Mario Zen visited Asia for the first time. He arrived in Hong Kong to work as a buyer for some Italian customers and explored a supply market which was well known by western multinationals purchasing electrical appliances and products. He then started building a network of relationships and contacts with Chinese manufacturers. Since the early 1990s, the western demand for low-level electronic materials has started to decline, in parallel with the rise of Japanese and Korean producers who transferred their production to China, achieving huge cost advantages. But the demand for other types of product has increased, highlighting the need to have reliable oriental inter-mediaries who could guarantee the quality standards and lead-times required by western buyers.

Thanks to his knowledge of the oriental market and his network of contacts, Mario Zen was requested by utensils firms and Personal Protection Devices manufacturers to monitor orders, control shipments and source new suppliers. To manage these services better and to cope with growing volumes, he realized the need to obtain a local base and a local partner. After a long period of research and some fruitless trials, Mario Zen found the right partner. His name was Mr Pen and he worked for a Chinese foreign trade company, but he had a strong entrepreneurial vocation and had long been looking for the opportunity to set up his own business. In 1998 he abandoned the trade company and founded a company in Suzhou specializing in Personal Protection Devices. Mr Pen's target was to attack foreign markets with these products, but he faced great difficulties in coping with very different geographic and cultural realities. Mario Zen and Mr Pen thus developed close relationships and a fruitful collaboration, whereby each one helped the other to understand better the home market and settle there. Mr Pen's company became the sourcing base in Asia for ZenAsia, which then became the commercial bridgehead for the Chinese company. The first customers of ZenAsia were Italian wholesalers and distributors who imported big volumes from China. The company provided them with logistics services, in particular quality and container control to avoid the costs and delays associated with intercontinental shipments of defective materials. Similar services were subsequently requested of ZenAsia by other small and medium-sized firms which already practiced sourcing activities in China or which intended to start them. The demand was so high that ZenAsia decided to move a good part of the business towards them, since small companies represented a more suitable target for the services in which ZenAsia was specializing.

In fact, the wholesalers' principal aim is to achieve price competitiveness, while they are only interested in the general characteristics of the product (functionality, colour, etc); small manufacturing firms instead ask suppliers to provide technical and technological adaptations on products and processes, are more sensitive to quality issues and more willing to provide precise and detailed specifications. They therefore ask logistics services providers to guarantee a continuous monitoring of Chinese manufacturers. The decision to focus on this target was a winning one: in a few years ZenAsia had sales of 20 million Euros. Its customers were mainly small and medium-sized Italian firms and the codes of supply covered an ample number of sectors: from components for wooden furniture to electromechanical components, from clothing to shoes, from house furniture to metal hardware and tools. China was the main sourcing base, but the services offered were also available in other Far East countries, such as Taiwan, South Korea, Japan, Vietnam, India. There are actually 350 Asian suppliers.

The organization

The main office is based in Italy in S. Zenone degli Ezzelini, which is the points of contact with Italian customers. Another unit has been established in China, in Suzhou; it employs a Chinese workforce, some of which have administrative roles, others whose task is to monitor Chinese manufacturers. These personnel currently speak English. ZenAsia's activity in China is operated in liaison with a Chinese (from the legal point of view) company; this offers advantages in the event of legal issues relevant to product quality or forgery (as we will discuss better later). According to a common model for small units, the entrepreneur has a wide array of tasks: from the relationship with suppliers and customers, to the approval of new vendors, to the overall coordination of activities. Figure CS5.1 shows the company organizational chart, while Figure CS5.2 highlights the geographical localization of the Chinese local office.

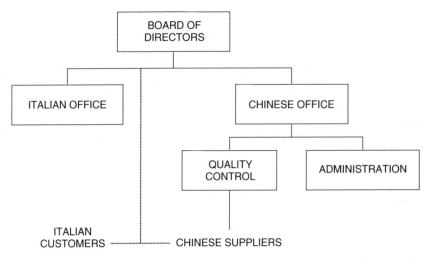

Figure CS5.1   ZenAsia's organizational structure

Figure CS5.2   Geographical localization of the Chinese office

The company is planning to open a new branch in Spain, where some wholesalers of house tools and utensils are interested in logistics services supporting sourcing activities in China.

ZenAsia's Chinese offices are located in Suzhou, a city in the Jangsu region, 100 km from Shanghai. This area mirrors the economic and commercial model of Hong Kong and the Guangzhou region, the region which experienced the first and most powerful industrialization phase. Shanghai is now the economic capital of China, and therefore has higher costs than nearby regions. Labour and production costs are decidedly lower in Suzhou, and the distance from the Shanghai harbour is short. It is not by chance that many Taiwanese, Korean and western joint ventures settled here. Therefore ZenAsia, in addition to exploiting the support of Mr Pen's company, can rely on a continuously growing economic environment and on an ample base of potential suppliers.

The services provided

The services provided by ZenAsia are listed here and described further below.

- Sourcing
  - product sourcing;
  - vendor search;
  - search for a partner for co-operation (and development of OEM productions).
- Negotiation
  - document acquisition;
  - initial samples acquisition;
  - consultancies for the best contractual terms and conditions and purchase and payment terms.
- Manufacturing
  - control of production development;
  - development, production and final control of pallets and packaging;
  - on line quality control;
  - manufacturing times check.
- Quality control
  - pre-shipment quality and quantity control (for the pre-shipment base inspection procedure refer to Annex 2);
  - final sample acquisition;
  - final inspection report.
- Shipments and logistics
  - definition of fares and shipments from Chinese harbours;
  - logistics and assistance for the shipment of materials and customs operations.
- After-sales service
  - assistance for complaints relevant to imported products;
  - re-order assistance.

Sourcing

ZenAsia uses three channels to source new suppliers: the internet, expos and foreign trade companies (FTC). With respect to this third channel, it is interesting to notice how effective is this source of information. These large state companies in fact maintain relationships with multiple local manufacturers, generally the smaller ones. For many of them FTCs are the only access to foreign markets, which implies intermediation charges between 5 per cent and 10 per cent. While in the past export was only suitable for these big companies, today, at least in different sectors, foreign trade rights can be obtained by other bodies as well. FTCs have often allowed ZenAsia to source valid suppliers, with whom it has managed direct relationships.

Negotiation

According to ZenAsia, this is the most critical activity, because it does not only concern the allocation of an order and the definition of its specifications, but also the possibility for organizations to meet and interface with each other. It helps to build a relational context, beyond defining an agreement on a number of formal terms and conditions. Such dynamics are not familiar to western operators, who are often culturally unprepared to negotiate and misunderstand the behaviour of their Chinese counterpart. A frequent element of disorientation is pricing: Chinese suppliers tend to be explicit only in advanced negotiations, subjecting it to a number of other variables and postponing it at the suggestion of western counterparts. Another important aspect during negotiations is constituted by the volumes required, on which ZenAsia is particularly sensitive since it mainly interfaces with small and medium-sized customers. Chinese manufacturers, according to the company's experience, mainly pursue big numbers, either to obtain the economies of scale necessary to safeguard profit margins from the low prices imposed by customers, or because different sectors are accustomed to sell to big distribution chains, especially North American ones. Therefore it is not simple to accept the idea that even a small customer can represent a good opportunity, if this relationship will originate regular and lasting purchases. To obtain the supplier's trust it is necessary 'to sell' the Italian or European company, illustrating its profile, references and requirements. We should highlight that approximately 80 per cent of the suppliers with whom ZenAsia collaborates are privately owned. The company has in fact noticed two main issues when dealing with state-owned companies: the high turnover of personnel on the one hand, and their limited technical knowledge on the other. The capability to understand the specifications and maintain adequate technical dialogue is considered a necessary condition to start any supply relationship. The first interactions usually take place with the Chinese manufacturer's export manager, who generally speaks English but does not always have a technical culture and therefore may be supported by Chinese technicians. The availability of local personnel has nevertheless sensitively reduced, even if not cancelled, the communication problems with suppliers which ZenAsia experienced in the past. The cultural and linguistic mediation of this personnel is fundamental, since the latter performs an important activity of translation of the technical specifications and other documents.

Preliminary auditing

Visiting suppliers' premises is necessary during selection and evaluation to verify their actual suitability. Such activity can also be performed during the following phases, to monitor the agreed standards over time. Preliminary auditing is performed by ZenAsia's Chinese personnel, on the basis of detailed supervisory instructions provided by western customers. It will require detailed information on sales, markets currently served, products, number and characteristics of specific production machinery, productive capability, but it will also require information on the productive and labour organization, the cleanness of premises, the availability of a showroom. The specifications of investigation defined by the customer therefore determine the characteristics and structure of the report which shall be prepared by inspectors. An example of such report is displayed in Annex 1.

Quality controls constitute the most critical activity among those performed by ZenAsia. The characteristics of supervisory phases, i.e. the objects, phases and instruments of control, are entirely defined by the customer: ZenAsia's inspectors must follow in detail the instructions relevant to the products to sample, the parameters to be measured and instruments to use. The Italian customer is provided with photographic documentation of the plant, machinery, showroom and, eventually, product samples. It is useful to underline that in this delicate phase ZenAsia only performs data collection tasks, without interpretations or judgements on the qualitative profile analysed. Such judgements are only reserved to the customer, who knows precisely the utilization and the corresponding technical requirements of the product. In this way, ZenAsia protects itself with respect to its customers, leaving them responsible to accept, modify or reject a batch and taking responsibility only for the reliability of its measurements. Moreover, even if ZenAsia's controllers have a technical background (mainly in electronics and mechanics) to perform supervisory tasks, it is evident that they cannot substitute the customer's technicians in some evaluations of detail. According to the needs, quality control can concern productive inputs, the production process or the finished product: the extension of control is evidently accompanied to different levels of costs.

Transport and shipment

The shipment of products from productive plants to ZenAsia's warehouse in Shanghai is usually under the responsibility of Chinese suppliers, according to free on board delivery terms. In the event of repeated damages to the products or delivery delays, ZenAsia recurs to well-established Chinese forwarding agents. Such cases are rare, despite the insufficiency of the road network. For sea transport, and therefore inter-continental transfers, ZenAsia has ratified contracts with important international logistics agents.

The management of transport is one of the most qualifying and researched activities, for two reasons:

1 the cost advantage which ZenAsia can offer, thanks to the economies of scale related to the possibility of cumulative volumes directed to multiple customers. Only smaller batches pose some problems, since it is not worthwhile to ship a single container;
2 the management of documents and customs clearance, which require familiarity with Chinese laws and practice.

The harbour infrastructures are deemed excellent, thanks to the continuous extensions and modernizations which they have enjoyed. To keep good standards of reliability and advantageous tariffs, government authorities left much leeway to European and American forwarding agents. The practices and operations of shipment have been made much quicker in recent years, because harbours are active at any hour of the day. It is interesting to note how the transfer of a container from Venice to Shanghai costs less than half as much as one on the opposite route. According to the costs, times and availability of freight, ZenAsia chooses from time to time one of two sea freight means:

1 *direct lines*. The cargo-container ship departs from Shanghai and reaches the Italian harbour in four weeks on average;
2 *indirect lines*. Containers are transported from Shanghai to some big Mediterranean harbours (Pireo, Gioia Tauro, Haifa), where they are embarked on smaller tonnage ships directed towards Venice, Genoa, Trieste.

Negotiation process and operative aspects

The negotiation process after which the long term agreement is defined is quite complex but carefully tailored and improved through long experience. It is therefore worth analysing it briefly.

Phase 1

It has reduced costs and consists of the sourcing of potential suppliers. On the customer's request to verify the possibility of sourcing a specific type of product in China, ZenAsia activates its local network. The list of suppliers compatible with the customer's requests is defined utilizing the aforementioned information sources. In cooperation with the customer, the analysis is then narrowed to three or more suppliers whose premises are visited. The preliminary audit allows the definition of a detailed profile of the manufacturer, with photographic documentation. On the basis of this information, the customer preliminary knows the offer for the required products. A usually carefully considered parameter concerns the references of potential suppliers: the Italian customer is thus interested to know who are the other customers served and to control the product samples. This information is checked by ZenAsia, for instance consulting the export documents of the potential supplier. The Italian customer, who doesn't yet know the identity of the potential Chinese supplier but has sufficient information to perform a preliminary evaluation, can thus decide whether to proceed to the following phase or to stop.

Phase 2

This phase comprises the activities necessary to accomplish the sample order and deliver it. Its sub-phases are described below.

- *Delivery of preliminary documentation.* The information relating to potential suppliers that is relevant to the company is transferred to the customer, together with a copy of their catalogues.
- *Development and realization of the samples.* ZenAsia receives from the customer the complete technical specifications, drawings (whenever possible) and eventual samples of the products. This material is provided to the selected Chinese suppliers, to allow them to develop the counter-samples.
- *Field support to technical personnel in China.* ZenAsia can provide its technicians to the Chinese manufacturer; these will maintain a constant link with the Italian mother company and the customer. These technicians have the task of controlling product development at the Chinese plants. ZenAsia China's office is also in charge of supervising the various operations and eventually of translating the technical documents from Chinese to English.
- *Shipment of samples.* ZenAsia China receives the samples in its Suzhou office. It performs a preliminary control, taking digital pictures of the requested details, transferring the entire documentation via e-mail to the customer and waiting for them to request the shipment. In this way it can avoid any waste of time and the costs related to shipments of samples which clearly do not conform to expectations.
- *Analysis of the samples.* After the analysis of the samples, the customer will decide whether: a) to request other samples; b) to perform directly an audit of the selected manufacturers; c) to authorize the first trial order. In the last case, the customer defines with ZenAsia Italy the specifications of the order: quantity, prices, technical characteristics, packaging, shipping

mark, delivery time, certifications, inspections, payment terms, export documents, after-sale warranty, transportation type, final destination. A preliminary contract between the Italian customer and the Chinese company is then drafted, possibly defining aspects related to intellectual property rights and particular exclusives. If the Italian company highlights precise needs for legal protection, the contract can define ZenAsia China as the customer's legal representative. Eventual successive legal disputes will therefore happen between Chinese parties.

- *On-line quality control.* At the customer's request, ZenAsia China monitors the productive aspects and performs on-line quality control on the goods directly, i.e. through its own personnel, or through a local third party.
- *Shipment.* Upon the customer's request, ZenAsia coordinates door-to-door transport of the trial order. This service comprises the management of the shipment documents, the collection of documents, customs clearance operations and delivery to the final warehouse.
- *Pre-shipment inspection.* Before the shipment, ZenAsia performs pre-shipment inspection and tests on the order, according to the customer's instructions. After these operations, ZenAsia e-mails a copy of the inspection sheet together with the digital images of the required details (Annex 2). Moreover, if required, it sends via courier samples extracted from the outgoing batch. The Italian customer then performs any necessary inspection of the documents received and requires ZenAsia to: a) confirm the shipment; b) delay it for eventual modifications; c) cancel it.
- *Final check.* Upon goods receipt, ZenAsia and the Italian customer perform the last check on the order and draw a conclusive evaluation of the supplier.

Once again, the Italian customer decides whether to stop at this level or proceed to the next phase.

Phase 3

In this phase the medium–long term relationships between western customers and Chinese suppliers are well defined and managed. After completing vendor selection and monitoring activities, the customer can now establish a direct relationship with a qualified Asiatic manufacturer. But the customer rarely renounces ZenAsia's intermediation: its technical–productive overseeing, the control that it performs on the Chinese manufacturers, the management of the complex logistics procedures are often indispensable for the customer.

The fundamental points of phase 3 are described below.

- *Definition of the final conditions of purchase.* On the basis of the estimated medium–long term requirements, ZenAsia agrees with the customer the

contractual 'ideal' terms and conditions which it shall negotiate with the Chinese manufacturer: prices, payments, packaging, warranty, etc.
- *Final contract*. ZenAsia defines the agreement with the manufacturer. The final contract is underwritten by the latter and the Italian buyer.
- *Dissemination of orders*. ZenAsia is provided with the orders by the customer and forwards them to the manufacturers and its branch in China. The latter can thus check the relevant completion.
- *Instructions for inspection*. At the same time, the customer delivers to ZenAsia the inspection order, which provides instructions for on-line and pre-shipment inspections and eventual functional tests. In the meantime the scheduling of inspections is defined in liaison with the Chinese manufacturer.
- *Payment*. Particular attention is reserved to define payment terms with the Chinese supplier.
- *Controls and shipments*. The previous procedure is replicated on the trial order.
- *After-sales assistance*. In cases of complaints for missing quantities, damage or non-conformance, ZenAsia Italy and ZenAsia China ensure assistance to the Italian customer.

Italian customers can still delegate ZenAsia to develop eventual new productions or to search for new sources of supply. In any case, the sourcing of new vendors and new articles is an activity which ZenAsia performs continuously, through the participation at exhibitions or other events.

The request of services such as those just described is experiencing a continuous growth, especially thanks to small and medium-sized customers. According to ZenAsia, the support which these units receive from specialized institutions (national institutions for international commerce, chambers of commerce, etc.) has in fact a prevalently informational validity. These institutions therefore create useful occasions for matching demand and supply and offer legal support for contracts. However, there is still the problem of identifying which offers are really qualified and of monitoring the completion of an order which is realized in a geographically and culturally distant context. In other words, there is the requirement to monitor these productions and transports in situ, delegating its own decentralized units or third parties. Intermediation is the most suitable solution for small units, since the volumes purchased or the limited resources available do not justify an investment in dedicated infrastructures. Alternatively, intermediaries can achieve economies of scale and specialization regarding these activities, especially transport. It is evident that over and above the demand for these services there is an extraordinarily competitive growth of Chinese supply. According to ZenAsia's experience, the price/quality ratio of Chinese products has decidedly increased in many sectors. So it is not surprising that China represents the most attractive market in the world for foreign investments, even if their Italian content remains limited. For instance, in the Suzhou area, where foreign investments are among the highest in China, Italian investors are rare: while their presence is well established in the clothing and shoes sector, it is still at an exploration phase for electromechanical, mechanical and wooden furniture. According to ZenAsia's experience, Italian companies complain about delays and management inaccuracy. Behind the different negative experiences denounced by our operators there has been a lack of planning and an insufficient knowledge of this particular context.

Other aspects

In this section it may be useful to highlight again the experience and the evaluations of this company with respect to some context-related aspects: geographical and sector heterogeneity of the Chinese industry, characteristics of supply, infrastructure conditions and forgery issues.

The economic condition of China is heterogeneous and presents strong differences among regions. While the internal regions have mainly remained rural, coastal areas have instead experienced a rapid industrialization process and often have a sector specialization: textiles in the Shenyang and Dalian areas (in the Liaoning region), mechanics in Tianji, electronics in Jangsu, small domestic electrical appliances in Zeijiang. Moreover, there are also 'geographical' specializations: the Fujian area focuses on the Taiwanese demand, while the Guangzhou area is preferred by the manufacturers based in Hong Kong (in the Guangdong region, a leading region for consumer electronics). To reduce the strong differences between internal and coastal areas, the territorial authorities are offering various forms of incentives to foreign operators, often competing with each other. With respect to the average profile of Chinese manufacturers, even in this case we face very different situations. Together with 'excellent' units, which have developed an organizational and managerial level comparable with that of the best western companies (which often favoured or drove their development), we find very underdeveloped units, especially relating to information systems utilization. Many units have been recently founded and privatized, and their young age is often accompanied by violent dimensional development trend. These companies therefore need organizational redefinition, more technical and managerial culture, investments for plant and machinery expenditure. They are still 'primitive' units, for which the western interlocutor needs patience and support. But they show flexibility and the capability to learn if they receive precise, punctual and constant directives. Regarding the availability of raw materials, ZenAsia considers it as ample and capable to satisfy most of the requirements. This variable constitutes a comparative advantage for China with respect to other Asian emerging markets, such as India and Vietnam, where the availability of productive inputs generally appears lower. With respect to the communications infrastructures, China has made great progress in recent years thanks to a huge programme of public investment. Thanks to the great spread of the mobile phone network, internet connection is affordable for every unit and e-mails and telephone are the most common instruments of communication. Some companies have also developed their own web sites to advertize their catalogues, but e-commerce practices have not yet been developed.

The wisest procurement policy consists of buying in China single components manufactured according to western specifications; they offer unit cost advantages, and at the same time the spread of sourcing tasks obstructs the acquisition of competences regarding the whole production process. Patent registering is necessary in China, and possibly the support of a local operator so that eventual legal disputes happen only between Chinese parties.

Annex 1

Example of a report compiled by ZenAsia's personnel on a visit to a Chinese lamps supplier. Information in square brackets is confidential and does not form part of this annex.

- *Elements of company identification*
  - Company name
  - Address
  - Telephone and fax numbers
  - E-mail
  - Website
  - Contacts
- *Structural characteristics.* This company, founded in 1991, initially supplied lamp accessories to many big companies in the sector. Since then it has started to produce lamps thanks to the purchase of other machinery. It gradually grew and now it has 40,000 square metre for offices and manufacturing, which includes the new warehouse and the assembly line. The most important structural elements are described below.
  - Personnel: about 600 employees
  - Assembly: six assembly lines for lamps; two lines for the manufacture of electrical components; a division for the finished components process; an independent assembly line for industrial lamps.
  - Capacity: four groups of high-pressure fusion machinery of 400T and two lines of plastics materials electrostatic spraying; it has a daily productive capacity of about 3,000 lamps
  - Warehouse: 2,000 square metres utilized
- *Company property.* It is privately owned and has a risk capital of 10 million reminbi.

- *Real nature of the company.* It is really a manufacturing company: in fact it has divisions producing lamps, headlights and electrical components. [The photographs of details are enclosed].
- *Foreign markets.* The company has already exported to the USA, southeast Asia (Indonesia, Thailand), the Middle East (Arabia, Qatar) and Europe (the United Kingdom and Germany) HIP, ESL a large number of the lamps produced; it has not yet entered the Italian market. With respect to the exports to Europe, they comprise not only the empty container packed separately as a spare part, but also the complete lamp with EC-valid certificate.
- *Eventual productions in OEM.* It produces in OEM for [confidential].
- *Monthly volume of export.* With respect to the lamps, the company exports [confidential] lamps each month.
- *Product Certification.* There are different types of lamps, reflectors, etc. which are EC-certified. EC certification will also be applied to any new article required by the customer.
- *ISO Certification.* The company developed ISO 9001 certification in 2001.
- *Level of quality control.* The company does not have a regular inspection process, since its only control is performed at line-end. [The enclosed photograph shows the production line]
- *Origin of raw materials utilized.* The majority of raw materials utilized has a domestic origin, and only some light-reflecting materials are imported to China.
- *Zone of origin of imported materials.* Some light-reflecting materials for reflectors are imported from Germany. The imported light-reflecting materials will be applied to all the products exported.
- *Total amount of sales.* According to the data provided by the export manager, 70 per cent of sales concern export, 30 per cent the domestic market. The total amount of sales is about 20 million dollars.

[The report is accompanied by photographic documentation.]

Annex 2

Basic procedure for pre-shipment inspection

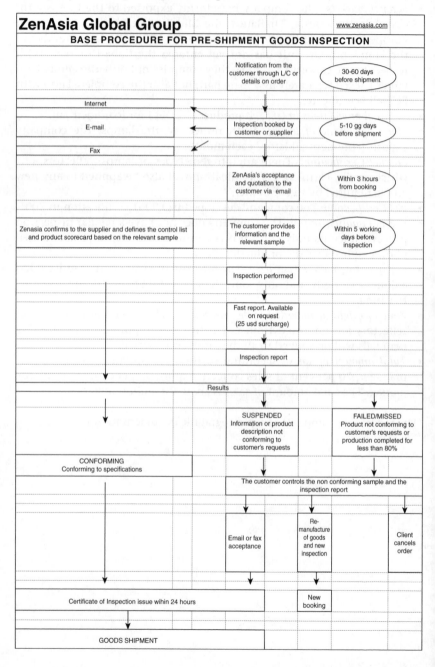

Bibliography

Accenture, 'Executive Insights Into The Growing Use of Procurement Outsourcing. 2003 Procurement Survey', Accenture, 2003

Ambler T., Styles C., Xiucun W., 'The effects of channel relationships and guanxi on the performance of inter-province export ventures in the People's Republic of China'; *International Journal of Research in Marketing*, 1999, Vol. 16, pp. 75–87

Andersen O. and Buvik A. 'Inter-firm co-ordination: international versus domestic buyer–seller relationships'; *Omega – the international journal of management science* Vol. 29 2001 pp. 207–19

Arnold U. 'Organization of global sourcing: ways towards an optimal degree of centralization'; *European Journal of Purchasing & Supply Management* No. 5 1999 pp. 167–74

Arnold U. 'New dimentions of outsourcing: a combination of transaction cost economics and the core competencies concept'; *European Journal of Purchasing & Supply Management* No. 6 2000 pp. 23–9

Babbar S. and Prasad S. 'International purchasing, inventory management and logistics research. An assessment and agenda'; *International Purchasing* Vol. 28 No. 6. 1998 pp. 403–33

Beamish B., 'The Characteristics of Joint Ventures in the People's Republic of China'; *Journal of International Marketing*, pp. 29–48, February 1993

Bennet D., Xiaming Liu, Parker D., Fred Steward, Kirit Vaidya, 'Technology transfer to China: a study of strategy in 20 EU industrial countries', 2000

Birindelli e Associati, 'Quadro di riferimento legislativo e fiscale per gli operatori economici stranieri nella Repubblica Popolare Cinese', Il Sole 24 Ore, 2004

Birou L. and Fawcett S. 'International purchasing: benefits, requirements and challenges'; *International Journal of Purchasing and Materials Management,* Spring 1993 pp. 28–37

Björkman I., Kock S., 'Social relationships and business networks: the case of Western companies in China'; *International Business Review*, 1995, Vol. 4, No. 4, pp. 519–35

Björkman I., Lu Y., 'The management of human-resources in Chinese–Western Joint Ventures'; *Journal of World Business*, 1999, Vol. 34, No. 3, pp. 306–24

Bozarth C., Handfield R. and Das A. 'Stages of global sourcing strategy evolution: an exploratory study'; *Journal of Operations Management*, Vol. 16, 1998 pp. 241–55

Caddick J.R. and Dale B.G. 'Sourcing from less developed countries: a case study'; *Journal of Purchasing And Materials Management*, Fall 1987 pp. 17–23

Camera di Commercio, Industria, Artigianato ed Agricoltura di Bolzano, 'Guida al deposito di domande di brevetto e modello d'utilità', pp. 5–7, 2004

Canigiani E., 'Introduzione allo studio dei marchi cinesi e delle traduzioni dei nomi dei marchi stranieri in cinese', *Mondo Cinese* no. 106, 2001

Carmel E., Agarwal R., 'The maturation of offshore sourcing of information technology work', MIS Quarterly Executive Vol. 1, No. 2/June 2002, 76

Carter J. And Narasimhan R. 'Purchasing in the international marketplace: implications for operations'; *Journal of Purchasing and Materials Management*, Summer 1990 pp. 2–11

Carter J. and Vickery S. 'Currency exchange rates: the impact on global sourcing'; *Journal of Purchasing and Materials Management*, Fall 1989 pp. 19–25

Carter J.R., Pearson J.N., Peng L., 'Logistics barriers to international operations: the case of the People's Republic of China'; *Journal of Business Logistics*, 1997, Vol. 18, No. 2, pp. 129–45

Carter, J.R., L. Smeltzer, and R. Narasimhan, 'The Role of Buyer and Supplier Relationships in Integrating TQM Through the Supply Chain'; *European Journal of Purchasing & Supply Management*, Vol. 4, No. 4, pp. 223–34, 1998

Chadee D.D., Qiu F., 'Foreign ownership of equity joint ventures in China: a pooled cross-section-time series analysis'; *Journal of Business Research*, 2001, Vol. 52, pp. 123–33

Chadee D.D., Qiu F., Rose E.L., 'FDI location at the subnational level: a study of EJVs in China'; *Journal of Business Research*, 2003, Vol. 56, pp. 835–45

Chadwick, T and Rajagopal, S. 'Strategic supply management: an implementation toolkit', Butterworth-Heinemann, Oxford, UK, 1995

Chase R.B. Zhang A. 'Operations management: internationalization and interdisciplinary integration'; *International Journal of Operations & Production Management*, Vol. 18, No. 7, 1998, pp. 663–7

Chen X., Sun C., 'Technology transfer to China: alliances of Chinese enterprises with western technology exporters'; *Technovation*, 2000, Vol. 20, pp. 353–62

Chen M., 'Asian Management Systems', Thomson Learning, 2004, pp. 44–55

Chin K.-S., Pun K.-F., Xu Y., Chan J.S., 'An AHP based study of critical factors for TQM implementation in Shangai manufacturing industries'; *Technovation*, 2002, Vol. 22, pp. 707–15

Chow D., 'Counterfeiting in the People's Republic of China'; *Washington University Law Quarterly*, vol. 78, no. 1, pp. 3–52, 2000

Chung W.W.C., Yam A.Y.K., Chan M.F.S., 'Networks enterprise: a new business model for global sourcing'; *International Journal of Production Economics*, 2004, Vol. 87, pp. 267–80

Cohen M.A. and Mallik S. 'Global supply chain: research and applications'; *Production and Operations Management*, Fall 1997 Vol. 6, No. 3, pp. 193–210

Comba D., Garelli S., 'I contratti internazionali', *Il Sole* 24 Ore, 2003, pp. 529–72

D'Agnolo G., Dal Colle A. 'Cina: guida al commercio estero e agli investimenti', Giuffrè editore, 2001

Daly P.S., Cui L.X., 'E-logistics in China: basic problems, manageable concerns and intractable solutions'; *Industrial Marketing Management*, 2003, Vol. 32, pp. 235–42

Davies H., Leung T.K.P., Luk S.T.K., Wong Y., 'The benefits of "Guanxi" '; *Industrial Marketing Management*, 1995, Vol. 24, pp. 207–14

Davies H, 'A Roadmap for China's Mergers and Acquisitions'; *The China Business Review*, pp. 12–18, August 2003

De Meyer A., 'Technology transfer into China: preparing for a New Era'; *European Management Journal*, 2001, Vol. 19, No. 2, pp. 140–4

De Toni A., Nassimbeni G., 'Just-In-Time purchasing: an empirical study of operational practices, supplier development and performance', *OMEGA – International Journal of Management Science*, Vol. 28, no. 6, 2000, pp. 631–51

De Toni A., Nassimbeni G., 'Buyer–supplier operation practices, sourcing policies and plant performances: Results of an empirical research'; *International Journal of Production Research*, Vol. 37, no. 9, 1999, 597–619

Deli Yang, 'Insights from the P.R. China of Multinational Intellectual Property Inflows', Bradford University School of Management, 2004

Deng P., 'WFOEs: The Most Popular Entry Mode into China'; *Business Horizons*, 2001, Vol. 44, No. 4, pp. 63–72

Domeach J., 'Dove va la Cina?' Carocci Editore, 2003

Ellram L. and Billington C. 'Purchasing leverage considerations in the outsourcing decision'; *European Journal of Purchasing & Supply Management* No. 7, 2001, pp. 15–27

Fagan M.L., 1991, 'A guide to global soucing', *Journal of Business Strategy*, March/April, 21–6

Fawcett S., Birou L. and Cofield Taylor B. 'Supporting global operations through logistics and purchasing'; *International Journal of Physical Distribution & Logistics Management*, Vol. 23, No. 4, 1993 pp. 3–11

Fraering M. and Prasad S. 'International sourcing and logistics: an integrated model'; *Management Decision*, Vol. 12, No. 6, 1999 pp. 451–9

Frear C.R., Arguire M.S., Metclaf L.E., 1995, 'Country segmentation on the basis of international purchasing patterns', *Journal of Business & Industrial Purchasing*, Vol. 10, No. 2, pp. 59–68

Gallant R., 'The small fry take on China', *The China Business Review*, pp. 30–6, February 2003

Gao T., 'Ethnic Chinese networks and international investment: evidence from inward FDI in China'; *Journal of Asian Economics*, 2003, Vol. 14, pp. 611–29

Gaudenzi Sirotti A., 'Il nuovo diritto d'autore'; Maggioli Editore, 2003, pp. 27–205

Giunipero L.C. and Monczka R.M. 'Organizational approaches to managing international sourcing'; *International Journal of Physical Distribution & Logistics Management*, Vol. 20, No.4, 1990 pp. 3–12

Goldstein B., 'WTO: Year Two Begins', *The China Business Review*, pp. 16–22, February 2003

Goodall K. and Warner M., 'Human resources in sino-foreign joint ventures'; *International Journal of Human Resource Management*, pp. 569–4, August 1997

Haley U.C.V., 'Assessing and controlling business risks in China'; *Journal of International Management*, 2003, Vol. 9, pp. 237–52

Handfield R. 'US global sourcing: patterns of development'; *International Journal of Operations & Production Management*, Vol. 14, No. 6, 1994 pp. 40–51

Heytens A., 'Human Resources and the Transition to Sole Foreign Ownership'; *The China Business Review*, pp. 36–40, December 2001

Herbig P. and O'Hara B. 'International procurement practices: a matter of relationships'; *Management Decision*, Vol. 34, No. 4, 1996 pp. 41–5

Hofstede, Geert (1983) 'National cultures in four dimensions: a research-based theory of cultural differences among nations'; *International Studies of Management and Organization*, XIII (1–2): 46–74

Holt D.H., 'A comparative study of values among Chinese and US entrepreneurs: pragmatic convergence between contrasting cultures'; *Journal of Business Venturing*, 1997, Vol. 12, pp. 483–505

HKTDC Research Department, 'Protection against Intellectual Property Rights Infringement', *Guide to Doing Business in China*, 2003

Huang G., 'On the Modernization of Chinese Family Business', in Jiang Yi-wei and Min Jian-shu (eds), *Ancient Management Practices* Economic Management Press, 1989, pp. 133

Humphreys P., Mak K.L. and Yeung C.M. 'A just-in-time evaluation strategy for international procurement', *Supply Chain Management*, Vol. 3, No. 4, 1998 pp. 175–86

Humpreys P.K., Lai M.K., Sculli D., 'An inter-organizational information system for supply chain management'; *International Journal of Production Economics*, 2001, Vol. 70, pp. 245–55

Hu H.C., 'The Chinese Concepts of Face', *American Anthropologist*, 1944, pp. 45–64

Kaufmann P. and Carter C., 'International Purchasing and Supply Management: A Comparison of US and German Practices'; *Journal of Supply Chain Management*, 2000, 38, pp. 4–17

Kogut, Bruce and Singh, Harry (1988) 'The effect of national culture on the choice of entry mode'; *Journal of International Business Studies*, 19(3): 411–32

Kotabe M. and Murray J. 'Linking product and process innovations and modes of international sourcing in global competition: a case of foreign multinational firms'; *Journal of International Business Studies*, Third quarter, 1990 pp. 387–407

Kotabe M. and Swan S. 'Offshore sourcing: reaction, maturation, and consolidation of US multinationals'; *Journal of International Business Studies*, First quarter, 1994 pp. 115–39

Kotabe M. 'The relationship between offshore sourcing and innovativeness of US multinational firms: an empirical investigation'; *Journal of International Business Studies*, Fourth quarter 1990 pp. 622–38

Kühnle H., Martinetz J., 'Experiences and Concepts for the German Bicycle Industry'; EU–China Conference on International Sourcing and Supply Chain Management, Proceedings, Beijing, April 2004; pp.89–93

Lancioni R., Schau H.J., Smith M.F., 'Internet impacts on supply chain management'; *Industrial Marketing Management*, 2003, Vol. 32, pp. 173–5

Levy D. 'International sourcing and supply chain stability'; *Journal of International Business Studies, Second quarter* 1995 pp. 343–60

Li J., Lam K., Qian G., 'Does the culture affect behaviour and performance of firms? The case of Joint Ventures in China'; *Journal of International Business Studies*, 2001, Vol. 32, No. 1, pp. 115–31

Li J., Qian G., Lam K., Wang D., 'Breaking into China: strategic considerations for multinational corporations'; *Long Range Planning*, 2000, Vol. 33, pp. 673–87

Liu X., Burridge P., Sinclair P.J.N., 'Relationships between economic growth, foreign direct investment and trade: evidence from China'; *Applied Economics*, 2002, Vol. 34, pp. 1433–40

Liu X., Wang C., Wei Y., 'Causal links between foreign direct investment and trade in China'; *China Economic Review*, 2001, Vol. 12, pp. 190–202

Liu Z., 'Foreign direct investment and technology spillover: evidence from China'; *Journal of Comparative Economics*, 2002, Vol. 30, pp. 579–602

Locke D. *Global supply management: a guide to international purchasing* (1996) Irwin Professional (USA)

Luo Y., 'Evaluating the performance of strategic alliances in China'; *Long Range Planning*, 1996, Vol. 29, No. 4, pp. 534–42

Luo Y., 'Pioneering in China: risks and benefits'; *Long Range Planning*, 1997, Vol. 30, No. 5, pp. 768–76

Luo Y., 'The structure–performance relationship in a transitional economy: an empirical study of multinational alliances in China'; *Journal of Business Research*, 1999, Vol. 46, pp. 15–30

Mattson M. and Salehi-Sangari E. 'Decision making in purchases of equipment and materials: a four-country comparison'; *International Journal of Physical Distribution & Logistics Management*, Vol. 23, No. 8, 1993 pp. 16–30

Meijboom B. and Dekkers K. 'International manufacturing: the role of global sourcing'; *Journal of International Business Studies* 1997 pp. 167–72

Meijboom B. 'Production to order and international operations'; *International Journal of Operations & Production Management*, 1999 pp. 602–19

Min H., Galle W, 1991, 'International purchasing strategies of multinational US firms'; *International Journal of Purchasing and Materials Management*, 27(3), pp. 9–18

Monczka R. and Trent R.J., 'Worldwide sourcing: assessment and execution'; *International Journal of Purchasing and Materials Management*. Fall 1992 pp. 9–19

Monczka, R.M., and Trent, R.J. (1991), 'Global sourcing: A development approach'; *International Journal of Purchasing and Materials Management*, Spring, pp. 2–8

Murray J., Kotabe M. and Wildt A. 'Strategic and financial performance implications on global sourcing strategy: a contingency analysis'; *Journal of International Business Studies*, First quarter 1995 pp.181–203

National Centre for Science and Technology Evaluation (China), 'International Sourcing Strategies for China, deliverable 2.2'; September 2003

Nassimbeni G., 'International sourcing: empirical evidences from a sample of Italian firms'; Proceedings of the Ist Euroma-Poms Conference 'One World? One view of OM'; June 2003, SGEditoriali Padova, pp. 733–42

Nassimbeni G., 'Local manufacturing systems and global economy: are they compatible? The case of the Italian eyewear district', *Journal of Operations Management*, Vol. 21, 2003, pp. 151–71

Nassimbeni G., Sartor M., 'Sourcing Strategies from China', 13th IPSERA Conference, University of Catania, April, 2004, pp. 609–18

Nassimbeni G., Sartor M., 'Procurement Policies and Practices from Chinese Supply Market'; 2004 Euroma Annual Conference: 'Operations Management as a change agent', Fontainebleau, June 2004, Vol.1, pp. 891–901

Nassimbeni G., Sartor M., 'Sourcing Strategies for China', EU–China Conference on International Sourcing and Supply Chain Management, 'Proceedings, Beijing, April 2004; pp 79–88

Nellore R., Chanaron J. and Soderquist E. 'Lean supply and price-based global sourcing-the interconnection'; *European Journal of Purchasing & Supply Management* No. 7 2001 pp. 101–10

Nellore S. Soderquist K. 'Strategic outsourcing through specifications'; *Omega – the International Journal of Management Science* Vol. 28, 2000 pp. 525–40

Norton P. Chao H. 'Mergers and Acquisitions in China', *The China Business Review*, pp. 46–53, October 2001

Padolecchia S., 'Business in Cina'; *IL Sole* 24 Ore, 2003

Pan Y., Li X., 'Alliance of foreign firms in equity joint ventures in China'; *International Business Review*, 1998, Vol. 7, pp. 329–50

Pattlock T., 'Protection of Intellectual Property in China', German–Chinese Business Forum, 5 June 2003, pp. 32–4

Pike D., Farley J., Robb D., 'Manufacturing and supply chain management in China: a survey of State, Collective-, and privately-owned enterprises'; *European Management Journal*, 2000, Vol. 18, No. 6, pp. 577–89

Pike D., Farley J., Robb D., 'Manufacturing Technology and Operations in China: a survey of State-Owned Enterprises, Private firms, Joint Ventures and Wholly-Owned Foreign subsidiaries'; *European Management Journal*, 2002, Vol. 20, No. 4, pp. 356–75

Pye L., 'Chinese Commercial Negotiating Style', Quorum Books, 1982

Prasad S., Babbar S. and Calis A. 'International operations management and operations management research: a comparative analysis'; *Omega – the International Journal of Management Science*, Vol. 28, 2000, pp. 97–110

Rao K. And Young R. 'Global supply chains: factors influencing outsourcing of logistics functions'; *International Journal of Physical Distribution & Logistics Management*, Vol. 24, No. 6, 1994 pp. 11–19

Redding S.G., Ng M., 'The Role of "Face" in the Organizational Perceptions of Chinese Managers'; *Organizational Studies*, 1982, pp. 207

Rozemeijer F. 'How to manage corporate purchasing synergy in a decentralized company? Towards design rules for managing and organizing purchasing synergy in decentralized companies'; *European Journal of Purchasing & Supply Management* No. 6 2000 pp. 5–12

Salvagni C., 'Marchi, brevetti e Know-how', *Finanze e Lavoro Editore*, 2003, pp. 7–116

Scully, J.I. & Fawcett, S.E. 'International Procurement Strategies: Challenges and opportunities for the small firm', *Product and inventory Management Journal*, 1994 Second Quarter, pp. 39–46

Selmer J., 'Culture shock in China? Adjustment of western expatriate business managers'; *International Business Review*, 1999, Vol. 8, pp. 515–34

Shi Y. and Gregory M. 'International manufacturing networks – to develop competitive capabilities'; *Journal of Operations Management*, No. 16, 1998, pp. 195–214

Shi Y., 'Technological capabilities and international production strategy of firms: the case of foreign direct investment in China'; *Journal of World Business*, 2001, Vol. 36, No. 2, pp. 184–204

Smith, J.M. (1999) 'Item selection for global purchasing'; *European Journal of Purchasing and Supply Management*, No. 5, pp. 117–27

Spekman J., Spear J. and Kamuff J. 'Towards more effective sourcing and supplier management'; *European Journal of Purchasing & Supply Management* No. 5 1999 pp. 103–16

Sun Q., Tong W., Yu Q., 'Determinants of foreign direct investment across China'; *Journal of International Money and Finance*, 2002, Vol. 21, pp. 79–113

Sutter K., 'Investors Growing Pains', *The China Business Review*, pp. 14–17, December 2000

Swamidass P. 'Import sourcing dynamics: an integrative perspective'; *Journal of International Business Studies*, Fourth quarter 1993 pp. 671–991

Swamidass P. and Kotabe M. 'Component sourcing strategies of multinationals: an empirical study of European and Japanese multinationals'; *Journal of International Business Studies*, First quarter 1993 pp. 81–99

Tavano F., 'Brevettare un'idea e goderne i diritti'; Edizioni FAG, 2004, pp. 29–92

Thomas T. Moga, 'The TRIPs agreement and China'; *The China Business Review*, pp. 12–18, November–December, 2002

Thompson E.R., 'Clustering of foreign direct investment and enhanced technology transfer: evidence from Hong Kong garment firms in China'; *World Development*, 2002, Vol. 30, No. 5, pp. 873–89

Trainer T., 'The fight against trademark counterfeiting', *The China Business Review*, Vol. 29, No. 6, pp. 3–9, November–December 2002

Trent R.J., Monczka R.M., 2002, 'Pursuing competitive advantage through integrated global sourcing'; Academy of Management Executive, 16(2), 66–80

Tseng H.C., Ip W.H., Ng K.C, 'A model for an integrated manufacturing system implementation in China: a case study'; *Journal of Engineering and Technology Management*, 1999, Vol. 16, pp. 83–101

Wang W., 'China's role and strategy in the Integration of global procurement and supply chain management'; EU–China Conference on International Sourcing and Supply Chain Management, Proceedings, Beijing, April 2004; pp. 73–9

Warner M., 'Foreign investors' choices in China: going it alone or in partnership?'; *Human Systems Management*, pp. 137–49, October 2002

Weber M., 'Il miracolo cinese', *Il Mulino*, 2003

World Trade Organization, 'WTO: International trade statistics 2003'; 2003

Wright D.T. and Burns N.D. 'New organization structures for global business: an empirical study'; *International Journal of Operations & Production Management*, 1998, pp. 896–923

Wu X., 'Foreign direct investment, intellectual property rights and wage inequality in China'; *China Economic Review*, 2000, Vol. 11, pp. 361–84

Zizhen B., 'Intellectual property protection in China', *Economic Reform Today*, No. 1, 1996, pp. 87–91

Web-sites

Istituto Nazionale per il Commercio Estero (*www.ice.it*):
- 'Porti della Cina'
- 'Cina: i trasporti marittimi di container'
- Ufficio Pechino: 'Profili province'
- Ufficio Shanghai: 'Profili province'
- Ufficio Canton: 'Profili province'

National Bureau of Statistics of China (*http://www.stats.gov.cn*):
- 'Investment in Fixed Assets by Industry'
- 'Total Volume of Transportation'

China–Italy Trade (*http://www.china-italy-trade.net*):
- 'Infrastrutture e Servizi'
- 'Auto e veicoli industriali – Il mercato'
- 'I consumi nelle grandi città'
- 'Il cargo aereo'
- 'Il trasporto su ruota'
- 'Trasporti e logistica'
- 'Trasporti via nave'
- 'Logistica e trasporti: l'evoluzione in atto'
- 'Progetti in fase di esame presso la ADB'

Istituto italo-cinese (*http://www.china-italy.com*):
- 'Ferrovie, anno zero'
- 'Alta velocità'
- 'Liberalizzazione merci su rotaia'
- 'Il Porto di Canton'
- 'Nordovest: 4 mila chilometri di nuove ferrovie'
- 'Aeroporti, crescono i piccoli, si rafforzano i grandi'
- 'Treni veloci: il made in China raggiunge 305 chilometri orari'
- 'Ferrovie'
- 'Logistica'
- '10 grandi progetti per la China occidentale'
- '20 milioni di container via mare'

China Data Center (*http://chinadatacenter.org*)

Camera di Commercio Italo-Cinese (*www.china-italy.com*)

DHL (*www.dhl.com*)

China Data Center (*www.chinadatacenter.com*)

The Italian Embassy in the People's Republic of China (*http://www.italianembassy.org.cn*)

Index